Unification Through Division

Unification Through Division

Histories of the Divisions of the American Psychological Association

VOLUME V

EDITED BY

Donald A. Dewsbury

AMERICAN PSYCHOLOGICAL ASSOCIATION
WASHINGTON, DC

Published by
American Psychological Association
750 First Street, NE
Washington, DC 20002

Copies may be ordered from
APA Order Department
P.O. Box 92984
Washington, DC 20090-2984

In the UK and Europe, copies may be ordered from
American Psychological Association
3 Henrietta Street
Covent Garden, London
WC2E 8LU England

Typeset in Goudy by World Composition Services, Inc., Sterling, VA

Printer: Goodway Graphics, Springfield, VA
Cover Designer: Minker Design, Bethesda, MD
Editor and Production Manager: Debbie K. Hardin, Reston, VA

The opinions and statements published are the responsibility of the authors, and such opinions and statements do not necessarily represent the policies of the APA.

Library of Congress Cataloging-in-Publication Data
Unification through division : histories of the divisions of the
  American Psychological Association / Donald A. Dewsbury, editor.
      p. cm.
    Includes bibliographic references and index.
    ISBN 1-55798-683-5
    1. American Psychological Association—History. I. Dewsbury,
  Donald A., 1939–
  BF11.U55 1999
  150'.6073—dc20   96-41480
                                                                         CIP

British Library Cataloguing-in-Publication Data
A CIP record is available from the British Library.

Printed in the United States of America
First Edition

CONTENTS

DIVISIONS OF THE AMERICAN PSYCHOLOGICAL ASSOCIATION

Number	Name
1.	Society for General Psychology
2.	Society for the Teaching of Psychology
3.	Experimental Psychology
5.	Evaluation, Measurement, and Statistics
6.	Behavioral Neuroscience and Comparative Psychology
7.	Developmental Psychology
8.	Society for Personality and Social Psychology
9.	Society for the Psychological Study of Social Issues (SPSSI)
10.	Psychology and the Arts
12.	Society of Clinical Psychology
13.	Consulting Psychology
14.	Society for Industrial and Organizational Psychology
15.	Educational Psychology
16.	School Psychology
17.	Counseling Psychology
18.	Psychologists in Public Service
19.	Military Psychology
20.	Adult Development and Aging
21.	Applied Experimental and Engineering Psychology
22.	Rehabilitation Psychology
23.	Society for Consumer Psychology
24.	Theoretical and Philosophical Psychology
25.	Experimental Analysis of Behavior

(*continued*)

Number	Name
26.	History of Psychology
27.	Society for Community Research and Action: Division of Community Psychology
28.	Psychopharmacology and Substance Abuse
29.	Psychotherapy
30.	Psychological Hypnosis
31.	State Psychological Association Affairs
32.	Humanistic Psychology
33.	Mental Retardation and Developmental Disabilities
34.	Population and Environmental Psychology
35.	Society for the Psychology of Women
36.	Psychology of Religion
37.	Child, Youth, and Family Services
38.	Health Psychology
39.	Psychoanalysis
40.	Clinical Neuropsychology
41.	American Psychology–Law Society
42.	Psychologists in Independent Practice
43.	Family Psychology
44.	Society for the Psychological Study of Lesbian, Gay, and Bisexual Issues
45.	Society for the Psychological Study of Ethnic Minority Issues
46.	Media Psychology
47.	Exercise and Sport Psychology
48.	Society for the Study of Peace, Conflict and Violence: Peace Psychology Division
49.	Group Psychology and Group Psychotherapy
50.	Addictions
51.	Society for the Psychological Study of Men and Masculinity
52.	International Psychology
53.	Clinical Child Psychology
54.	Society of Pediatric Psychology
55.	American Society for the Advancement of Pharmacotherapy

Note: There are no Divisions 4 or 11.

CONTRIBUTORS

Christopher M. Aanstoos, University of West Georgia

James R. Council, North Dakota State University

Donald A. Dewsbury, University of Florida

Arthur J. Drucker, Silver Spring, MD

Paul A. Gade, U.S. Army Research Institute

Melvin A. Gravitz, George Washington University Medical Center

Thomas Greening, Los Angeles, CA

Raymond F. Hanbury, Jr., Manasquan, NJ

Ernest R. Hilgard, Stanford University

Paul C. Larson, Chicago School of Professional Psychology

Eugene E. Levitt, Indiana University School of Medicine

Ann C. Marcotte, Brown University School of Medicine

Antonio E. Puente, University of North Carolina—Wilmington

James M. Richards, Jr., Psychocrostics, Green Valley, AZ

Paul R. Sachs, Professional Psychology Group, Bala Cynwyd, PA

Ilene Serlin, Saybrook Institute, San Francisco, CA

Jalie A. Tucker, University of Alabama at Birmingham

Rudy E. Vuchinich, Auburn University

INTRODUCTION

DONALD A. DEWSBURY

This is the fifth volume in a series that was planned to include the histories of as many of the American Psychological Association's (APA) 52 divisions as possible. More than 55 years ago (1946) the APA was reorganized around a set of divisions structured to represent the diverse interests of constituent groups of psychologists within the organization at that time. Although the number of divisions has grown since, the basic structure remains intact. It is through these divisions that the unity of the APA was reestablished. By providing homes for groups with similar interests in research, practice, and policy, the divisions can work more effectively on many problems of local interest than can the APA as a whole. Because they are smaller, the divisions are more flexible and can change more readily as fields change. So effective have these divisions been that some psychologists identify more closely with these interest groups than with the parent organization.

In Volumes I through IV we presented the first 34 division histories of the set (Dewsbury, 1996, 1997, 1998, 1999). In this volume we include seven more chapters. This brings the set to completion with 41 of the 52 APA divisions.

The project began with a survey of existing divisions' histories, some of which had just been written for the 1992 centennial celebration of the APA. From that survey, and word of mouth, we located authors for chapters dealing with many of the divisions. The first four volumes include chapters whose authors could meet the first deadlines for inclusion; this volume includes contributions from a fifth group of authors. We considered the possibility of holding chapters to publish a set of volumes with coherent themes, rather than the mix of diverse divisions, as in the present volume. However, the advantages of such coherence seemed outweighed by the disadvantages of holding some chapters for several years as other authors' work and the original chapters grew stale. The diversity of each volume is characteristic of the complexity of psychology.

I hope that these chapters will be of interest to diverse readerships. Division members should be aware of the histories of their divisions and understand where they stand in the webs and cascades of developing psychology. Historians of psychology and nonpsychologists alike will find much information on the evolving fabric of the discipline of psychology. The hope is that any reader interested in understanding the complexity of this field will benefit from these chapters.

THE APA BEFORE WORLD WAR II

The APA was founded in G. Stanley Hall's living room at Clark University in July 1892, and held its first annual convention in Philadelphia in December of that year. Throughout its history, the APA has been the primary organization of psychologists in North America (see Evans, Sexton, & Cadwallader, 1992). However, throughout its history various interest groups of psychologists, on the sides of both basic research and practice, have formed their own organizations, either inside or outside of the APA. Beginning in 1904 Edward B. Titchener's Experimentalists, later the Society of Experimental Psychologists, was one such alternative organization for experimental psychologists (Boring, 1967). During the 1920s another group of experimental psychologists formed to conduct round tables within the framework of the APA.

From the practice side, the American Association of Clinical Psychologists was founded in 1917 and became a section of the APA 2 years later. When the American Association of Applied Psychology (AAAP) was founded in 1937, the APA clinical section was disbanded and joined sections on consulting, educational, and industrial psychology as the clinical section of the AAAP.

Thus when World War II broke out psychology lacked a unified presence. The Emergency Committee in Psychology was formed by the Division of Anthropology and Psychology of the National Research Council in 1940 to help mobilize psychologists for the war effort. It was from the Subcommittee on Survey and Planning of the Emergency Committee that Robert M.

Yerkes and other psychologists began a push to reunify the APA, the AAAP, and various other smaller organizations into a single voice for psychology. An Intersociety Constitutional Convention was convened on May 29, 1943, in New York City to effect the reorganization. The result was a revised constitution and set of bylaws for the APA, which became an organization whose stated purpose was not only to advance psychology as a science but also as a practice that could be used in the promotion of human welfare. Membership requirements were changed to accommodate practitioners whose efforts often did not lead to publication. Most critically, for the present purposes, the divisional structure was conceived as a way to maintain diverse interest groups within the broader structure of the new APA. Both the APA and the AAAP officially approved the reorganization in September 1944, and the new APA was inaugurated on September 6, 1945.

Psychologists were canvassed for their division interests with a preliminary list of 19 proposed divisions (Recommendations, 1943), and the results were used to modify the proposed list into a revised set of 19 charter divisions arranged in a modified hierarchy (Doll, 1946; Hilgard, 1945a). Temporary division chairs and secretaries were appointed (Hilgard, 1945b) and elections of the first officers were held in 1945. The divisions were up and running.

This basic structure has seen minor modifications over the past 50 years, but has remained largely intact. Perhaps the greatest challenge to the integrity of the APA has come with the formation in 1988 of the American Psychological Society, a group of academic, applied, and experimental psychologists that has challenged the hegemony of the APA. One can only hope that another unification will soon come to pass.

FROM 1945 TO THE PRESENT

Psychology in North America has changed dramatically in the 50 years since the division structure was adopted. I summarize the changes as follows:

- *Growth*   The membership has grown from approximately 3200 in 1943 to more than 80,000 50 years later.
- *Specialization*   Psychology has become more specialized, with few general psychologists and many psychologists limiting their interests to relatively narrow areas.
- *Fractionation* With increased specialization there have emerged many smaller societies and organizations that vie with the larger umbrella groups for psychologists' loyalties.
- *Professionalization*   There has been a dramatic shift from a dominance of basic science in psychology to an overwhelming numerical dominance of those with practice interests.

- *External politization*   Psychologists have become more involved with matters of policy outside of the APA and psychology in general, including interactions with governmental agencies at all levels.
- *Internal politization*   There has been an increase in the political structure and activity within the APA.
- *Feminization*   There has been a substantial increase in the number of women in psychology and the roles they play.
- *Diversification*   There has been an increase in representation and activity from members of diverse racial and ethnic groups.
- *Internationalization*   There is increased recognition of the importance of psychology as it is developing outside of North America.
- *Cognitivization*   The field has become more cognitively oriented.
- *Expansion*   Psychologists have expanded their spheres of activity into areas not previously covered, as in the increased conduct of therapy and the drive for prescription privileges.
- *Legalization*   Both the practice and science of psychology have, like many functions in the United States, become entwined with the courts, litigation, and lawyers.
- *Breakup of global theories*   The global theories of personality, learning, and other processes so prevalent 50 years ago have largely disappeared.
- *Aging*   The membership of the APA has been getting older, with an increasing proportion of psychologists at or past traditional retirement ages.

The divisions have evolved in synchrony with these broader trends, both helping to effect the changes and being affected by them. The themes just elaborated should stand out as one reads the chapters of this volume. There are many problems for divisions created by the growth, specialization, and fractionation of psychology over this period. Most of these problems have affected all divisions to some degree, but some are more apparent in the histories than others. As will be apparent, these problems have led to both conflict and cooperation within divisions, among divisions, and with groups outside of psychology.

The shifting balance between science and practice can be seen in the dominance of practice orientations in the formation of many of the newer divisions and in the evolution of some of the older divisions, such as Division 25 (Experimental Analysis of Behavior). The increased presence of psychologists in policy matters is apparent in the formation of the divisions of Child, Youth, and Family Services (37) and of the Society for the Study of Peace, Conflict & Violence (48). The expansion of psychology is especially apparent

as the members of the Division of Psychoanalysis (39) interact with physicians in defining appropriate spheres of activity.

AN OVERVIEW OF THE CHAPTERS

The divisions represented in this volume are diverse but all have
appreciable applied components, illustrating the importance of concerns
about the application of psychological knowledge. They range from the
military to humanism and hypnosis to addictions. All have strong connec-
tions to fields outside of psychology.

In chapter 1 Paul Gade and Arthur Drucker provide a history of
Division 19 (Military Psychology). A section on military psychology was
established by the American Association for Applied Psychology shortly
before its amalgamation into the APA, and the old section became a new
division. The division has been embedded in controversy throughout much
of its history. Perhaps the most serious conflict occurred during the Vietnam
War, when another division introduced a resolution for the abolition of
Division 19. The division also was involved in a controversial demonstration
project concerning prescription privileges for psychologists, has been in
conflict over the issue of gay men and lesbians in the military, and disagreed
with the APA Council of Representatives' banning of the military services
from advertising jobs in APA publications. In spite of these controversies,
the division has survived and accomplished much.

In chapter 2 Paul Larson and Paul Sachs trace the history of Division
22 (Rehabilitation Psychology). The American rehabilitation movement
evolved from private charitable organizations, state–federal partnerships,
and federal veteran's programs. Psychologists concerned with rehabilitation
came from these three streams to found the National Council on the Psychological Aspects of Disability, the forerunner of Division 22. Conferences,
such as those held at Princeton and Clark Universities, were especially
important in shaping Division 22. Larson and Sachs show how events outside
of psychology, such as President Lyndon Johnson's Great Society and passage
of the Rehabilitation Act of 1973, affected the growth of the field in general
and the division in particular.

Writing on the development of Division 30 (Psychological Hypnosis)
in chapter 3, James Council, Melvin Gravitz, Ernest Hilgard, and Eugene
Levitt show how long a history the study of hypnosis has in psychology.
The authors trace the organizational background of the division, emphasize
the challenges it has faced, and look to the future and problems yet to be
resolved by the field and the division. Whereas most new divisions emerged
as the result of efforts of prominent leaders in the field who form an informal

network, then a specialized organization, and finally apply for division status, the formation of Division 30 was spearheaded by a young psychologist, Adel M. Mahran, who later fell into conflict with the more established leaders of the field. An interesting aspect of this history is the difficulty faced in even defining the nature of the phenomenon that defines the division.

So-called third-force psychology developed in reaction to the perceived hegemony of behaviorism and psychoanalysis in psychology with a focus on bringing a more humanistic approach to the field. In chapter 4 Christopher Aanstoos, Ilene Serlin, and Thomas Greening show how Division 32 (Humanistic Psychology) developed in this context. It is not surprising that the field coalesced during the 1960s, an era of great humanistic ferment. The division emerged from the Association for Humanistic Psychology and developed a full program of division activities. With the 1970s and 1980s, however, the popularity of humanistic approaches began to wane, partially as a result of a growing conservatism in the United States. During the 1980s questions of self-identity plagued the division, as they did numerous other divisions at various times. Projecting trends into the future the authors see efforts to bring more of a human science approach to psychology, to provide greater integration of the clinical and research wings of the division, and to relate its activities to emerging sociocultural developments, such as holistic health and ecology.

Another product of the 1960s is Division 34 (Population and Environmental Psychology). In chapter 5 James Richards shows how the field and division emerged not only from concerns about population growth and environmental degradation but other issues as well. If the concerns in Division 32 are for the human being as a whole, those of Division 34 are for the ecosystem as a functioning unit. A number of important events preceded the establishment of the division; these centered about the formation of the APA Task Force on Psychology, Family Planning, and Population Policy in 1969 and the conferences and workshops its members organized. Several important publications also appeared near the time of the formation of the division in 1973 and both influenced and were influenced by the division. A Task Force on the Environment and Behavior was formed the year after the division was organized. Division members have been prominent in these efforts to bring attention to issues of population and the environment.

As Antonio Puente and Ann Marcotte show in chapter 6 on Division 40 (Clinical Neuropsychology), the field has roots among clinical psychology, physiological psychology, the study of individual differences, and medicine. It encompasses the study and practice of brain–behavior relationships. Its antecedent organization was the International Neuropsychological Society, formed, like most such groups, from a meeting of like-minded psychologists. Puente and Marcotte review the many activities of the division and address some of the issues that have been focal. One major concern has been that of establishing standards for education and training in neuropsychology. As with other divisions, there has been concern over the definition of the field. The division has evolved with changing conditions. One interesting development is the formation of four advisory committees paralleling the directorates of the APA: science, education, practice, and public interest.

In chapter 7 Raymond Hanbury, Jalie Tucker, and Rudy Vuchinich provide a history of one of the newest APA divisions, Division 50 (Addictions). As substance abuse has become such a broad and high-profile problem around the world, it is appropriate that the APA has a division devoted to psychological issues related to addiction. The forerunner of this division was an organization with a name subject to misinterpretation, the Society of Psychologists in Substance Abuse, formed in 1975. Psychologists in the field were concentrated in Division 42 (Psychologists in Independent Practice) and worked through that division before the new division was formed. The division has strong ties to numerous other divisions as well. A *Policy Statement on Alcohol and Other Drug Abuse* was an important impetus in bringing APA focus on issues of addiction.

CONCLUSION

Reading these 41 chapters suggests a common pattern in which interest groups form and become progressively more organized until a petition is developed to coalesce into a new APA division. Another common theme is the impact of events outside of the division on its growth and development. It also becomes clear how closely intertwined are practice and research endeavors in many of the divisions. It is interesting to see how may divisions have struggled with their identities and definitions. As the divisions mature, one sees the changing of the guard in most divisions, as the older leaders become less active and are replaced by younger, able successors.

REFERENCES

Boring, E. G. (1967). Titchener's Experimentalists. *Journal of the History of the Behavioral Sciences, 3*, 315–325.

Dewsbury, D. A. (1996). *Unification through division: Histories of the divisions of the American Psychological Association* (Vol. I). Washington, DC: American Psychological Association.

Dewsbury, D. A. (1997). *Unification through division: Histories of the divisions of the American Psychological Association* (Vol. II). Washington, DC: American Psychological Association.

Dewsbury, D. A. (1998). *Unification through division: Histories of the divisions of the American Psychological Association* (Vol. III). Washington, DC: American Psychological Association.

Dewsbury, D. A. (1999). *Unification through division: Histories of the divisions of the American Psychological Association* (Vol. IV). Washington, DC: American Psychological Association.

Doll, E. A. (1946). The divisional structure of the APA. *American Psychologist, 1,* 336–345.

Evans, R. B., Sexton, V. S., & Cadwallader, T. C. (Eds.). (1992). *100 years of the American Psychological Association.* Washington, DC: American Psychological Association.

Hilgard, E. R. (1945a). Psychologists' preferences for divisions under the proposed APA by-laws. *Psychological Bulletin, 42,* 20–26.

Hilgard, E. R. (1945b). Temporary chairmen and secretaries for proposed APA divisions. *Psychological Bulletin, 42,* 294–296.

Recommendations of the Intersociety Constitutional Convention of Psychologists: IV. Sample blank for survey of opinion on the proposed by-laws. (1943). *Psychological Bulletin, 40,* 646–647.

1

A HISTORY OF DIVISION 19 (MILITARY PSYCHOLOGY)

PAUL A. GADE and ARTHUR J. DRUCKER

War and the preparation for war have been key ingredients in the growth and prosperity of American psychology and of the American Psychological Association (APA) in particular. The most rapid growth of early psychology occurred during World War I. Although the APA only had about 200 members at the start of the war, more than 400 psychologists participated in the World War I war effort (Capshew & Hilgard, 1992). World War II produced phenomenal growth in applied psychology and a reorganization of the APA that forever changed the face of psychology.

WAR AND REMEMBRANCE: MILITARY PSYCHOLOGY COMES OF AGE IN WORLD WAR I

World War I consumed psychology. For example, all but one of the papers at the 1918 APA annual meeting was on the war effort. Robert M.

The authors thank Kerry Gruber for her assistance in gathering much of the information we used from the Melton Library and the Library of Congress and for her help in corresponding with former division officers. The views, opinions, and findings contained in this article are solely those of the authors and should not be construed as an official Department of the Army or DoD position, policy, or decision, unless so designated by other official documentation.

Yerkes, who was the president of the APA when World War I started, was the driving force behind organizing psychology to apply its scientific principles to the war effort. In 1917, he received a commission as an Army major in the Sanitary Corps and a mandate to organize and direct psychological examining for the Army (Zeidner & Drucker, 1988). He led many prominent psychologists of the day in conceptualizing and executing the Army's successful recruit selection and classification testing program. During the war, nearly two million men were tested with either the Army Alpha or Beta tests developed by Yerkes and his colleagues (Zeidner & Drucker, 1988). Because of Yerkes's preeminence in establishing psychology as a vital contributor to the war effort, he is considered by many to be the father of military psychology (Cronin, 1998; McGuire, 1990; Zeidner & Drucker, 1988).

After World War I, applied psychology flourished as psychologists armed with their wartime experiences and successes moved into the civilian world. Testing was psychology's most significant accomplishment during the war, and as such it became the panacea for all ills, particularly for those within education. Psychology as an applied science had arrived.

Between World War I and World War II, the early enthusiasm within the APA for applied psychology faded with the field's inability to deal as effectively with the social issues of the Great Depression and the rise of fascism as it had with the war effort. The APA retreated to its prewar academic isolationism, once again affirming that the purpose of the APA was to foster the development of psychology as a science, in effect turning a deaf ear to the applied needs of clinical and consulting psychologists. Attempting to fill the void left by the APA's retreat into academia, psychologists established new applied psychology associations, such as the Society for the Psychological Study of Social Issues (SPSSI) and, more important for military psychology and Division 19, the American Association for Applied Psychology (AAAP). It was within the AAAP that Division 19, Military Psychology, was conceived. If the AAAP could be considered to be the mother of Division 19, its father would surely be World War II. For it was within the execution of psychology's participation in that war effort that the need for a separate group called military psychologists was recognized within the AAAP.

WORLD WAR II AND THE BIRTH OF DIVISION 19

As the world prepared for war in 1939, the National Research Council (NRC), Division of Anthropology and Psychology, voted to establish a committee on Public Service in the Event of War, later renamed the Committee on the Selection and Training of Military Personnel. The APA also organized an emergency committee on the war effort, as did the AAAP; however, it was the NRC that pulled together these disparate national committees into one united psychology effort—the Emergency Committee on Psychology.

As in World War I, Yerkes played a key role in American psychology's war effort, organizing a conference on long-range planning of psychology in early 1942. Participants were prominent psychologists and members of the APA and the AAAP. A major outcome was the Inter-Society Constitutional Convention (Capshaw & Hilgard, 1992). The convention produced a plan to reorganize the APA, permitting special interest groups such as the AAAP, the SPSSI, and the Psychometric Society to be represented. All five sections of the AAAP, including the newly formed Military Psychology Section, would become charter divisions within the APA. The new organization of the APA was realized in 1944 when both the APA and the AAAP members ratified the plan. The new APA began operation in September 1945 but did not technically get underway until 1946 with the election of new division officers (Olson, 1945).

THE AMERICAN ASSOCIATION FOR APPLIED PSYCHOLOGY: THE MOTHER OF DIVISION 19

The AAAP was founded in 1937–1938 as a national organization to promote applied psychology. It had grown out of a federation of several applied psychology organizations, such as the powerful New York-based Association of Consulting Psychologists (ACP). The ACP and other applied groups had come into existence as a result of the APA's failure to serve applied psychologists' needs for professional certification and educational opportunities. The ACP was the nucleus of the newly formed AAAP; its president, Douglas Fryer, served as the first president of the AAAP (Benjamin, 1997b).

The original four sections of the AAAP formed the new APA charter divisions of Clinical Psychology (12), Educational Psychology (15), Industrial and Business Psychology (14; now the Society of Industrial and Organizational Psychology), and the division of Consulting Psychology (13). The fifth section of the AAAP, the Military Section, was added in 1943 as Military Psychology, also one of the charter divisions (19) under the grandfathering agreement between the APA and the AAAP.

The petition to the board of governors of the AAAP to establish the military section was only three and one half lines long and merely asked the governors to establish a military psychology section without any rationale for doing so. Perhaps the petitioners felt that the large number of psychologists in uniform was reason enough. The signers of the petition were C. M.

Louttit, C. Gilbert Wrenn, Gwendolen Schneidler, Roger M. Bellows, Donald E. Baier, Marion W. Richardson, Mortin A. Seidenfeld, John G. Jenkins, and Charles C. Limburg (Louttit et al., 1943). The petition contains only signatures; no signer's name is typed or printed. The surname of "Charles C. Limburg" is unclear but presumed to be that of Charles C. Limburg who was a member of the APA after World War II (APA, 1957) and the same Charles Limburg who served at U.S. Air Force Headquarters after World War II (L. G. Humphries, personal communication, June 29, 1998).

The board of governors recommended that the AAAP approve the petition, and an amendment establishing the military section passed at the annual association meeting in September 1943. At the recommendation of the board of governors, the association appointed Maj. T. Willard Harrell chair of the newly formed section and Lt. Col. Gilbert Wrenn as the section secretary. Both were to serve one-year terms and were authorized to organize the military section. The association also appropriated $50 for the newly formed military section to use in carrying out its organizational work (Bryan, 1943). Neither individual completed his terms. Lieutenant Wrenn was called to duty outside the United States and Lt. Gwendolen Schneidler was appointed by the AAAP board of governors to complete Lieutenant Wrenn's term (Bryan, 1944a). A similar fate befell Major Harrell in May 1944, when he also was assigned overseas. The AAAP president, A. T. Poffenberger, appointed Maj. Paul M. Fitts to complete Major Harrell's term as chair (Bryan, 1944b).

The first meeting of the military section was held in Washington, DC, on November 18, 1943. It was already apparent at this meeting that the APA and the AAAP were likely to merge in a reconstituted APA. The members who attended the first military section meeting were Maj. Baier, Lt. Col. Robert Bernreuter, Capt. Fitts, Jr., Comdr. Charles Ford, Lt. Roy Hackman, Maj. Thomas Harrell, Lt. Comdr. J. Q. Holsopple, Lt. Comdr. John Jenkins, Comdr. C. M. Louttit, Lt. (JG), Mildred Mitchell, Lt. T. Earnest Newland, Lt. (JG), Charles Vaughn, and Lt. Col. Gilbert Wrenn. It appears that the primary accomplishment of this meeting was to establish the purpose of the military section, which according to the minutes of that meeting was "to encourage professional relationships among psychologists in the armed services, and to provide for the continued availability to the armed services of technical advances in psychology during and after the war period." (p. 1). Nonetheless, the initial membership of the military section was limited to AAAP members on active duty in the armed services and included about 100 psychologists (Wrenn, 1943).

To complete the mission of organizing the military section as laid out by the board of governors of the AAAP, two committees were formed. The Committee on Organization chaired by Maj. Roger M. Bellows was to revise and submit a set of bylaws for the military section and prepare for approval, should it become necessary, a set of bylaws for the military division of the reconstituted APA. The nominating committee, chaired by Lt. Col. L. Shaffer, was to nominate candidates and conduct the section's first election of officers, prior to the September 1944 annual meeting of the AAAP. The first elected chair of the military section was Cdr. C. M. Louttit, who had been president of the AAAP in 1943. Lt. Cdr. William A. Hunt was elected secretary of the section. Members-at-large to AAAP council elected were Comdr. John G. Jenkins, Lt. Comdr. Jack W. Dunlap, and Lt. Col. Marion Richardson. Elected to the board of editors were Lt. Comdr. Gilbert Wrenn, Lt. Comdr. E. Lowell Kelly, Lt. Hugh M. Bell, and Lt. Col. Arthur M. Melton.

As part of the APA reorganization, Chauncey M. "Mac" Louttit automatically became the temporary chair of the charter division of military psychology. Louttit had been a prominent figure in the clinical section of the AAAP, had been president of the AAAP in 1943, and was then the chair of its military section at the time the AAAP was absorbed into the new APA structure. Louttit had been the first Navy psychologist to come on active duty during the buildup prior to World War II (McGuire, 1990). At the time of his appointment as temporary Division 19 chair, Louttit was serving as the commanding officer of the Service School, Naval Training Center, Bainbridge, Maryland.

As shown in Table 1, John G. Jenkins was the first Division 19 chair (the office that was to become "president") elected under the new APA division structure. In 1952 the title of the position changed to president during Frank Geldard's tenure (Bray, 1952). Jenkins and his successors, Melton and Geldard, served two-year terms until the 1952 bylaws changes established the office of president-elect. During World War II, Jenkins had served in the Navy as the director of the Medical Section of the Bureau of Aeronautics, leaving the service as a captain at the end of the war to return to the University of Maryland (McGuire, 1990). During the time that Jenkins served as the Division 19 chair, he, along with Walter Bingham and Dael Wolfle, was responsible for incorporating the American Board of Examiners in Professional Psychology (ABEPP) as an entity related to, but separate from, the APA. Jenkins had also chaired the influential NRC Committee on the Selection and Training of Military Personnel as it prepared for World War II in 1939.

Alterations to the bylaws between 1946 and 1952 produced other significant changes in the division. The first was a change in the stated purposes of the division. The primary purpose of the division was now stated to be "to encourage professional relationships among psychologists interested in the application of psychological knowledge and techniques to military problems" ("The Military Division," 1946–50). This subtle but important change opened membership to those who were interested in military issues but who were not necessarily in the military. The secondary purpose, "to

TABLE 1
Past Presidents of Division 19

Years	Presidents	Years	Presidents
1946–1948[a]	John G. Jenkins	1975–1976	Arthur J. Drucker
1948–1950[a]	Arthur W. Melton	1976–1977	Earl I. Jones
1950–1952[a]	Frank A. Geldard	1977–1978	Paul D. Nelson
1952–1953	Paul M. Fitts	1978–1979	Elaine N. Taylor
1953–1954	Jack W. Dunlap	1979–1980	Robert R. Mackie
1954–1955	Philip H. Dubois	1980–1981	E. Ralph Dusek
1955–1956	Robert L. Thorndike	1981–1982	James K. Arima
1956–1957	Charles W. Bray	1982–1983	Robert Nichols
1957–1958	Lloyd G. Humphreys	1983–1984	A. David Mangelsdorff
1958–1959	George K. Bennett	1984–1985	Martin F. Wiskoff
1959–1960	Franklin V. Taylor	1985–1986	Randall M. Chambers
1960–1961	Robert M. Gagné	1986–1987	Joyce L. Shields
1961–1962	John C. Flanagan	1987–1988	Francis J. Fishburne
1962–1963	Walter Grether	1988–1989	Timothy B. Jeffrey
1963–1964	John T. Dailey	1989–1990	W. Steven Sellman
1964–1965	Meredith Crawford	1990–1991	Jared B. Jobe
1965–1966	Richard Trumbull	1991–1992	Richard W. Bloom
1966–1967	Philip Sperling	1992–1993	Brian K. Waters
1967–1968	William McClelland	1993–1994	Paul A. Gade
1968–1969	Launor Carter	1994–1995	Stephen L. Goldberg
1969–1970	J. E. Uhlaner	1995–1996	Gerald P. Krueger
1970–1971	Saul B. Sells	1996–1997	Russell J. Hibler
1971–1972	Gordon A. Eckstrand	1997–1998	Deirdre J. Knapp
1972–1973	Julien M. Christensen	1998–1999	James E. Griffith
1973–1974	Howard A. McFann	1999–2000	Janice Laurence
1974–1975	Earl A. Alluisi		

[a] Each of the first three division chairs served a two-year term. Changes to the bylaws in 1952 replaced the title "chairman" with "president" and divided presidential service into three one-year terms for president-elect, president, and past-president.

provide for the continued availability to the armed services of technical advances in psychology following the war period" (Bray, 1952) was similar to that of the initial division bylaws, merely dropping the word "during" when referring to the war effort. The second significant change to the bylaws in 1952 established three classes of members: fellows, associates, and life members.

DIVISION SIZE AND MEMBERSHIP

According to Dewsbury (1997), membership is the most common issue among all divisions—and Division 19 is no exception. Since the beginning, the leadership has been concerned with recruiting new members to sustain the division. As Figure 1 shows, the size of Division 19 has always been smaller than the mean size of APA divisions overall. Until recently, Division

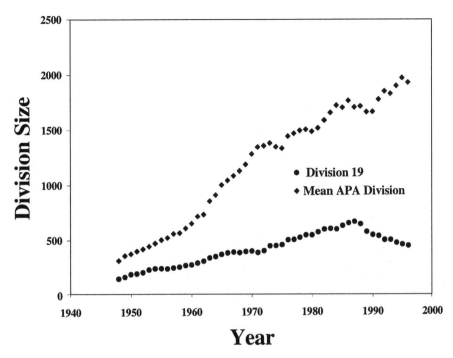

Figure 1. Size of Division 19 Compared to APA Mean Division Membership Size by Year.

19 has shown a growth pattern similar to the division average. The 1990s down trend is most likely a result of the accelerated downsizing of the military services. This downsizing decreased the numbers not only of uniformed clinical and research psychologists but also at agencies that employ civilian research psychologists and sponsor research that employs contract psychologists as well. For example, the U.S. Army Research Institute for the Behavioral and Social Sciences was cut in budget and personnel for behavioral research by about 50% in September 1997. The Navy Personnel Research and Development Center, the Navy's primary laboratory for personnel and training research, suffered a similar fate along with the Air Force's Armstrong Human Resources Laboratory. A loss of membership was to be expected with such deep cuts in the Department of Defense (DoD) sponsorship of military psychology. The American Psychological Society (APS) has also taken its toll on Division 19 members. More than a few military researchers opted to leave the APA because of high dues and the current APA ban on advertising by any DoD agency (see the discussion under "Gay Men and Lesbians in the Military").

This decline led to a diminishing voice of Division 19 within the APA. This decrease of Division 19's input within the APA began in 1971 when the division lost one of its two seats on the APA Council of

Representatives. Moreover, in the past 10 years, the division lost its remaining seat and vote on the Council in 1992 and 1993 as a result of apportionment balloting. As a result, in 1974 and again in 1993, Division 19's leadership seriously considered merging with Division 21 (Applied Experimental and Engineering Psychology), which has suffered a similar decline in membership. On both occasions, Division 19 leadership determined that such a merger was premature, difficult, and not in the best interest of the division membership.

The division has managed to keep its head above water since 1994, retaining its seat on the Council through a concerted annual effort to have as many members as possible cast all their apportionment votes for Division 19. A recent change in the APA bylaws that provides every division, regardless of size, with a minimum of one seat on the Council, has assured Division 19 that it will have at least a small voice within the APA.

An aging membership appears to be the next serious challenge to the continuation of the division. Division 19 may yet be forced to merge with another small division with overlapping interests, such as Division 21, to maintain a critical mass of members.

THE APA IN CONFLICT WITH MILITARY PSYCHOLOGY

Through the years there have been several conflicts between the APA and Division 19. Perhaps the most serious threat to the division came during the Vietnam War. In 1969 Division 8 (Society for Personality and Social Psychology) proposed a resolution to the APA Council to study whether the existence within the APA of a division of military psychology was consistent with the APA's commitment to advancing psychology as a means of promoting human welfare (APA, 1969). There is no record of any discussion or voting on the resolution in the Council. However, the fact that the issue was even raised was disturbing to the members and leaders of Division 19. In response, Division 19 president J. E. Uhlaner established a special division committee on the Role of Military Psychology in a Transitioning American Society to study the issues surrounding the attack on Division 19 at the 1969 meeting and to recommend appropriate division action. The committee recommended that a letter be sent to the APA Council urging that each of the "professional"—in other words, applied—divisions within the APA conduct a self-study to assess the impact of a transitional society on their "professional aspects." The committee also developed and cosponsored with Divisions 8 (Society for Personality and Social Psychology) and 14 (Society for Industrial and Organizational Psychology) a symposium titled, "Psycho-technology and Its Impact on Psychology" for the 1970 APA convention (APA, 1970; Nadel, 1971).

The issue of the appropriateness of a military psychology division within the APA smoldered for several years after this, appearing in various discussions of new ethical standards being developed by the APA with inputs from the divisions. Much of this consternation about the appropriateness of a military psychology division, no doubt, was a result of the zeitgeist of the unpopular Vietnam War. Eventually the war ended and so too the controversy over the existence of Division 19. Support for the hypothesis that involvement in an unpopular war may have been the basis for attempts to eliminate Division 19 was seen in the APA's reaction to the military and military psychology during the much more popular Persian Gulf War in 1991. Here the APA formed a task force under the direction of APA president Charles Spielberger to help military service members deal with wartime issues and especially the aftermath of the war (DeAngelis, 1991a, 1991b, 1991c, & 1991d). Furthermore, the APA, the Council of Representatives, and President Spielberger formally acknowledged the contributions of uniformed military psychologists to the Gulf War in a ceremony at the 1991 APA annual meeting (APA, 1991b). It is interesting to note that apparently Division 19 was never asked to participate in organizing or running the task force.

The DoD Psychopharmacology Demonstration Project

Patrick DeLeon, whom many consider to be the father of prescription privileges for psychologists, is an active fellow of Division 19. DeLeon, in his role as an assistant to Sen. Daniel Inouye, was instrumental in implementing the DoD Psychopharmacology Demonstration Project. The project was designed to train a few uniformed clinical psychologists to prescribe and use psychotropic drugs in therapy and to demonstrate that they could do so to the satisfaction of the medical community (Levant & Abeles, 1997). In addition to DeLeon, Greg Laskow and several other Division 19 members also made significant contributions to the success of the demonstration project.

Gay Men and Lesbians in the Military

Another controversy that has put Division 19 in a difficult position within the APA and the Council of Representatives is the issue surrounding the U.S. Military's ban against openly homosexual individuals enlisting and serving in the military services. Initially the Committee on Lesbian and Gay Concerns (CLGC) argued that the DoD policy on gay men and lesbians was in violation of the APA's policy of nondiscrimination and that DoD agencies should be banned from using the APA convention and APA publications to advertise for job openings and internships. The CLGC reasoned that the DoD was not an equal opportunity employer because there was no job-related justification for the military's discrimination against gay men and lesbians. At the suggestion of CLGC and the Society for the Psychological Study of Lesbian, Gay, and Bisexual Issues (Division 44), beginning in 1992, the Council of Representatives banned the military services from advertising jobs and conducting job placement interviews at the annual convention. They also set in motion a mechanism to impose a similar ban on advertising in the APA Monitor if the DoD restrictions on gay men and lesbians serving in the military were not lifted by December 1992 (APA, 1991a). In a special mail-out vote, a majority of Division 19 members said they supported lifting the DoD prohibition on gay men and lesbians serving in the military; however, the Division 19 leadership opposed the advertising ban from the beginning (Jobe, 1991). Despite Division 19 objections, and those of others within the APA leadership, on August 18, 1991, the Council voted overwhelmingly for the advertising ban; it went into effect in January 1993 (McCarthy, 1991).

Since the "don't ask, don't tell" policy was signed into law by President Bill Clinton in 1993, the division leadership has worked diligently, but thus far unsuccessfully, to have the advertising ban removed. In the fall of 1993, Division 19 president Paul Gade met with the CLGC in an attempt to open a dialogue on the issue. Gade argued that "don't ask, don't tell" was now the law of the land, passed by Congress and signed by the president, thus no longer merely a DoD policy (Gade, 1993). The members of CLGC, although sympathetic, were not moved to support Division 19's efforts to remove the ban on DoD advertising.

The CLGC asked Division 19 to "give us something" in return for their support for, or at least nonobjection to, the APA's removing the advertising ban (Gade, 1993). When asked to clarify what they meant, CLGC members said that it was up to the military psychologists to suggest something. The administration of Division 19 attempted to satisfy this demand by first conducting a preconvention workshop on gay men and lesbians in the military with Division 44 at the 1994 APA meeting. The Division 19 organizers of the workshop jointly published, with the Division 44 participants, a book based on that workshop (Herek, Jobe, & Carney, 1996). Finally, Division 19 conducted a series of discussions with representatives from Division 44 and the CLGC at the APA annual meetings and by telephone. These meetings ended in 1995 at the APA meeting in New York when an impasse was reached in the discussions, and the ban on DoD advertising still remains in effect. The inability of Division 19 leaders to successfully end the advertising ban remains a sore point with many Division 19 members and even resulted in the resignations of several members from the division and from the APA.

RELATIONSHIPS WITH OTHER APA DIVISIONS
AND PROFESSIONAL ORGANIZATIONS

Division 19 and Division 14 (Society for Industrial and Organizational Psychology) have traditionally shared a close relationship, especially in the earlier years when they shared presidents. These presidents include John G. Jenkins, George K. Bennett, and Jack W. Dunlap (Benjamin, 1997a). Dual membership in both divisions is less evident now, and it is rare for a president of one division to have been the president of another division as well. However, Divisions 14 and 19 continue to cosponsor symposia at almost every annual convention.

Seven presidents of Division 21 (Applied Experimental and Engineering Psychology), particularly early presidents, also served as presidents of Division 19—Paul M. Fitts, Franklin Taylor, Walter Grether, Julian Christensen, Arthur W. Melton, Earl A. Alluisi, and E. Ralph Dusek. Divisions 19 and 21 have become closer during recent years and, as mentioned earlier, on occasion have considered merging to maintain a critical mass within the APA Council, as memberships in both divisions have shrunk. In the years in which Division 19 lost its lone seat on the Council, Division 21 agreed to represent Division 19's interests. When Division 21 lost its lone seat on Council, Division 19 returned the favor. At the annual APA conventions, Divisions 19 and 21 have cosponsored many paper sessions and symposia and frequently have held joint social hours as well. More recently, Divisions 19 and 21 have been cosponsors, along with the Potomac Chapter of the Human Factors and Ergonomic Society, of an annual spring science symposium held in Washington, DC.

Division 19 has maintained a liaison with Division 35 (Psychology of Women) initiated during Division 35's inception. The Women and Minorities Committee of Division 19 has been the primary source for maintaining the relationship between the two divisions.

Relationships between Division 19 and Division 44 (Society for the Psychological Study of Lesbian, Gay, and Bisexual Issues) and the CLGC have been, at best, tenuous. As early as 1989, the two divisions were exploring common interests—or perhaps common difficulties is a more appropriate description. Divisions 19 and 44 jointly sponsored a symposium at the 1989 APA annual convention titled "Should Lesbians and Gays Be Given Security Clearances by the U.S. Government?" The symposium, chaired by Dick Bloom of Division 19, was actually a debate between Greg Herek, representing the pro side of the question, and Theodore Blau, former APA president, representing the con (R. W. Bloom, personal communication, July 22, 1998; Division 19, 1989). Although the two divisions and CLGC seemed to draw together more closely when they attempted to seek an amicable solution to the DoD advertising ban, even then the relationship was an uneasy one.

Formal collaboration between Divisions 19 and 48 (Society for the Study of Peace, Conflict, & Violence) seems to have begun when the president-elect of Division 19, Dick Bloom, was invited to be the discussant at a Division 48 discussion hour at the 1990 APA convention (R. W. Bloom, personal communication, July 22, 1998). Subsequent to this initial outreach, at a jointly sponsored symposium during the 1994 APA annual meeting, members of both Divisions 19 and 48 seemed pleasantly surprised to find a common interest and a common ground in peace operations. This initial symposium led to additional and productive joint symposia on peace-keeping at the 1995 and 1996 annual meetings.

Perhaps this is a more natural relationship than one might think, paralleled, for example, in the American Sociological Association, where military and peace interests are represented in one interest group: War and Peace.

Division 19 has had a long working relationship and maintains a formal liaison with the Inter-University Seminar on Armed Forces and Society (IUS). Several Division 19 members are also fellows in the IUS. Paul Nelson served on the editorial board of *Armed Forces & Society*, the IUS quarterly journal. H. Wallace "Wally" Sinaiko and Paul Gade served on the IUS Advisory Council and were regional coordinators for the Washington, DC, area in the late 1980s and early 1990s. The primary function of the regional coordinator was to arrange four or five meetings per year at which guest speakers addressed topics relevant to armed forces and society. Jointly sponsored Division 19 and IUS paper sessions have been held at several APA annual conventions (R. Nichols personal communication, July 4, 1998).

PUBLICATIONS

Although Division 19 has had several newsletters, the first recorded newsletter found on file at the APA headquarters was dated March 1971. The editor of that newsletter was J. Daniel Lyons. The newsletter grew; a banner heading and a logo were added to the fall 1979 issue as the newsletter began to take on the formal, professional appearance it has today. As an interesting aside, the official division logo, used on the newsletter and other official publications and documents, was selected from three candidate logos presented with a call for member votes in the fall 1978 issue of the newsletter (Taylor, 1978). The response was anything but overwhelming. Only 24 members voted, and only 11 voted for the winning candidate.

Today's newsletter, *The Military Psychologist*, was established as the official Division 19 newsletter in 1984. The first editors were Jared B. Jobe,

John E. Morrison, and Stephen L. Goldberg. Jobe and Goldberg each became president of the division subsequent to their service as newsletter editors.

One of the great success stories of Division 19 has been its refereed journal publication, *Military Psychology*. Although the journal had a difficult birth, it is alive and well today, producing a profit for the division every year. Attempts to start a journal date back to the early 1980s. In 1984 the division attempted to publish the journal as a subsection of the *Journal of Applied Social Psychology*, but that effort failed after one issue because there were not enough manuscripts (Division 19, Spring 1984, Spring 1986). The journal was revived in 1986 with Martin "Marty" Wiskoff as the founding editor (Division 19, Fall/Winter 1986). After the APA approved the division's publication plans, an agreement to publish *Military Psychology* was signed with Lawrence Erlbaum Associates in 1987, and the first issue was published in 1989. Under the able stewardship of its founding editor, Marty Wiskoff, *Military Psychology* has flourished. The journal has become a respected publication that has very successfully filled its niche as an outlet for high-quality, applied military psychology research. In addition, *Military Psychology* has become a much-needed source of revenue for Division 19. Recently, the journal conducted an outreach program to gather articles from the clinical constituency of the division, and the editorial board plans to feature clinical articles as a regular part of the journal.

AWARDS

Five awards have been established as official Division 19 awards: the Presidential Award, The Lifetime Achievement Award, the Military Psychology Award, the Early Career Achievement Award, and the Yerkes Award.

The Presidential Award is presented to the outgoing president for service to the division following his or her presidential address at the annual convention. It is not clear from historical records when this award and tradition was established, but it is known to have been in effect for at least two decades.

Although lifetime service or long-term contributions to military psychology and Division 19 had been recognized as early as 1979 when a posthumous award was made to William A. McClelland, the Lifetime Achievement Award was not officially established in the division until 1994. This award was instituted by the division to honor, on an as-needed basis, the exceptional contributions of military psychologists during a career in military psychology. The first three recipients were John C. Flanagan (1994); Julius E. Uhlaner (1995); John Kobrick (1997); Capt. Larry W. Bailey, U.S.

Navy Reserve (1998); and John D. Meisz, U.S. Army Human Engineering Laboratory (1999).

The Military Psychology Award was established in 1974 to recognize outstanding contributions of mid-career military psychologists in research, practice, or in other activities that advance the field of military psychology. The award is presented as needed and can be presented to an individual or group of individuals. More than one award can be made in any year. The first award was not conferred until 1975. Past recipients of the Military Psychology Award are given in Table 2.

The Robert M. Yerkes Award was instituted by the division to honor nonpsychologists who made outstanding contributions to military psychology. Although an award similar to this was given as a special Division 19 award in 1986 to Sen. Daniel K. Inouye, the award was not officially established and named until 1987. Recipients have been the Hon. Craig Alder-

TABLE 2
Military Psychology Award Recipients

Years	Recipients
1975	Robert Levit, David Alden, Jean Erickson, and Berton Beaton, Honeywell Corporation
1976	Meredith P. Crawford and the Human Resources Research Organization
1978	Jesse Orlansky, Institute for Defense Analyses
1978	John P. Foley, John J. K. Klesch, Robert C. Johnson, and Donald L. Thomas, U.S. Air Force Human Resources Laboratory
1978	J. Patrick Ford, Roy C. Campbell, James H. Harris, William C. Osborn, and Charlotte H. Campbell, Western Division of the Human Resources Research Organization
1979	Cecil B. Harris, Lieutenant Colonel, Medical Service Corps, U.S. Army
1979	Fred E. Fielder, Professor of Psychology, University of Washington
1979	Laurie Broedling, Linda Doherty, Delbert Nebeker, and Robert Penn, Navy Personnel Research and Development Center
1980	Robert S. Nichols, Colonel, Medical Service Corps, U.S. Army
1982	A. David Mangelsdorff, Academy of Health Sciences, U.S. Army
1985	Frank Rath, Lieutenant Colonel, Medical Service Corps, U.S. Army; and Alvin Wootin, Lieutenant Colonel, Medical Service, U.S. Air Force
1987	Timothy B. Jeffrey, Lieutenant Colonel, Medical Service Corps, U.S. Army
1989	Martin F. Wiskoff, Defense Personnel Security Research and Education Center
1989	Patrick DeLeon, Legislative Assistant to Sen. Daniel Inouye
1990	Newell Kent Eaton, U.S. Army Research Institute for the Behavioral and Social Sciences
1996	Gregory Laskow, Lieutenant Colonel, Medical Service Corps, U.S. Army
1997	Ricky L. Campise, Major, U.S. Air Force, Malcom Grow Medical Center
1998	Larry James, Lieutenant Colonel, U.S. Army
1999	James R. McBride and Brian K. Waters, Human Resources Research Organization; and W. A. Sands, Navy Personnel Research and Development Center

man, Deputy Under Secretary for Defense (1987); Gen. Maxwell R. Thurman, Vice Chief of Staff, U.S. Army (1988); Irving M. Greenberg, Logistics Management Institute (1991); Manny Radomski, Canadian Defense and Civilian Institute of Environmental Medicine (1996); Sen. Daniel K. Inouye, United States Senate (1997); Elizabeth Dole, American Red Cross (1998); and Frances Grafton, U.S. Army Research Institute (1999).

In 1998, the division established the Early Career Achievement Award to recognize outstanding pyschologists with five or fewer years of experience in military psychology. The first Early Career Achievement Award was presented to Winston Bennett, Jr., U.S. Air Force, in 1999.

PRESIDENTIAL ADDRESSES

According to division folklore, the presidential address by the outgoing president is a tradition that dates back to the beginning. The earliest recorded presidential address was "Dimensions of Simulation" by Meredith Crawford at the annual meeting in Chicago in September 1965 (Crawford, 1966). This address and several others were subsequently published in refereed journals (Gagné, 1962; Manglesdorff, 1985; Uhlaner, 1972).

PRECONVENTION WORKSHOPS

From 1983 to 1994 preconvention workshops became a convention tradition, usually held on the Thursday before a Friday convention start date from 10:00 a.m. to 5:00 p.m. Initially the workshops were run by the Selection and Training Committee, renamed the Education Committee in 1989. Beginning around 1992, the workshops were generally run by whoever had a good idea for the workshop and was willing to devote the time and effort to do the job.

Edward Eddows conducted the first recorded preconvention workshop in 1983 on the topic "Computerized Adaptive Testing." The workshop was free to anyone wishing to attend. The next preconvention workshop was run by Brian Waters in 1985 in Los Angeles on "The Use of Computers in Military Personnel Assessment"—the last free preconvention workshop the division would hold. In 1986, Waters again ran the preconvention workshop, this year titled, "Applications of Artificial Intelligence." Participants were charged a $25 fee. In 1987 and 1988, Richard Bloom conducted very successful back-to-back workshops on "Psychology and National Security Affairs." The fee for this and all workshops thereafter was $50. Both workshops were well-attended. Christine Jaggi's workshop before the 1990 convention in Boston was on "Women in the Military." The 1991 preconvention workshop topic for that year was appropriately "The Role of Psychology in Operation Desert Storm and Its Aftermath," developed by Deirdre Knapp. Before the 1992 convention, Paul Gade's well-attended workshop on the "History of Military Psychology," in Washington, DC, netted the division revenue of $500.

In 1993, Jim Griffith conducted a preconvention workshop on "Sexual Harassment in the Military." In view of the scandals revolving around issues of sexual harassment in the late 1990s, Griffith seems to have been prescient in choosing this topic. This was the first Division 19 preconvention workshop to offer continuing education credits to participants.

The 1994 preconvention workshop, titled "Gays and Lesbians in the Military: Psychological Perspectives on Implementing the New Policy on Gays and Lesbians in the Military," was cosponsored by Division 44 (Society for the Psychological Study of Lesbian, Gay, and Bisexual Issues) and Division 19 and, like the workshop the preceding year, offered participants continuing education credits. The workshop was run by Jared Jobe and Ralph Carney of Division 19 and by Greg Herek of Division 44. Although the workshop was not well-attended by members of either division, the papers presented were excellent and were published as a book (Herek et al., 1996).

The series ended in 1995 when Carney led a workshop on "HIV Positives in the Military." Because this workshop was also not well-attended, a dwindling interest in division-sponsored preconvention workshops was presumed and no workshops have been held since.

In the spring of 1996, Division 19 cosponsored, along with Division 21 (Applied Experimental and Engineering Psychology) and the Potomac Chapter of the Human Factors and Ergonomics Society, a mid-year science symposium, jointly sponsoring the event again in 1997 and 1998. It appears that this joint annual symposium has, for the time being, supplanted the preconvention workshop as the division's primary educational activity.

CONVENTION PROGRAMS

Convention programs in the years immediately following World War II were largely consumed with reporting the results of research programs that had been conducted during the war or shortly thereafter. Aviation psychology programs in both the Army and the Navy were major contributors (APA, 1946). As the division moved away from the war, the subject matter of the annual convention program broadened to include topics of human engineering, aptitude measurement, job analysis, psychomotor performance, leadership and morale, and performance or "criterion" measurement. However, the presence and influence of aviation issues was still apparent in the work that was reported in the 1950s and 1960s. For example, much of the human engineering work reported on issues concerning cockpit and instrument design (APA, 1951).

In the early 1970s, the convention program still contained papers on military ergonomics, but more social psychological issues were beginning to emerge as well. For example, the 1973 program contained paper sessions on race relations in the Army, psychosocial research on drug abuse in the Army, counseling and personality, organizational analysis, and attitude and survey research in the military (Prather, 1973). Although issues of organizational development or effectiveness and race relations seem to have been particularly salient during the early 1970s, traditional issues concerning selection and classification testing, leadership and motivation, and pilot training continued to be included in convention programs. In the mid- to late 1970s, computerized adaptive testing emerged as a new subject in the convention programs, as did new training issues such as embedded training. Race relations and social psychological issues were still strongly represented, as exemplified by an invited address at the 1975 annual meeting on "the military in evolving society" by the noted military sociologist Morris Janowitz (Division 19, 1975).

A structural shift in the type of convention presentations took place in the early 1970s. Before 1973, paper sessions were the usual form for presentation at the annual APA meetings. Beginning in 1973, the symposium—organized around a specific, integrated theme—became the dominant form of Division 19 convention presentation by a margin of about two to one. Although this shift seems to have been unplanned, it seems likely that it occurred because of difficulties encountered by those developing the convention programs in forming paper sessions that had a common theme. This move to the symposium as the dominant convention format persists today and seems to have been reinforced by the advent of the poster-session format, first used by the division at the 1985 convention, because this format permits papers on a variety of topics to be presented in a single session.

In the 1980s convention programs reflected concerns with military recruiting, selection and classification of recruits, and soldier retention. However, measuring military performance was the most dominant theme of convention symposia and paper sessions of the 1980s. For example, 11 of the 28 symposia and 6 of the 13 paper sessions in for the annual meetings between 1983 to 1985 were devoted to performance-measurement issues (Division 19, 1983; 1984, Summer; 1985). Many of Division 19 convention papers and symposia during the later 1980s were based on the emerging findings from the Army's large selection research project, "Project A." Computerized testing, especially adaptive testing, was a frequent theme in symposia and paper sessions, and sessions on artificial intelligence and expert systems emerged during the 1980s as well. Clinical issues during the 1980s increasingly focused on mental health issues in the military and on issues of assessing and maintaining the well-being of soldiers. As a harbinger of things to come in the 1990s, one of the highlights of the 1989 convention was a lively debate session on whether gay men and lesbians should be given security clearances, as discussed earlier in the chapter (Division 19, Summer, 1989).

Convention programs in the 1990s seem to have been dominated by issues and research about women performing in nontraditional military occupations (especially combat), sexual harassment, gay men and lesbians serving at all, the Gulf War, and by the issues surrounding military downsizing and new military roles in peace-keeping and disaster relief. For example, joint symposia on peace-keeping issues and research were held with Division 48 (Society for the Study of Peace, Conflict, & Violence) at the 1994, 1995, and 1996 conventions (Carney, 1996; Division 19, 1994; 1995). A joint symposium with Division 44 (Society for the Psychological Study of Lesbian, Gay, & Bisexual Issues) on sexual orientation and U.S. military policy resulted in some lively discussions among the members of the audience and the participants at the 1994 convention (Knapp, Summer 1994). At the 1998 convention, a discussion session on gender integration in the armed forces provided a historical perspective and a focus on issues surrounding the military service of women (Division 19, 1998).

History and historical perspectives also played a major role in the conventions of the 1990s, beginning with the 1990 convention at which the contributions of military psychology to the history of psychology were discussed in relation to the 100th anniversary celebration of the APA (Georgoulakis, Fiducia, Williams, & Harris, 1992). Because Division 19 is one of the original APA divisions, division history presentations played a small but important role in the convention presentations of 1996 and 1997 in celebration of the 50th anniversary of the APA divisions (Carney, 1996; Division 19, 1997).

From the clinical perspective, the highlight of the 1990s conventions centered on the psychopharmacology demonstration project. A symposium was held at the 1995 convention at the demonstration project's initiation (Division 19, 1995). A subsequent miniconvention on prescription privileges for psychologists at the 1997 convention, sponsored by Division 19, discussed issues in extending the prescription privileges in the military demonstration project to other trained psychologists (Levant & Abeles, 1997).

CONCLUSION

As one of the original APA divisions, Division 19 has had a long but sometimes uneasy relationship within the APA. Table 3 summarizes some

TABLE 3
Significant Events in the History of Division 19

Years	Events
1945	Division 19 founded; grandfathered as one of the five AAAP sections. John G. Jenkins elected first president (chair).
1952	Bylaws changed. Members no longer need to be in the military. Title of chair changed to president and presidential service divided into three one-year terms of president-elect, president, and past president.
1969	Division 8 challenges Council to decide whether the existence of a division of military psychology is consistent with APA philosophy of promoting human welfare.
1971	First recorded newsletter is published; J. Daniel Lyons, first editor.
1974	Military Psychology Award established.
1977	Elaine N. Taylor elected as first female president (1978–1979).
1978	Division logo established, first appears on the masthead of the newsletter in the spring 1979 issue.
1984	Newsletter, *The Military Psychologist,* officially established; Jared B. Jobe, John E. Morrison, and Stephen L. Goldberg first editors.
1986	Division journal *Military Psychology* established; Martin Wiskoff founding editor.
1987	Robert M. Yerkes Award established. The Hon. Craig Alderman, Deputy Under Secretary for Defense, is first recipient.
1989	First quarterly issue of *Military Psychology* is published.
1993	APA ban on DoD advertising implemented.
1994	Joint Workshop on Gays in the Military with Division 44; results in a book, *Out in Force: Sexual Orientation and the Military,* published in 1996 by the University of Chicago Press.
1994	Lifetime Achievement Award established; John C. Flanagan, first recipient.
1995	DoD Psychopharmacology Demonstration project implemented.
1996	Division receives its first revenues from *Military Psychology.*
1998	Early Career Achievement Award established; Winston Bennett, Jr., first recipient in 1999

of the most salient events in the history of the division. If it were not for the fact that so many psychologists were consumed by the war effort during World War II, it seems doubtful that the Division of Military Psychology would have been conceived, let alone born within the AAAP. Furthermore, had it not been one of the grandfathered divisions from the AAAP, it seems improbable that the APA would have invented it.

The Cold War employment of psychologists helped the division sustain its strength after World War II and the Korean War. Even so, the APA was more than a little uneasy with the ethics of having a division of military psychology during the unpopular Vietnam War.

Today, the division's life is threatened by severe post-Cold War military downsizing. And yet the division not only survives but in many ways flourishes. The military's leadership in running peace-keeping operations has made the military and the psychologists who work for the military perhaps more relevant and more in harmony with APA ethics than they have been since the end of World War II. It has also opened up new potential alliances with organizations such as Division 48 (Society for the Study of Peace, Conflict, & Violence). In addition, the division journal, *Military Psychology*, is providing a useful function in the applied and academic worlds. The DoD psychopharmacology project has paved the way for a new era of clinical practice. However, the division once again finds itself at odds with the APA over the issue of the APA's ban on DoD advertising.

It seems that controversy and contradiction are destined to follow Division 19 for as long as it exists. The paradox continues; for in an APA-wide era of conflict between clinical and academic, research-oriented psychology, Division 19 finds itself with approximately equal numbers of clinical and applied research psychologists. The division's clinical and research psychologists get along well—and in fact they support one another.

Division 19 came into existence because it had relevance for so many psychologists in the war effort. Perhaps the division will continue to endure, if for no other reason than because it has relevance for research and clinical psychologists who must address the political and social issues of the post-Cold War era.

REFERENCES

American Psychological Association. (1946). Division of Military Psychology. *The American Psychologist, 1*, 292–294.

American Psychological Association. (1951). Program arranged by the Division of Military Psychology. *The American Psychologist, 5*, 386–394.

American Psychological Association. (1957). *The 1957 directory of the American Psychological Association.* Washington, DC: Author.

American Psychological Association. (1969, August 29–30). *Resolution submitted to APA council by Herbert C. Kelman (representative of Division 8): On assessing the implications of psychological activities for human welfare.* Annual report of the Board of Governors, section V, heading A (Available from the Arthur Melton Library of the American Psychological Association, Washington, DC).

American Psychological Association. (1970, September 3–8). 78th annual convention program, American Psychological Association, Miami Beach, Florida, p. 69 (Available from the Arthur Melton Library of the American Psychological Association, Washington, DC).

American Psychological Association. (1991a, June 21–23). *Resolution on the U.S. Department of Defense policy on sexual orientation and advertising in APA publications.* Board of Directors Minutes, pp. 16–17 (Available from the Arthur Melton Library of the American Psychological Association, Washington, DC).

American Psychological Association. (1991b, October). Psychologists honored by APA for their services in the war in the Persian Gulf. *The APA Monitor, 22,* 9.

Benjamin, L. T., Jr. (1997a). A history of Division 14 (The Society for Industrial and Organizational Psychology). In D. A. Dewsbury (Ed.), *Unification through division: Histories of the divisions of the American Psychological Association* (Vol. II, pp. 101–126). Washington, DC: American Psychological Association.

Benjamin, L. T., Jr. (1997b). The origin of the species: History of the beginnings of American Psychological Association divisions. *American Psychologist, 52,* 725–732.

Bray, C. (1952, September 2). American Psychological Association, Division of Military Psychology, Minutes of the annual business meeting (Box 599, Manuscript Division, U.S. Library of Congress, Madison Building, Washington, DC).

Bryan, A. I. (1943, October 10). Letter from Alice I. Bryan, Executive Secretary, AAAP, to Major T. Willard Harlem (Box 696, Manuscript Division, U.S. Library of Congress, Madison Building, Washington, DC).

Bryan, A. I. (1944a, March 3). Letter from Alice I. Bryan, Executive Secretary, AAAP, to Lieutenant Gwendolen G. Schneidler. (Box 696, Manuscript Division, U.S. Library of Congress, Madison Building, Washington, DC).

Bryan, A. I. (1944b, May 20). Letter from Alice I. Bryan, Executive Secretary, AAAP, to Major Paul Fitts (Box 696, Manuscript Division, U.S. Library of Congress, Madison Building, Washington, DC.).

Capshew, J. H., & Hilgard, E. R. (1992). The power of service: World War II and professional reform in the American Psychological Association. In R. W. Evans, V. S. Sexton, & T. C. Cadwallader (Eds.), *The American Psychological Association: A historical perspective* (pp. 149–175). Washington, DC: American Psychological Association.

Carney, R. (1996, Summer). 1996 APA convention activities: Division 19. *The Military Psychologist, 12,* 12–17 (Available from the Arthur Melton Library of the American Psychological Association, Washington, DC).

Crawford, M. P. (1966). Dimensions of simulation. *American Psychologist, 21,* 788–796.

Cronin, C. J. (1998). *An introduction to military psychology.* In C. J. Cronin (Ed.), *Military psychology: An introduction* (p. 3). Needham Heights, MA: Simon & Schuster.

DeAngelis, T. (1991a, February). Role of psychologists in the Gulf is demanding. *The APA Monitor, 22,* 1.

DeAngelis, T. (1991b, February). Back home, Div. 29 aids troops' families. *The APA Monitor, 22,* 18.

DeAngelis, T. (1991c, February). Gas warfare has psychological effects. *The APA Monitor, 22,* 18.

DeAngelis, T. (1991d, July). APA brochure outlines re-entry issues. *The APA Monitor, 22,* 22–23.

Dewsbury, D. A. (1997). On the evolution of divisions. *American Psychologist, 52*, 733–741.

Division 19. (1975, Summer). Program for annual meeting–Division 19. *Military Psychology Newsletter*, pp. 7–15 (Available from the Arthur Melton Library of the American Psychological Association, Washington, DC).

Division 19. (1983, Summer). 1983 APA convention Division 19 program. *Military Psychology Newsletter*, pp. 2–3 (Available from the Arthur Melton Library of the American Psychological Association, Washington, DC).

Division 19. (1984, Spring). Journal of military psychology reminder. *Military Psychology Newsletter*, p. 7 (Available from the Arthur Melton Library of the American Psychological Association, Washington, DC).

Division 19. (1984, Summer). 1984 APA convention Division 19 program. *Military Psychology Newsletter*, pp. 2–3 (Available from the Arthur Melton Library of the American Psychological Association, Washington, DC).

Division 19. (1985, Summer). Division 19 convention program. *The Military Psychologist, 1*, 4–9 (Available from the Arthur Melton Library of the American Psychological Association, Washington, DC).

Division 19. (1986, Spring). Minutes of the Division 19 mid-winter meeting. *The Military Psychologist, 2*, 2 (Available from the Arthur Melton Library of the American Psychological Association, Washington, DC).

Division 19. (1986, Fall/Winter). Military psychology journal. *The Military Psychologist, 2*, 15 (Available from the Arthur Melton Library of the American Psychological Association, Washington, DC).

Division 19. (1989, Summer). Summary of sessions and participants for Division 19: 1989 APA convention. *The Military Psychologist, 5*, 3–4 (Available from the Arthur Melton Library of the American Psychological Association, Washington, DC).

Division 19. (1994, Summer). Division 19 convention program. *The Military Psychologist, 10*, 11. (Available from the Arthur Melton Library of the American Psychological Association, Washington, DC).

Division 19. (1995, Summer). Division 19 convention program. *The Military Psychologist, 11*, 13–16 (Available from the Arthur Melton Library of the American Psychological Association, Washington, DC).

Division 19. (1997, Summer). 1997 APA convention Division 19 program overview. *The Military Psychologist, 13*, 17. (Available from the Arthur Melton Library of the American Psychological Association, Washington, DC).

Division 19. (1998, Summer). 1998 APA convention activities: Division 19. *The Military Psychologist, 14*, 9–17 (Available from the Arthur Melton Library of the American Psychological Association, Washington, DC).

Gade, P. (1993, Fall/Winter). President's message. *The Military Psychologist, 10*, 3–4 (Available from the Arthur Melton Library of the American Psychological Association, Washington, DC).

Gagné, R. M. (1962). Military training and principles of learning. *American Psychologist*, 17, 83–91.

Georgoulakis, J. M., Fiducia, D. A., Williams, D., & Harris, J. H. (1992, Summer). Convention program: Division of Military Psychology program committee. *The Military Psychologist*, 8, 9–18 (Available from the Arthur Melton Library of the American Psychological Association, Washington, DC).

Herek, G. M., Jobe, J. B., & Carney, R. M. (Eds.). (1996). *Out in force: Sexual orientation and the military*. Chicago: University of Chicago Press.

Jobe, J. (1991, Summer). President's message. *The Military Psychologist*, 7, 1–3 (Available from the Arthur Melton Library of the American Psychological Association, Washington, DC).

Knapp, D. (1994, Summer). Division 19 convention program. *The Military Psychologist*, 10, 10–15 (Available from the Arthur Melton Library of the American Psychological Association, Washington, DC).

Levant, R. F., & Abeles, N. (1997, Summer). Mini-convention on psychopharmocology. *The Military Psychologist*, 13, 16 (Available from the Arthur Melton Library of the American Psychological Association, Washington, DC).

Louttit, C. M., Wrenn, C. G., Schneidler, G., Bellows, R. M., Baier, D. E., Richardson, M. W., Seidenfeld, M. A., Jenkins, J. G., & Limburg, C. C. (1943, April 7). Petition to the board governors of the American Association for Applied Psychology to establish a military section (Records of the Military Section of the AAAP are contained in Box 696, Manuscript Division, U.S. Library of Congress, Madison Building, Washington, DC).

Manglesdorff, A. D. (1985). Lessons learned and forgotten: The need for prevention and mental health interventions in disaster preparedness. *Journal of Community Psychology*, 13, 239–257.

McCarthy, K. (1991, October). Council bans military ads after '92. *The APA Monitor 22*, 7.

McGuire, F. L. (1990). *Psychology aweigh!: A history of clinical psychology in the United States Navy, 1900–1988*. Washington, DC: American Psychological Association.

Mitary Division of the American Psychological Association, The. (1946–1950). *By-laws* (Box 598, Manuscript Division, U.S. Library of Congress).

Nadel, A. B. (1971, March). Report of the Special Committee on the Role of Military Psychology in a Transitioning American Society. *Military Psychology Newsletter*, p. 5 (Available from the Arthur Melton Library of the American Psychological Association, Washington, DC).

Olson, W. C. (1945). Notice: Cancellation of the fifty-third annual meeting of the American Psychological Association and provisions for a meeting of officers. *Psychological Bulletin*, 42, 409.

Prather, D. C. (1973, June). Division of Military Psychology American Psychological Association program 1973. *Military Psychology Newsletter*, pp. 3–8 (Available from the Arthur Melton Library of the American Psychological Association, Washington, DC).

Taylor, E. (1978, Fall). Proposed logos for Division 19. *Military Psychology Newsletter*. p. 10 (Available from the Arthur Melton Library of the American Psychological Association, Washington, DC).

Uhlaner, J. E. (1972). Human performance effectiveness and the systems measurement bed. *Journal of Applied Psychology, 56*, 202–210.

Wrenn, C. G. (1943, November 18). Minutes of the Meeting of the Military Psychology Section (Records of the Military Section of AAAP are contained in Box 696, Manuscript Division, U.S. Library of Congress, Madison Building, Washington, DC).

Zeidner, J., & Drucker, A. J. (1988). *Behavioral science in the Army: A corporate history of the Army Research Institute*. Alexandria, VA: U.S. Army Research Institute for the Behavioral and Social Sciences.

2

A HISTORY OF DIVISION 22 (REHABILITATION PSYCHOLOGY)

PAUL C. LARSON and PAUL R. SACHS

History is never, in any rich sense, the immediate crudity of what happens, but the much finer complexity of what we read into it and think of in connection with it.

—Henry James

Henry James's reflections on history are an apt starting point for an examination of the history of the Division of Rehabilitation Psychology. The bare bones details, however, do not provide a full and rich picture of the important themes that the history represents. The larger picture is the story of how psychologists became interested in the problems of physical and mental impairments and how they came to be committed to working with people who have those conditions to help them live a fuller, more meaningful life.

Psychologists, both inside and outside the profession, have been viewed as "mental health" professionals. Rehabilitation psychology represents a departure from that typical viewpoint and one that is gaining increasing interest and relevancy as the older mind–body dualism gives way to a more holistic integration of the physical and psychological aspects of life. Thus the history of the emergence of rehabilitation psychology and its organizational voice, Division 22, is an important part of the development of psychologist as a "health care professional" (Sullivan, 1995), addressing both the body and the mind.

The involvement by American psychologists with problems of physical illness and disability goes back to the early part of the century. Shepard Ivory Franz (1847–1933) instituted training programs for aphasic patients at McLean Hospital and pioneered some early work on brain–behavior relationships (Reisman, 1991). Later, in his APA presidential address, Franz emphasized that the psychological effects of brain damage need not be permanent—a hopeful note that continues to be sounded by Division 22 members. But organized efforts would await a later period.

THE CONTEXT OF REHABILITATION PSYCHOLOGY

Rehabilitation psychology needs to be put in context of the emergence of rehabilitation in general in the decades between the two world wars. As Oberman (1965) noted, there were at least three streams that fed into the development of vocational rehabilitation, and by implication, rehabilitation in general. One of those streams is the role of private charitable organizations and agencies, another is the development of the state–federal partnership for vocational rehabilitation, and another is the federal effort to provide for the needs of veterans with disabilities.

The founders of Division 22 generally came from one or another of the streams feeding into the development of rehabilitation, working in private or public agencies that provided services in this period. Among them were Jane Shover and Phyllis Bartelme, two of the founders of the organizational forerunner of Division 22, who were employed by the National Society of Crippled Children and Adults (NCPAPD Newsletter, 1953).

Charitable organizations were among the first to contribute to the field of rehabilitation psychology. Beginning in the early Middle Ages the Church established hospitals to provide care to the sick and disabled who had no families to care for them. The reform efforts during the 19th and 20th centuries saw such organizations as the Red Cross, the National Tuberculosis Foundation, Goodwill Industries, and the Easter Seal Society, among many others, address the needs of persons with disability (Oberman, 1965). The dominant ethic sustaining these efforts was charity, and the dominant expectation of the recipient was to be humble and grateful toward their benefactors.

Beginning in the 19th century, governmental organizations were set up to care for some types of persons with disability; people with mental illness or mental retardation, and children who were deaf or blind (Oberman, 1965). The beginning of vocational rehabilitation came with the Act to Provide for Vocational Rehabilitation of Persons Disabled in Industry or Otherwise and Their Return to Civil Employment (1920), which expanded the role of the Federal Board of Vocational Education to include civilians as well as veterans and set up the beginnings of the state–federal partnership in funding vocational rehabilitation efforts. From the very beginning the definition of disability emphasized the return to work as a goal. *Persons disabled* the statute defined as "any person by reason of a defect or infirmity whether congenital or acquired by accident, injury or disease, is, or may be expected to be, totally or partially incapacitated for remunerative occupation" (Act to Provide for Vocational Rehabilitation of Persons Disabled in Industry or Otherwise and Their Return to Civil Employment, 41 U.S. at 735). Each state now has an agency whose primary mission is to help persons with disability reach their potential for employment or independent living.

Among the founders of Division 22 who were involved at the federal side of this partnership was Dr. James Garrett. In his capacity in the associate director of the Office of Vocational Rehabilitation (OVR) in the Department of Health, Education and Welfare, he sponsored the first two conferences (held at Princeton and Clark University) that defined the emerging field of rehabilitation psychology. He also was responsible for the publication of an early pamphlet on the psychological aspects of disability (*NCPAPD Newsletter*, 1953).

War has stimulated periods of growth in rehabilitation psychology as a result of the increased need to care for large numbers of disabled veterans returning from war. Efforts to care for American veterans who became disabled begin in the period following the Civil War. In 1921 several agencies were consolidated into the Veterans Bureau, which later became the Veterans Administration, and now the Department of Veterans Affairs. This agency was critical in developing clinical psychology as a profession and in placing psychologists in rehabilitation settings (Reisman, 1991). Robert Waldrop, chief of vocational counseling in the VA, was one of the founding members of Division 22 and the NCPAD, its forerunner. The role of the VA system on the growth of both the fields of clinical and counseling psychology in general as well as the field of rehabilitation psychology is immense and fundamental. Without training and employment opportunities, profesional psychology would be considerably smaller as a field.

ORGANIZATIONAL ANCESTOR

The organizational beginning of Division 22 was the National Council on the Psychological Aspects of Disability (NCPAD). As noted previously, this group was convened by Jane Shover and Phyllis Bartelme, who called together psychologists working with persons with disabilities at several APA annual meetings between 1949 and 1951. In that year the group formally organized as a special interest group within the APA. By the next year it had became the National Council on the Psychological Aspects of Physical Disability (NCPAPD), which remained the name until 1956, when largely for the sake of convenience it was shortened to its original name. The name change reflects the tension between those whose work was primarily with physical disabilities and those who saw rehabilitation in a broader perspective that included mental disabilities. Many felt that the persons interested in the latter had adequate outlets through Division 12 (Society of Clinical Psychology) and wanted to emphasize the situation of those with physical conditions. The early role of NCPAD was primarily as a focus of activity during the annual meetings of the APA, but as time went on and more people became involved, there was a greater perceived need for organizational structure to manage the business between annual meetings.

Despite its growth, the members of NCPAD were ambivalent about making the next step, seeking divisional status within the APA. A vote of the membership in 1955 (*NCPAPD Newsletter*, 1956) resulted in only 7 in favor of divisional status, 29 in favor of continuing as a special interest group, and 13 in favor of affiliating with another division (15 in favor of a proposal to affiliate with Division 17, Counseling Psychology). Even as late as the fall of 1957, on the eve of becoming a division, a similar vote was 38 in favor, 16 against seeking divisional status (*NCPAD Newsletter*, p. 1). But that same fall 155 of the 180 members of NCPAD signed a petition for division status. The APA board of directors recommended granting divisional status to the Council of Representatives, who then voted at the APA annual meeting in August 1958, and Division 22 was officially born. (See Table 4 for a list of officers from 1958–1959 to the present.)

PROFESSIONAL IDENTITY

In American psychology the history of the evolution of professional identity can be traced by looking at various conferences, usually sponsored by the APA, to discuss the concerns and articulate the emerging consensus within a field. For example, the historic Boulder conference in 1949 marks the beginning of modern clinical psychology (Ramie, 1950); the Northwestern conference in 1951 marks the beginnings of modern counseling psychology (Whitely, 1980).

The origin of rehabilitation psychology was similarly defined by the conference held at Princeton, New Jersey, February 3 to 7, 1958, on the role of psychology and psychologists in rehabilitation. The conference was cosponsored by the APA and the U.S. Department of Health, Education and Welfare. The proceedings of the Princeton Conference, as it was known, were recorded by Beatrice Wright (1959) and published by the APA as *Psychology and Rehabilitation*. This is an excellent reflection of the thoughts

TABLE 4
Officers of Division 22

Years	President[a]	Secretary	Treasurer	Council Representatives
1958–1959	Frederick A. Whitehouse	William Gellman (1958–1960)	Sidney Fishman (1958–1960)	Phyllis F. Bartelme, Morton A. Seidenfeld
1959–1960	Lee Meyerson			Phyllis F. Bartelme, Morton A. Seidenfeld
1960–1961	James F. Garrett	Leonard Pearson[b] (1960–1963)		Morton A. Seidenfeld, Robert S. Waldrop
1961–1962	Salvatore DiMichael			Leonard Pearson, Robert S. Waldrop, Mildred C. Templin, Shalom E. Vineberg
1962–1963	Beatrice A. Wright			Leonard Pearson, Robert S. Waldrop, Mildred C. Templin, Shalom E. Vineberg
1963–1964	Joseph M. Wepman	Morton Seidenfeld (1963–1966)	Joseph Stubbins (1963–1966)	Shalom E. Vineberg, Leonard V. Wendland, Salvatore G. DiMichael, Morton Seidenfeld
1964–1965	Leonard Diller			Salvatore G. DiMichael, Morton A. Seidenfeld, Harold Chenven, Leonard Pearson
1965–1966	William Gellman			Salvatore G. DiMichael, Morton A. Seidenfeld, Harold Chenven, Walter S. Neff
1966–1967	Leonard Pearson	John R. Barry (1966–1969)	Gerald W. Green (1966–1968)	Harold Chenven, Walter S. Neff, Beatrice A. Wright, John R. Barry
1967–1968	Walter S. Neff			Beatrice A. Wright, John R. Barry, James F. Garrett, M. Erik Wright
1968–1969	Tamara Dembo		Joan H. Criswell (1968–1971)	John R. Barry, James F. Garrett, M. Erik Wright, Frederick A. Whitehouse
1969–1970	William M. Cruikshank	Wilbert E. Fordyce (1969–1972)		James F. Garrett, M. Erik Wright, Frederick A. Whitehouse
1970–1971	William M. Usdane			Frederick A. Whitehouse, Tamara Dembo, Wilbert E. Fordyce
1971–1972	Donald Brieland		Durand F. Jacobs (1971–1974)	Tamara Dembo, Wilbert E. Fordyce, John E. Jordan

(continued)

TABLE 4
(continued)

Years	President[a]	Secretary	Treasurer	Council Representatives
1972–1973	John R. Barry	Raymond A. Ehrle (1972–1975)		John E. Jordan (1972–1974)
1973–1974	Wilbert E. Fordyce			
1974–1975	Nancy J. Kerr		Rose Lynn Sherr (1974–1977)	Alan Frankel
1975–1976	Franklin Shontz	Herbert H. Zaretsky (1975–1978)		Richard J. Morris
1976–1977	Durand F. Jacobs			Durand F. Jacobs (1976–1979)
1977–1978	Jerome Siller		Richard Morris (1977–1980)	
1978–1979	Rose Lynn Sherr	Myron Eisenberg (1978–1980)		Rose Lynn Sherr
1979–1980	Herbert H. Zaretsky			
1980–1981	John Muthard	Laurence P. Ince	Lawrence B. Feinberg (1980–1983)	Earl A. Alluisi
1981–1982	Myron G. Eisenberg	Roberta B. Trieschman (1981–1984)		Rose Lynn Sherr
1982–1983	Leonard G. Perlman			
1983–1984	George N. Wright		Nancy M. Crewe (1983–1986)	Mary A. Jansen (1983–1985)
1984–1985	Lawrence B. Feinberg	Rita Nakcen Gugel (1984–1987)		
1985–1986	Roy C. Grzesiak			Herbert H. Zretsky (1985–1988)
1986–1987	Richard J. Morris		Rochelle V. Habeck (1986–1989)	

Year				
1987–1988	Nancy M. Crewe	Paul Leung (1987–1990)		
1988–1989	Robert T. Fraser			Roy Grzesiak
1989–1990	Bernard Brucker	Paul Leung	Daniel E. Rohe (1989–1992)	Richard Morris (1989–1991)
1990–1991	Susanne M. Bruyere	Barry P. Nierenberg (1990–1993)		
1991–1992	Mitchel Rosenthal			
1992–1993	Paul Leung		Thomas Czerlinsky (1992–1995)	Herbert H. Zaretsky (1992–1996)
1993–1994	Robert Gleuckauf	Dennis C. Harper (1993–1996)		
1994–1995	Bruce M. Caplan			
1995–1996	Robert G. Frank			
1996–1997	Marie DiCowden	Cathay A. Redd (1996–1999)	Paul Alston (1996–1998)	Mitchell Rosenthal (1996–1998)
1997–1998	Dennis C. Harper			
1998–1999	Barry Nierenberg		Dawn Ehde	Mitchell Rosenthal, John D. Corrigan

[a]The office of past-president and president-elect should be referenced by noting the president of the year preceding or succeeding the year of interest.
[b]In this year the offices of secretary and treasurer were merged.

at the time concerning the professionalization of rehabilitation psychology and helps us to understand the goals, viewpoints, and methods of this emerging specialty.

The scope and nature of rehabilitation were two of the important topics discussed. The degree to which rehabilitation should include mental disorders or remain focused on physical disorders was at issue. The tension concerning the name of the National Council reflects this debate.

In part the debate on the scope of rehabilitation was a result of the multidisciplinary character of rehabilitation. Rehabilitation medicine, or psychiatry, was emerging as a medical specialty at the same time. The role of physical therapists, nurses, and social workers, among others, was also important. It was clear from the start that rehabilitation psychology, more than most professional specialties, involved extensive day-to-day contact with other professionals from a very wide range of training with very different vantage points on the problems of disability. Indeed, an entire chapter in the proceedings was devoted to "Interprofessional Relations." As Wright noted, rehabilitation "is not the sole province of any one profession. It is rather an expression of a system of values and attitudes toward the person with a disability and his place in society" (1959, p. 10). A key value was a belief that "purposeful activity" (p. 12) should replace the idleness of mere "convalescence" (pp. 12–13).

Another major characteristic of rehabilitation psychology was its vocational focus. Although the overall adjustment of a person at an individual level and in other social roles such as family life was a major concern, work was recognized as a major source of economic and psychological independence. There were statutory mandates to provide vocational rehabilitation services to disabled veterans and nonveterans, and the agencies created to fulfill these mandates brought psychologists and vocational counselors into the forefront of rehabilitation. The vocational guidance movement stimulated by the returning veterans of World War I is a common ancestor to both Divisions 17 (Counseling Psychology) and 22. However, even in 1958 the concept of vocational rehabilitation had been broadened to include "sheltered and homebound employment as well as homemaking" (Wright, 1959, p. 16). It was also noted that pending legislation, if passed, would, establish a program of "independent living," thus heralding changes that were to play larger roles in the field of rehabilitation in later decades.

The roles and functions of psychology in a rehabilitation setting were also discussed. It is important to note that an equal percentage of participants (46.3%) were based in academia and in "institutions for the handicapped" (Wright, 1959, p. 32). Thus a large number at the conference reflect the people who train the clinicians as well as the clinicians themselves. It is not surprising that administration and consultation activities were the highest in frequency (all at 73.2%); testing and evaluation were next with 68.5% and counseling and psychotherapy at 67.5%; teaching and research were 65.6 and 61.0%, respectively. The next most frequent activity, improving public attitudes toward disability, dropped to 47.1%, and others trailed off after that. There was also a recognition that the clients seen reflected a spectrum of adjustment and that addressing their needs required going beyond the "consulting room" attitude, and emphasis on psychopathology that was seen to be typical of a more mental health focus.

Finally, the training of rehabilitation psychologists was discussed. Following the earlier decisions in clinical and counseling psychology, the doctoral level of training was seen as the most appropriate. The broad outline of curriculum, including practicum and internship experiences, was consistent with the consensus within professional psychology. In addition, needed coursework to acquaint the student with the particular issues regarding disability was discussed. The needs that were highlighted and the frequency of their endorsement by participants in the conference were "Psychological aspects of disability (82%), Medical information (58%), Community relations (51%) and Social work orientation (32%)" (Wright, 1959, p. 53). Reference was also made to the particular need to cover "somatopsychology," a term earlier coined by researchers to describe the study of the impact of physique and visible disability on psychological functioning (Dembo, Leviton, & Wright, 1956/1975).

DEVELOPMENTS

A year after the Princeton conference, another conference sponsored by the Office of Vocational Rehabilitation (OVR) was held at Clark University (Leviton, 1959). A more formal set of presentations and papers was used as starting points for discussion. One of the interesting papers was aimed at guiding the direction of research efforts and was sponsored by the OVR as the major federal granting agency (Myerson, 1959). Myerson noted the prevalence of "one-shot" investigations and urged more sustained programs of research by individual investigators. This goal fortunately has been largely met by a growing number of people who author multiple studies having a coherent focus during their careers in rehabilitation psychology. Another need noted was more outlets for research. Division 22's journal, *Rehabilitation Psychology*, was an outgrowth of this goal. Another salient point was Myerson's call for more "comprehensive theories of illness, disability and rehabilitation" (p. 16). After reviewing the extant theories he observed that an integrated theory would have to integrate facts about the person, the disability, the social setting, the rehabilitation process itself, and the "flexibility or amenability to change of each characteristic" (p. 23).

One of the pioneering studies on the psychological aspects of disability was conducted by three founding Division 22 members. Dembo, Leviton, and Wright (1956/1975) sought out veterans and others who had lost limbs in the war or were otherwise visibly different (e.g., scarring, etc.). They then interviewed them and sometimes significant others concerning their adaptation to the changes in physical appearance and function and the reactions of others to their visible disability. Dembo and her colleagues coined the term somatopsychology to refer to the ways in which apparent and obvious physical difference has a psychosocial impact on self and others. This social–psychological framework has been a major theme throughout the history of rehabilitation psychology.

Another important work from this period summarized the history of literature on psychological adjustment to physical disability (Barker, Wright, Myerson, & Gonick, 1953). Its further significance is in its reflection of the key role played by Kurt Lewin in the psychology and social psychology of disability. His field theory approach to psychology emphasized the holistic interaction between individual and environment, which was a concept of great relevance to studying how the visible physical differences of amputees led to changed reactions of self and others, which ultimately affected the adjustment of the affected individuals. Among the students of Lewin were Roger Barker, Tamara Dembo, and Beatrice Wright. Wright and Dembo went on to assume the presidency of Division 22, and Wright's (1983) book *Physical Disability—A Psychosocial Approach*, remains a classic textbook in the field of the psychology of disability.

The Lewinian emphasis on the person–environment interaction is reflected in several ways. The individual disability is understood in terms of the impact that the disability has on that individual him- or herself and on that individual's opportunity to integrate into the community at large. In the Barker et al. (1953) monograph, one can literally encounter the topological drawings that illustrate Lewin's conception of "life space." There are few examples in the research literature of this graphic device in research, though the heuristic value of the concept it illustrates is much larger. Though Lewin's theory has decreased in influence in recent years, it is clearly one of the major forerunners of all modern forms of holism, including general systems theory, which has become more popular since the 1960s and the growth of cognitive psychology.

Lewin's field theory has certainly not been the only theoretical position represented in research by Division 22 members. In his presidential message summarizing some of the division's history Morris (1986) noted that behavioral research conducted by such members as Lee Myerson, Wilbert Fordyce, and Nancy Kerr have made important contributions as well. Psychodynamic or psychoanalytic theories have had little influence on rehabilitation psychology. Analysts who founded psychosomatic medicine, such as Franz Alexander, were interested in how medical disease was initiated by unconscious conflict, but among rehabilitation psychologists the interest was on the coping and adaptational implications of visible disability. Part of the reason for this is that psychoanalysis never gained the following among psychologists as it did among psychiatrists (Reisman, 1991).

Another significant development in this early period is the close association between rehabilitation psychologists and Division 17 (Counseling Psychology). As noted previously, the growth in both clinical and counseling psychology were largely stimulated by the influx of training funds and jobs within the VA system in the decade following World War II. One of the historically distinguishing features of counseling psychology has been its emphasis on working with people who are psychologically normal and who are undergoing significant life-stage transitions. Both rehabilitation and counseling psychology share an emphasis on the vocational role and its importance in not only economic but psychological independence. In 1958 one of the leading organizational alternatives to evolving as a separate division was to affiliate as a special interest group within Division 17.

Rehabilitation psychology, like counseling psychology, has also been more sensitive to the differences between normalcy and pathology (Whitely, 1980). This is what Super (1980) termed the "hygiology" emphasis. Rehabilitation psychology has not presumed that having a disability in and of itself identifies an individual as experiencing psychopathology. Rather, the field has attempted to identify what factors influence an individual who has a disability to react in an adaptive or maladaptive manner to the circumstances imposed by his or her situation.

One of the most important contributions from a rehabilitation viewpoint is the emphasis on "functional capacities." Rather than emphasizing accuracy of diagnostic classification, the goal of returning people to a maximal degree of prior function has resulted in a focus on describing, measuring, and enhancing what the person can actually do. The broad range of issues covered under the rubric of "independent living" has forced rehabilitation psychologists to structure their relationships with clients around much more pragmatic goals.

COMING OF AGE

By the 1960s, rehabilitation psychology had emerged as a distinct specialty within professional psychology. This was also, of course, a major decade of social change, which included the intensifying struggle for civil rights and racial justice as well as President Lyndon Johnson's Great Society and the beginning of the Medicare program as a means of providing health care to elderly and disabled individuals. Especially the inauguration of

Medicare and Medicaid, its state–federal partnership for those not eligible for Medicare, expanded the services available to persons with disability, though it was not until much later that psychologists could participate as independent providers in this system.

By the time William Gellman (1966) gave his presidential address to Division 22 at the 1966 APA annual meeting, his comments reflected the many social changes underway at that time. He also noted the major changes in the labor market as Americans began to shift to an information-based economy and the dominance of the economy by a corporate culture influenced by large corporations. Gellman explored the implications for the rehabilitation of these changes. In particular he saw significant changes for persons with disability in the labor force—changes that would "devaluate or eliminate the economic potential of groups with limited education or training" p. 41). He also saw the impact of poverty, especially long-term intergenerational poverty, on the current models of rehabilitation. Just as the community mental health movement forced a shift away from exclusive reliance on individual psychotherapy, so he felt must rehabilitation "develop a greater variety of more appropriate services using positive ecological community forces" (p. 43). He also urged that rehabilitation increasingly adopt preventative and maintenance objectives. His address exemplifies the era of not only concern for serious social problems but the optimism of that age for the ability of applied psychology to ameliorate the pain in the lives of many more people, if not transform society through its impact on social policy.

In the 1970s a disability rights movement gained momentum, with an emphasis on the psychological issue of normalization and the social challenge against paternalism. This led to the passage of the Rehabilitation Act of 1973. The ethic behind this movement is one of empowerment rather than charity; persons are viewed as socially disadvantaged by physical and psychological barriers (Chubon, 1994; Nagler, 1993), and changing those environmental features is the major goal. One of the most important developments for persons with disabilities was the passage of the Americans With Disabilities Act (ADA) in 1990. An entire issue of *Rehabilitation Psychology* was dedicated to exploring the implications of this landmark legislation (Bruyere, 1993).

PUBLICATIONS

One of the marks of scholarly and professional maturity is the publication of a refereed professional journal. From its early incarnation as the NCPAD, the organization published a newsletter, which kept division members up to date on organizational matters, as well as the *Bulletin*, which presented more formal scientific and scholarly articles. Lee Myerson was the first editor of the *Bulletin*. He recognized the need to further improve the quality of the journal and the research contained in it if the division was to truly emerge as an important source of knowledge and assistance to practitioners. From volume 16 to 18, it was titled *Psychological Aspects of Disability*. In 1971 a long relationship with Springer Publishing began, and the editorship was passed to Mary Jansen, and then in 1987 with volume 32 to Myron Eisenberg. The title also changed to the present one, *Rehabilitation Psychology*. The editorship has now been passed to Bruce Caplan, and the American Psychological Association is currently the publisher. It remains one of the two official publications of the division (the other is the *Newsletter*).

By 1970 the time was ripe for a conference on the psychological aspects of disability; one was sponsored by the APA and held in Monterey in October of that year. In addition to the 73 invited guests, the author of the preface to the proceedings observed that for the first time students participated in the conference (Neff, 1971). Chapters 1 to 11 in the proceedings were papers commissioned to reflect the state of our understanding of rehabilitation psychology at that point in time and included such traditional topics as physical disability and personality (Schontz, 1970) and the social psychology of disability (Kutner, 1970). Reflecting the growing sensitivity to minority group issues, two papers addressed both poverty and the impact of race and ethnicity on rehabilitation (Goldin, 1971; Gordon, 1971). In today's climate of multiculturalism, it is heartening to know that rehabilitation psychology had begun to recognize the importance of these broader social concerns, a trend that needs to continue.

One particularly interesting paper dealt with the social psychology of the rehabilitation process itself in the form of a study on professional–client relations in a rehabilitation hospital (Leviton, 1970). Leviton emphasized the fundamentally different perspectives of the provider and the client of services. The client of rehabilitation services is an insider to the experience of disability, whereas the provider is an outsider. The insider–outsider dimension was an idea advocated by Tamara Dembo and later incorporated in the classic book by her colleague Beatrice Wright (1983). Leviton referred to the impact of studies in medical sociology and lamented the slowness of psychology to recognize the need to look critically at the social structuring of the professional relationship. The impact of this discussion was to raise the possibility that rehabilitation psychologists might play a significant role as advocates for patients; this was first voiced at the conference and later articulated by M. Erik Wright (1971a). Wright also provided one of the earliest discussions of the role of self-help groups in the rehabilitation process (Wright, 1971b).

DIVISION AWARDS

By 1978 the division had matured enough to begin honoring its members who had distinguished themselves through research or service. The recipients are found in Table 5, and a review of the accomplishments of the various recipients is an excellent window on the issues that have been at the forefront of rehabilitation psychology.

The first recipient of the Distinguished Service Award for research contribution was James Garrett. In his position in the federal department of Health, Education, and Welfare, he was a key person in arranging sponsorship of the early conferences defining the field of rehabilitation psychology. He also edited one of the early handbooks on the psychological aspects of disability (Garrett, 1962). As early as 1952 Garrett was articulating the need to emphasize the capabilities of persons with disabilities, a theme that continues to be important (Garrett, 1952).

Other division members to receive this award are Tamara Dembo and Beatrice Wright, who were part of the early Lewinian tradition in rehabilitation psychology. Dembo, Wright, and their colleague Roger Barker were authors of the early research in the psychosocial aspects of disability. Dembo was an advocate for qualitative research even before the current revival of interest in these methodologies (Dembo, 1993). She also focused early attention on the importance of practical considerations of actual life problems and advocated actively involving the persons with disability in the rehabilitation process (Dembo, 1964, 1974). Wright has written extensively in the field of rehabilitation psychology and has also contributed to social psychology with a major summary of the literature on labeling theory (B. A. Wright, 1991); she has also discussed how person perception literature in social psychology can inform rehabilitation practice (B. A. Wright, 1975).

Beyond the Lewinian perspective other traditions have been represented among the recipients of the Distinguished Service Award. Durand (Dewey) Jacobs has written many articles on addictions and compulsive behavior, especially problem gambling. Out of this work came a general theory of addictions (1987). Wilber Fordyce pioneered behavioral approaches to chronic pain (Fordyce, 1968) and has contributed more than 20 articles expanding on this theme (Fordyce, 1988).

Two other recipients of the Distinguished Service Award, Nancy Kerr and Lee Myerson, collaborated on articles concerning the importance of independence for persons with disability (Kerr & Myerson, 1987) and research methodologies for rehabilitation (Myerson & Kerr, 1979). Myerson contributed numerous papers on aspects of rehabilitation of persons with mental retardation and sensory disabilities (Myerson, 1958).

The 1988 recipient of the Distinguished Service Award was George Wright, who wrote extensively on the topic of the competencies of rehabili-

TABLE 5
Division Awards

Years	Distinguished Service Award	Senior Distinguished Research Career (Roger Barker Award)	Early Career (James Garrett Award)	President Recognition
1978	James Garrett			
1979				
1980	Tamara Dembo			
1981	Beatrice Wright			
1982	Durand Jacobs			
1983				
1984	Leonard Diller			
1985	Douglas Fenderson			Roy Grzesiak
1986	Wilbert Fordyce			Rick Morris
1987	Nancy Kerr			Nancy Crewe
1988	George Wright	Brian Bolton		Bob Fraser
1989	Myron Eisenberg	Bill Anthony		Bernard Brucher
1990	Roberta Trieschman	Gary Bond	James Krause	Susanne Bruyere
1991	Lee Meyerson	Harold Yuker	Timothy Elliott	Mitch Rosenthal
1992	Herb Zaretsky	Wayne Gordon	Susan Buckelew	Paul Leung
1993	Nancy Crewe	Marcus Fuhrer	Fong Chan	
1994		Len Diller	Meg Nosek	
1995	Len Diller	Bob Frank	Tom Novack	
1996	Franklin Shontz		Peter Lichtenberg	

tation professionals and how to train and enhance them, and also contributed to the literature in cross-cultural psychology (G. N. Wright & Phillips, 1978). His textbook, *Total Rehabilitation* (Wright, 1980), now out of print, is a classic in the field. Through his long service as editor of *Rehabilitation Psychology*, Myron Eisenberg, the 1989 recipient of the Distinguished Service Award, has gained a mastery of the technical language in this field, contributing a dictionary of terms (Cammack & Eisenberg, 1995; Eisenberg, 1995). Herbert Zaretsky, the 1992 recipient of the award, has contributed studies over a wide range of areas, including tinnitus (Ince, Greene, Alba, & Zaretsky, 1987), and has edited a major volume on the medical aspects of disability (Eisenberg, Glueckauf, & Zaretsky, 1993).

The Roger Barker Award was initiated in 1988 to honor a senior colleague who had a distinguished career in research in rehabilitation psychology (named after another student of Kurt Lewin, who pioneered ecological psychology). Brian Bolton was the first recipient of this award. A prodigious researcher and author, Bolton has contributed or collaborated on more than 120 articles, books, and chapters in the field of rehabilitation. Among his more important works are a handbook of measurement and evaluation in rehabilitation (Bolton, 1976) and a book on psychosocial adaptation to disability (Bolton & Roessler, 1978).

William Anthony, recipient of the 1989 Barker Award, has published nearly 80 articles in the field of psychosocial rehabilitation of mental disabilities. The field of rehabilitation originally distinguished itself from the rest of clinical psychology by emphasizing a specific population, persons with physical disability. However, many of the same principles, values, and approaches developed for persons with physical disabilities have been successfully applied to persons with chronic mental illness. The combination of techniques and values from the one context applied to the other has been termed *psychosocial rehabilitation* (a journal with that name chronicles the developments in this field). Anthony's works over nearly 30 years (e.g., Anthony, Buell, Sharratt, & Althoff, 1972) have been influential in the development of psychosocial rehabilitation (Farkas & Anthony, 1989). The 1990 recipient of the Barker Award, Gary Bond, has also contributed more than 50 articles to the field of psychosocial rehabilitation. His work has emphasized "assertive community treatment (ACT) for the chronically mentally ill, which began to bring into outcome research an awareness of the need to include economic measures to better inform public policy decisions" (Bond, 1984, p. 356).

Bob Yuker received the award in 1991 for his long career interest in attitudes toward disability (Yuker, 1988, 1994). He developed the Attitudes Toward Persons With Disabilities scale (ATDP), which has been among the most widely used instruments in assessing such attitudes (Yuker & Block, 1986). The works of Wayne Gordon (recipient of the Barker Award in

1992; Gordon, 1987; Gordon & Hibbard, 1991)) and Leonard (Len) Diller (recipient of the Barker Award in 1994) have highlighted the growing field of neurorehabilitation (discussed later in the chapter).

The 1993 recipient of the Barker Award, Marcus Fuhrer along with Margaret Nosek, the 1995 winner of the Garret award, took up the theme of independence for persons with disabilities (Nosek & Fuhrer, 1992).

In 1990 the division instituted the James Garrett Award for early career achievement. Recipients must have conducted research in the field of rehabilitation psychology in the first 10 years following their doctorate. The first recipient of the award, James Krause (1990), had been involved in research involving spinal cord injury, which included an important long-term prospective study of predictors of survival (Krause, 1990). Tim Elliott (1991), the second winner of the award, has contributed research on the portrayal of persons with disabilities in films and television (Elliott & Byrd, 1982). Susan Buckelew, the 1991 recipient of the Garrett Award, has written about a number of issues in chronic pain, especially fibromyalgia, as well as collaborating on an article framing the cause of rehabilitation psychology as an opportunity to expand job possibilities for all of psychology (Frank, Gluck, & Buckelew, 1990). Fong Chan, the 1993 recipient, has been among the first non-European Americans to begin research on issues of disability and rehabilitation (Chan, Lam, Wong, Lueng, & Fang, 1988). He also has contributed extensively to the vocational evaluation literature. Thomas Novack, the 1994 recipient, is noted for his many contributions to the field of head injury rehabilitation. Margaret Nosek, the coauthor with Marcus Fuhrer of several articles on independence for persons with disabilities, was the winner of the 1994 Garrett Award. Her writings on independence have stemmed from a professional and disengaged perspective as well as from her own personal struggles—learning to use personal attendants and assistive devices and most important of all, limitations on resources (Division 22 Award Committee, 1994). Also in 1986 the division began honoring the past presidents of the division for their years of service. Most have served the division for many years in a variety of capacities and offices prior to their election as president.

NEUROREHABILITATION AND OTHER SPECIALTIES

There were significant advances in medical technology and the refinement of urban emergency treatment centers in the 1980s. The combined result of these two developments was an increase in the number of people surviving serious head injury, stroke, or other acute and often lethal neurological conditions. Dedicated head trauma rehabilitation arose to meet the need for helping the survivors and their families restore function and return to some semblance of community integration.

With the advent of "neuropsychological rehabilitation," which is the use of psychological principles and techniques to address the needs of persons with neurological disabilities, the interests of many rehabilitation psychologists became increasingly focused toward the specialty of neuropsychology as a result of working with persons with brain damage. Indeed, one of the largest areas of growth in job opportunities for persons trained in neuropsychology has been in rehabilitation settings. A growing number of Division 22 members are also affiliated with Division 41 (Clinical Neuropsychology). In some ways, rehabilitation has come full circle, because some of the first efforts at neuropsychological rehabilitation were conducted at the early part of the century by Goldstein and Gelb (Dembo, 1959) with brain-injured German veterans of World War I. Neuropsychology began primarily as an aid to diagnosis, and much work has been done by members of both Division 22 and Division 41 to enhance the use of psychological assessment data to diagnose brain damage. That is, diagnosis is most useful when it leads to interventions that aid the individual in recovering functional capacity. Thus preoccupation with refining the diagnostic process without expanding concerns to treatment options is like losing sight of the forest by paying too much attention to the trees. Wayne Gordon, the 1992 recipient of the Barker Award, has participated in the growth of the interdisciplinary field of cognitive rehabilitation (Gordon, 1987; Gordon & Hibbard, 1991).

One of the themes of neuropsychological rehabilitation has been to emphasize the relationship between the environment and the patient. Diller (1984), a leading figure in rehabilitation of brain injury, emphasized this ecological perspective. Classical neuropsychology focused more on the correlation between test performance and the presence or localization of a lesion. This awareness of the importance of the ecological relationship between person and environment is a continuation of the long tradition begun with Dembo, Barker, and Wright, noted previously.

SPECIAL INTEREST GROUPS

Many of the founding members of the division were involved in working with children, but it was not until 1987 that a formal special interest group was created for psychologists involved in pediatric rehabilitation. A pediatric social hour at the annual APA convention was an effective vehicle for bringing new members into the division, as well as providing a forum for networking and sharing ideas. From this beginning, the Pediatric Interest Group has been involved in testimony concerning legislation, initiating programs at the annual meeting, and developing policy guidelines for pediatric rehabilitation that have been adopted by a number of states. Pediatric rehabilitation has been but one of several special interest groups that have emerged as the field of rehabilitation psychology has grown in complexity and specialization.

There was dramatic growth in the 1970s and 1980s in rehabilitation and its diversification into subspecialties including but not limited to psychosocial rehabilitation of the chronically mentally ill, neurorehabilitation of traumatic head injury and stroke survivors, and the psychological management of chronic pain. The foregoing tour of issues via the accomplishments of recipients of the various awards bestowed by Division 22 indicate the complexity of the field.

CURRENT SITUATION AND FUTURE PROSPECTS

Perhaps the beginning of the current era can be pinpointed in the series of articles in the June 1990 issue of *American Psychologist* highlighting rehabilitation. In the article casting rehabilitation as an opportunity for psychology in general (Frank et al., 1990), the authors noted that there had been a rapid growth in the number of persons with disability. In part because of the aging of the American population and the improvement of health care, a larger number of individuals are both surviving into old age, where disabling conditions are more common, and surviving the disabilities and chronic conditions that had earlier resulted in death. These factors result in a larger number of people with needs that can be addressed by rehabilitation psychologists.

The article also heralds the changes in health care reimbursement. Frank and his colleagues saw the recent inclusion of psychologists as independent providers of service under Medicare as heralding a new era of possibilities. Although that was an important development, the attempts to control the costs of health care via managed care organizations and reforms in the reimbursement structure of Medicare have ushered in an era of uncertainty that Frank, Gluck, and Buckelew could not foresee. Despite these developments, no drastic curtailments of either reimbursement or services have occurred.

Managed care organizations have had a growing influence in reimbursement for services in the last decade in rehabilitation psychology, as they have for many other areas of professional psychology. Even government benefit programs such as Medicare and Medicaid have begun to encourage beneficiaries to use health maintenance organizations (HMOs) and other types of managed care.

In addition to managed care, with which all psychologists who are health care providers have to now deal, rehabilitation psychologists have felt the impact of private credentialing bodies. The Commission for Accreditation of Rehabilitation Facilities (CARF) is the major private credentialing body in this specialty area, and its standard mandating inclusion of psychologists on the inpatient rehabilitation team has aided growth in the job market for rehabilitation psychologists. One of the major sources for the increased job market for rehabilitation psychologists has been the accreditation standard promulgated by the CARF. In 1996 a proposed revision of CARF standards would have eliminated this particular requirement. This standard came under challenge. Rehabilitation psychologists and the APA responded and preserved the concept of the interdisciplinary team and psychology's role in it (Corrigan, 1997).

A significant sign of maturity in a professional specialty is the emergence of credentialing in that area. In 1995 the executive board of the division made an agreement to offer a diplomate in rehabilitation psychology through the American Board of Professional Psychology (ABPP). This decision reflects the increasing demands on rehabilitation psychologists, their diverse work roles, and the need for formal certification of their qualifications. The first diplomates in rehabilitation psychology were awarded in 1997.

DIAGNOSTIC SYSTEMS

All health care is rooted primarily in a medical model, for better or worse, and that invariably implies a diagnostic system. Psychology uses the *Diagnostic and Statistical Manual of Mental Disorders* (DSM-IV; American Psychiatric Association, 1994) for most of the mental health concerns. Medicine uses the ICD-10 (promulgated by the World Health Organization; WHO). The WHO (1980) also has an International Classification of Impairments, Handicaps and Disabilities (ICIHD), which covers the chronic problems resulting in disability and requiring rehabilitation. Two Division 22 members are part of the group revising the current classification (Liss & Kewman, 1996). This is important because of the need for consistency in terminology and reference points for describing the physical conditions and their resulting challenges to living. For many years the WHO has used *impairment, disability* and *handicap* in precise ways that clarify the nature of these phenomena. *Impairment* refers to the medical condition itself—the deficiency, difference, or defect in what is considered normal structure or function of the body. *Disability* refers to "any restriction or lack of ability to perform an activity within what is considered normal for a human being" (Liss & Kewman, 1996, p. 7). *Handicap* refers to the disadvantages encountered by individuals because of impairment or handicap and reflects the interaction between the physical level, the functional capacity level, and the level of social structures, support, and attitudes. This classification system has broad implications for practice, research, outcome evaluation, and of course policy making. It is significant that rehabilitation psychologists are involved in this important international endeavor.

As noted earlier, a major milestone in the movement for civil rights of persons with disabilities has been the passage of the Americans With Disabilities Act (ADA, 1990). Rehabilitation psychologists were very involved in providing testimony for passage of this legislation, as well as being involved after its passage in providing interpretive services to business and community groups regarding disabilities.

The division has developed special interest sections in Pediatric Rehabilitation (Leung, 1988). Marie DiCowden served as its chair until she became division president in 1996. There is also a special interest group on deafness, boasting 161 members as of 1996 (Pollard, 1996). In addition, new committees on integrated health and living have been added (DiCowden, 1997), bringing together interests in rehabilitation, wellness, psychospirituality, and alternative healing. The division has also moved into the computer era, with a Web site through the American Psychological Association (APA),[1] and a list server for rapid communication of notices via the Internet.[2]

CONCLUSION

Many challenges lie ahead for the division in the 21st century. Responding to the growing complexity of the field and the organization, a strategic planning committee was set up to formulate a long-term vision for the future (Harper, 1998). The impact of managed care and health care cost containment continues to have an impact on professional psychology in general and rehabilitation in particular. Yet practitioners continue to rise to the challenge and provide the needed care. The ubiquity of computers has resulted in increased visibility for the division through the Web site and increased ability of members to communicate with one another. The impact of the ADA continues to be significant, though the U.S. Supreme Court has now begun to limit the scope of the legislation (see *Sutton v. United Airlines*, 1999). Like the phoenix that was once the graphic logo of the division, human beings still transform what might be considered tragic and even catastrophic: the onset of a disabling medical condition. Rehabilitation psychologists continue to aid persons with disability to live fuller lives with access to all the benefits of society. The health of the division in this

---

[1] http://www.apap.org/divisions/div22/homepage.html.
[2] listserver@lists.acs.ohio-state.edu.

new century looks good, as it continues to provide a focus for psychology, disability, and rehabilitation.

REFERENCES

Americans With Disabilities Act of 1990. 42 U.S.C. § 1201 et seq., Public Law No. 101-336, 104 Stat. 327 (West, 1993).

American Psychiatric Association. (1994). *Diagnostic and statistical manual of mental disorders* (4th ed.). Washington, DC: Author.

An Act to Provide for Vocational Rehabilitation of Persons Disabled in Industry or Otherwise and Their Return to Civil Employment. (1920). Public Law No. 66-236, 41 Stat. 734 (1920).

Anthony, W. A., Buell, G. J., Sharratt, S., & Althoff, M. E. (1972). Efficacy of psychiatric rehabilitation. *Psychological Bulletin, 78*, 447–456.

Barker, R. G., Wright, B. A., Myerson, L., & Gonick, M. R. (1953). *Adjustment to physical handicap and illness: A survey of the social psychology of physique and disability.* New York: Social Research Council.

Bolton, B. (1976). *Handbook of measurement and evaluation in rehabilitation.* Baltimore: University Park Press.

Bolton, B., & Roessler, R. (Eds.). (1978). *Psychosocial Adjustment to Disability.* Baltimore: University Park Press.

Bond, G. R. (1984). An economic analysis of psychosocial rehabilitation. *Hospital and Community Psychiatry, 35*, 356–362.

Bruyere, S. M. (1993, Summer). Special Issue on the Implications of the Americans With Disabilities Act of 1990 for Psychologists [Special Issue]. *Rehabilitation Psychology, 38*(2).

Cammack, S., & Eisenberg, M. G. (Eds.). (1995). *Key words in physical rehabilitation: A guide to contemporary usage.* New York: Springer.

Chan, F. Lam, C. S., Wong, D., Leung, P., & Fang, X. Z. (1988). Counseling Chinese Americans with disability. *Journal of Applied Rehabilitation Counseling, 19*, 21–25.

Chubon, R. A. (1994). *Social and psychological foundations of rehabilitation.* Springfield, IL: Charles C. Thomas.

Corrigan, J. D. (1997). New CARF standards approved with revisions. *Rehabilitation Psychology News, 25*(1), 4.

Dembo, T. (1959). Introduction. In G. Leviton (Ed.), *The relationship between rehabilitation and psychology: Proceedings of a conference sponsored by the Office of Vocational Rehabilitation,* Worcester, MA, Clark University, June 11–13, 1959.

Dembo, T. (1964). Sensitivity of one person to another. *Rehabilitation Literature, 25*, 231–235.

Dembo, T. (1974). The paths to useful knowledge. *Rehabilitation Psychology, 21*, 124–128.

Dembo, T. (1993). Thoughts on qualitative determinants in psychology: A methodological study. *Journal of Russian and East European Psychology, 31*, 15–70.

Dembo, T., Leviton G. L., & Wright, B. A. (1956/1975). Adjustment to misfortune: A problem of social-psychological rehabilitation. *Artificial Limbs, 3*, 4–62 (Reprinted in *Rehabilitation Psychology*, 1975, 22, 1–100).

DiCowden, M. A. (1997). Integrated Health and Living Committee. *Rehabilitation Psychology News, 25*(1), 5.

Diller, L. (1970). Cognitive and motor aspects of handicapping conditions in the neurologically impaired. In W. Neff (Ed.), *Rehabilitation psychology*. Washington, DC: American Psychological Association.

Diller, L. (1984). Neuropsychological rehabilitation. In M. Meier, A. Benton, & L. Diller (Eds.), *Neuropsychological rehabilitation*. New York: Guilford Press.

Division 22 Awards Committee. (1994). James A. Garrett early career achievement award presented to Margaret A. Nosek, Ph.D. *Rehabilitation Psychology News, 22*(1), 4–5.

Eisenberg, M. G. (1995). *Dictionary of rehabilitation*. New York: Springer.

Eisenberg, M. G., Glueckauf, R. L., & Zaretsky, H. H. (Eds.). (1993). *Medical aspects of disability: A handbook for the rehabilitation professional*. New York: Springer.

Elliott, T. R., & Byrd, E. K. (1982). Media and disability. *Rehabilitation Literature, 43*(11, suppl. 12), 348–355.

Farkas, M. B., & Anthony, W. A. (Eds.). (1989). *Psychiatric rehabilitation programs: Putting theory into practice*. Baltimore: Johns Hopkins University Press.

Fordyce, W. E. (1968). An application of behavior modification technique to a problem of chronic pain. *Behavior Research and Therapy, 6*, 105–107.

Fordyce, W. E. (1988) Pain and suffering: A reappraisal. *American Psychologist, 43*, 276–283.

Frank R. G., Gluck, J. P., & Buckelew, S. (1990). Rehabilitation: Psychology's greatest opportunity. *American Psychologist, 45*, 757–761.

Garrett, J. F. (1952). Counsel the man—not the disability. *Crippled Child, 29*, 14–15.

Garrett, J. F. (Ed.). (1962). *Psychological practices with the physically disabled*. New York: Columbia University Press.

Gellman, W. (1966). Perspectives in rehabilitation. *Division 22 Bulletin, 13*(3), 40–47.

Goldin, G. J. (1970). Rehabilitation and poverty. In W. Neff (Ed.), *Rehabilitation psychology*. Washington, DC: American Psychological Association.

Gordon, W. A. (1987). Methodological considerations in cognitive remediation. In M. Maier & A. Benton (Eds.), *Neuropsychological Rehabilitation*. New York: Guilford Press.

Gordon, W. A., & Hibbard, M. R. (1991). The theory and practice of cognitive remediation. In J. Kreutzer & P. Wehman (Eds.), *Cognitive rehabilitation for persons with traumatic brain injury: A functional approach*. Baltimore: Paul H. Brookes.

Harper, D. C. (1998). Strategic planning for the Division of Rehabilitation Psychology. *Rehabilitation Psychology News, 26*(2), 1.

Ince, L. P., Greene, R. Y., Alba, A., & Zaretsky, H. H. (1987). A matching-to-sample feedback technique for training self-control of tinnitus. *Health Psychology, 6,* 173–182.

Jacobs, D. F. (1987). *A general theory of addictions: Applications to treatment and rehabilitation planning for pathological gamblers.* Springfield, IL: Charles C. Thomas.

Kerr, N., & Myerson, L. (1987). Independence as a goal and a value of people with physical disabilities: Some caveats. *Rehabilitation Psychology, 32,* 173–180.

Krause, J. (1990). Prediction of long-term survival of persons with spinal-cord injury: An 11-year prospective study. *Rehabilitation Psychology, 32,* 205–213.

Leung, P. (1988). Minutes—midwinter executive board meeting, Division 22. *Rehabilitation Psychology News, 16*(2), 13–15.

Leviton, G. L. (Ed.). (1959). *The relationship between rehabilitation and psychology: Proceedings of a conference sponsored by the Office of Vocational Rehabilitation,* Worcester, MA, Clark University, June 11–13, 1959.

Leviton, G. L. (1970). Professional–client relations in a rehabilitation hospital setting. In W. Neff (Ed.), *Rehabilitation Psychology.* Washington, DC: American Psychological Association.

Liss, M., & Kewman, D. G. (1996). Implications for rehabilitation psychology of the World Health Organization's International Classification of Impairments, Disabilities and Handicaps. (1980). *Rehabilitation Psychology News, 23*(2), 7–8.

Morris, R. J. (1986). President's message. *Rehabilitation Psychology News, 5*(1), 1.

Myerson, L. (1958). Psychological aspects of sensory disability. *Annals of the New York Academy of Science, 74,* 128–135.

Myerson, L. (1959). Theory and research in rehabilitation psychology. In G. Leviton (Ed.), *The relationship between rehabilitation and psychology: Proceedings of a conference sponsored by the Office of Vocational Rehabilitation,* Worcester, MA, Clark University, June 11–13, 1959.

Myerson, L., & Kerr, N. (1979). Research strategies for meaningful rehabilitation research. *Rehabilitation Psychology 26,* 228–238.

Nagler, M. (1993). The disabled: The acquisition of power. In M. Nagler (Ed.), *Perspectives on disability.* Palo Alto, CA: Health Markets Research.

NCPAPD Newsletter. (1953, Feb.). p. 3.

NCPAPD Newsletter. (1953, Aug.). p. 1.

Neff, W. S. (1971). *Rehabilitation psychology.* Washington, DC: American Psychological Association.

Nosek, M. A., & Fuhrer, M. J. (1992). Independence among people with disabilities: A heuristic model. *Rehabilitation Counseling Bulletin, 36,* 6–20.

Oberman, C. E. (1965). *A history of vocational rehabilitation in America.* Minneapolis, MN: T. S. Denison.

Pollard, R. (1996). Highlights for the special interest section on deafness. *Rehabilitation Psychology News, 24*(1), 14.

Raimy, V. C. (1950). *Training in Clinical Psychology*. Englewood Cliffs, NJ: Prentice-Hall.

Rehabilitation Act of 1973. (1973). 29 U.S.C. § 701-796, Public Law No. 93-112, 87 Stat. 355 (1973).

Reisman, J. M. (1991). *A History of Clinical Psychology* (2nd ed.). New York: Hemisphere.

Schontz, F. C. (1970). Physical disability and personality. In W. Neff (Ed.), *Rehabilitation psychology*. Washington, DC: American Psychological Association.

Sullivan, M. J. (1995). *The mind-body connection: Key to popular demand for psychological services*. Keynote address at Illinois Psychological Association, Chicago, November 10, 1995.

Super, D. (1980). From vocational guidance to counseling psychology. In J. Whitely (Ed.), *The History of Counseling Psychology*. Monterey, CA: Brooks/Cole.

Sutton v. United Air Lines. (1999). 1999 WL *407488.

Whitely, J. M. (1980). The historical development of counseling psychology: An introduction. In J. Whitely (Ed.), *The history of counseling psychology*. Monterey, CA: Brooks/Cole.

World Health Organization. (1980). *International Classification of Impairments, Disabilities and Handicaps*. Geneva, Switzerland: World Health Organization.

Wright, B. A. (1959). *Psychology and rehabilitation*. Washington, DC: American Psychological Association.

Wright, B. A. (1975). Social-psychological leads to enhance rehabilitation effectiveness. *Rehabilitation Counseling Bulletin, 18*(4), 214–223.

Wright, B. A. (1983). *Physical disability—A psychosocial approach* (2nd ed.). New York: Harper-Collins.

Wright, B. A. (1991). Labeling: The need for greater person-environment individuation. In C. Snyder and R. Donelson (Eds.), *Handbook of social and clinical psychology*. New York: Pergamon Press.

Wright, G. N. (1980). *Total rehabilitation*. Boston: Little, Brown.

Wright, G. N., & Phillips, J. D. (1978). Cultural variation in probabilistic thinking: Alternative ways of dealing with uncertainty. *Journal of Cross-cultural Psychology, 9*, 285–299.

Wright, M. E. (1971a). Advocacy: A new rehabilitation role function. *Psychological Aspects of Disability, 18*, 89–90.

Wright, M. E. (1971b). Self-help groups in the rehabilitation enterprise. *Psychological Aspects of Disability, 18*, 43–45.

Yuker, H. E. (Ed.). (1988). *Attitudes toward persons with disabilities*. New York: Springer.

Yuker, H. E. (1994). Variables that influence attitudes toward people with disabilities: Conclusions from the data. *Journal of Social Behavior and Personality*, 9, 9–22.

Yuker, H. E., & Block, J. R. (1986). *Research With Attitude Toward Disabled Persons Scales (ATDP) 1960–1985*. Hempstead, NY: Hofstra University Press.

3

A HISTORY OF DIVISION 30 (PSYCHOLOGICAL HYPNOSIS)

JAMES R. COUNCIL, MELVIN A. GRAVITZ,
ERNEST R. HILGARD, and EUGENE E. LEVITT

In 1960, Miller, Galanter, and Pribram wrote, "One of the seven wonders of psychology is that so striking a phenomenon as hypnosis has been neglected" (p. 103). By then, however, the stage had already been set for a major expansion of clinical and experimental hypnosis, a result in large part of contributions by psychologists. By the end of the 1960s, the American Psychological Association (APA) had established the Division of Psychological Hypnosis, and many of the psychologists noted in this section were involved in its formation and development. These include the following past presidents of the division: Ernest R. Hilgard, Milton V. Kline, Theodore X. Barber, John G. Watkins, Ronald E. Shor, Theodore R. Sarbin, Frederick Evans, John F. Chaves, and William C. Coe. This overview will

Certain of the material on the formation and early years of Division 30 comes from an invited address by Eugene E. Levitt, a founding member, past president, and archivist of the division. This document is titled "Twenty Years of Trances: A History of the Division of Psychological Hypnosis." It was presented at the annual meeting of the American Psychological Association in New Orleans on August 14, 1989. Dr. Levitt died in 1995, but because we have drawn at length from this paper, we have listed him as an author. We are grateful to his family for allowing us to do so. This and other material related to Division 30 have been archived with the APA in Washington, DC. We thank Sarah Jordan of APA Division Services for her invaluable assistance in gathering information about the division, and Donald Dewsbury for his editorial contributions.

introduce some of the key figures in hypnosis research and practice up to the time that Division 30 was established.

Hypnosis twines through the history of psychology and that of the United States. Benjamin Franklin, while ambassador to France in the 1780s, headed an investigation of mesmerism credited with conducting the first controlled experiments on human behavior (Kirsch, 1990). Although Franklin's research discredited Mesmer's theory, mesmerism soon crossed the Atlantic. By the mid-1800s, mesmerism was firmly established in the United States (see Crabtree, 1988), and mesmeric exhibitions were a popular American entertainment. In his autobiography, Mark Twain devoted a chapter to his experiences as a "mesmerized" participant in a show that visited Hannibal, Missouri, around 1850 (Clemens, 1959, pp. 50–58).

Thanks largely to James Braid, the eminent 19th-century English physician, hypnosis later acquired new respectability as well as its current name (Gravitz, 1997a; Hilgard, 1965). By the end of the century, its medical and psychological applications were attracting the attention of such luminaries as Sigmund Freud (e.g., Breuer & Freud, 1895, 1955) and William James. James (1890) included a chapter on hypnosis in *Principles of Psychology*, which undoubtedly helped establish hypnosis as an appropriate topic for scientific psychology.

Much of the late 19th- and early 20th-century work on hypnosis in the United States began in the Boston area, particularly at Harvard University where James spent his academic career. Prominent figures included Boris Sidis, who had been a student of James, and Morton Prince, who founded the Psychological Clinic at Harvard University. Prince was one of the foremost early investigators of multiple personality disorders, and his studies (e.g., Prince, 1905) were intimately connected with hypnosis. Prince also founded the *Journal of Abnormal Psychology* in 1906—since its founding this journal has been hospitable to hypnosis and has published important papers on the mechanisms, correlates, and applications of hypnosis.

William McDougall became interested in hypnosis research after joining the faculty at Harvard in 1920, and several of his students (William S. Taylor, Paul C. Young, George W. Estabrooks, and Frank A. Pattie) contributed significantly to the literature. The interest in hypnosis was enhanced when Henry A. Murray became director of the Psychological Clinic, and the succession at Harvard included Donald W. MacKinnon and Robert W. White.

White (1941) emphasized the contractual nature of hypnotic responses—that is, having agreed to experience and to participate in hypnosis, the participant attempts to conform to the expected hypnotic role as defined by the hypnotist's suggestions. This perspective eventually led to a major rift among hypnosis theorists, in which the traditional "altered-state" view was opposed by cognitive–behavior and social–psychological interpretations. One of White's students, Martin T. Orne, became prominent in the post-World War II generation, largely through his research designed to discriminate the "essence" of hypnosis from social-demand artifacts.

Other major pre-World War II figures include Clark L. Hull and Milton H. Erickson. Hull's interest in hypnosis began in 1923 while he was still at the University of Wisconsin. He is best known within the hypnosis community for his important book titled *Hypnosis and Suggestibility* (1933), which he wrote after moving to Yale University. This volume by a distinguished experimental psychologist did much to enhance the creditability of hypnosis within the scientific community. Erickson, a physician, was associated with Hull at the University of Wisconsin, but the major part of his career was spent in private practice in Phoenix, Arizona, from 1949 until his death in 1980. He became perhaps the most widely known practitioner and theorist in clinical hypnosis, and his influence has been perpetuated since his death by a large number of his admirers and disciples.

Particularly among health professionals, there was a resurgence of interest in hypnosis after World War II. This was evidenced by monographs on the hypnotic treatment of war neuroses by Brenman and Gill (1947), Kardininer (1947, with Herbert Spiegel), and Watkins (1949). Perhaps because hypnosis showed promise as a short-term therapeutic technique for traumatic reactions to combat, organized research funds became available following the war from the National Institute of Mental Health, the Office of Naval Research, the National Science Foundation, Ford Foundation, and other important sources. These funds supported laboratories devoted to scientific research in hypnosis and facilitated doctoral and postdoctoral training.

Before long, both clinical and experimental hypnosis began to be established in special centers. These included the Institute for Research in Hypnosis, established in New York City, which was founded by Milton V. Kline and Jerome Schneck in the 1950s, and the Morton Prince Clinic, which was associated with it. Orne, who had been trained in both psychology and psychiatry, established a laboratory in Harvard University in 1960, which moved in 1964 to the Institute of the Pennsylvania Hospital in Philadelphia under the name of the Unit for Experimental Psychiatry. In 1957 Hilgard received funds to open a Laboratory of Hypnosis Research at Stanford University in California. Hilgard remained active at Stanford into the 1980s, even though he retired in 1969. His accomplishments included, with the collaboration of Andre Weitzenhoffer, the development of psycho-metrically sound instruments that are still considered some of the best measures of hypnotic suggestibility (Weitzenhoffer & Hilgard, 1959, 1962). Hilgard also wrote several books that have had an international influence on hypnosis theory and application. These include *Hypnotic Susceptibility* (1965), *Divided Consciousness* (1977), and together with his wife and colleague Josephine, *Hypnosis in the Relief of Pain* (Hilgard & Hilgard, 1975).

It is unlikely that hypnosis could have sparked as much research interest as it has without controversy. In the 1950s, Theodore X. Barber and Theodore R. Sarbin developed alternative theories of hypnosis that continue to stimulate considerable research activity. Barber and a number of colleagues published more than 40 scientific research articles that were followed by his landmark book, *Hypnosis: A Scientific Approach* (1969). His laboratory at Medfield Hospital in Massachusetts trained and developed a number of prolific scientists, notably Nicholas P. Spanos and John F. Chaves. Their edited compilation, *Hypnosis: The Cognitive–Behavioral Perspective* (1989), is perhaps the best presentation of Barber's position as it has developed over the years. Sarbin's (1950) role-taking conceptualization was more social–psychologically based than Barber's, but it shared Barber's emphasis on how the participant perceives and responds to the demands of the hypnotic situation. Sarbin's best-known student is William C. Coe; their book, *Hypnosis: A Social Psychological Analysis of Influence Communication* (Sarbin & Coe, 1972), is considered to be a classic.

ORIGINS

Although hypnosis attracted scientific attention from its inception, it was slow to earn general professional recognition. However, by the 20th century hypnosis was gaining increasing credibility among clinical and academic health professionals. By the late 1940s the stage was set for the founding of professional organizations devoted to clinical and experimental hypnosis.

Organizational Background

In 1889 and 1900 two early congresses on hypnosis were held in Paris that attracted noted scholars and practitioners from around the world. Despite subsequent attempts to organize an international society of hypnosis, no such professional organizations were founded until after World War II (Watkins, 1995). In 1949, Jerome Schneck, an American psychiatrist, led the way for the establishment of the Society for Clinical and Experimental Hypnosis (SCEH), which quickly acquired a substantial following in the United States. The SCEH publishes the *International Journal of Clinical and Experimental Hypnosis*, which was edited for many years by Orne, and has been a primary outlet for significant research and clinical reports. Later the American Society of Clinical Hypnosis (ASCH) was founded in 1958 by

Milton Erickson and others who felt the need for a society that focused more on clinical practice than did the SCEH. Erickson also founded its journal, *The American Journal of Clinical Hypnosis,* and served as its editor until 1968. In 1959, a Canadian physician, Bernard Raginsky, took the lead in organizing the International Society for Clinical and Experimental Hypnosis and served as its founding president. In 1973, the international society was reorganized as the *International Society of Hypnosis* (ISH), with Hilgard as its first president.

The year 1960 saw the establishment of an important credentialing mechanism, the American Board of Examiners in Psychological Hypnosis (ABEPH). This board arose from a project by the ASCH and the SCEH to establish specialty boards in hypnosis, which also founded the American Board of Medical Hypnosis and the American Board of Hypnosis in Dentistry (Watkins, 1995). The ABPEH was soon recognized by the APA, which continues to list its diplomates in its membership directory (Hilgard, 1993). This board soon shortened its name to the American Board of Psychological Hypnosis (ABPH). Two classes of diplomates were established by the ABPH: those qualified for clinical hypnosis as practitioners and those qualified for experimental hypnosis as researchers (Hilgard, 1993). The former were also considered to have qualified as clinicians under the rules of the American Board of Professional Psychology (ABPP). At the present time, the ABPH is pursuing a move toward affiliation under the umbrella of the ABPP.

This was the organizational picture prior to the establishment of Division 30 as a component of the APA in 1969. Although psychologists have always been a substantial part of the overall membership of the SCEH, the ASCH, and the ISH, those groups are multidisciplinary, including among their membership medical, dental, psychological, and other health professionals. There had never before been an organization solely for psychologists interested in hypnosis.

Formation of the Division

During the summer of 1967, the "Notes and News" section of the *American Psychologist* published an announcement that heralded the establishment of APA Division 30, Psychological Hypnosis.

> A petition for a new APA Division in Psychological Hypnosis is in formation. Every Fellow, Member, or Associate who has interest in hypnosis, clinical or experimental, should take part in the establishment of such awaited division. [sic] The main purpose of the division is to establish an organizational unit for many efforts in the field of clinical and experimental hypnosis. . . .

The notion that the APA should create a division devoted to hypnosis originated with the young psychologist Adel M. Mahran. Mahran received his PhD degree from New York University in 1966, and placed this announcement the same year in which he became an APA member.

Mahran suggested to members who responded to the notice in the *American Psychologist* that they meet at the 1967 APA annual convention (Levitt, 1989). Although it is not known exactly how many individuals responded, Hilgard, Milton Kline, and Eugene Levitt met with Mahran at the convention that took place in Washington, DC, that year. In turn, they suggested other psychologists who should help form the division, and in September 1967 Mahran mailed invitations to Barber, Margaret Brenman, William E. Edmonston, Jesse Gordon, Perry London, Frederick Marcuse, Scott Moss, Joseph Reyher, Ronald Shor, and M. Erik Wright. All except Brenman eventually became active members and were among the early officers of the new division. According to Levitt (1989), Brenman and Orne were virtually the only well-known psychologists working in the area of hypnosis who did *not* join in the campaign for the new division or at least support it. However, Orne did participate in the division's 1970 program at the annual APA meeting, and he eventually became a member. By November of 1967, Mahran had set up an interim planning committee that consisted of Barber, Edmonston, Gordon, Hilgard, Kline, Marcuse, Shor, Reyher, Robert Woody, and Levitt, with Mahran as chair. Marcuse declined shortly after being appointed and was replaced by Henry Guze. Orne was a notable dissenter from these early formative efforts. In a letter to Levitt, Orne wrote that he saw no value in a division for hypnosis and was concerned that "border-line individuals" could use division membership as a clinical credential (Levitt, 1989). Orne's concern was heightened by the fact that Mahran was virtually unknown, as were his motives for putting so much energy into the effort to establish an APA division for hypnosis.

Problems relating to credentials influenced the framing of the division's first set of bylaws, which began in 1967. There was no bylaws committee as such, and the Interim Planning Committee proposed the first draft in the fall of 1967. Orne's reservations about the new division were reflected in this bylaws draft. For example, to be eligible for membership, a psychologist had to "prove one year of experience in hypnosis or a satisfactory completion of an introductory course in hypnosis in an accredited institute." There was, however, a provision for members lacking these credentials. They could join the new division for two years while they undertook to fulfill the proposed requirements, but if they failed to fulfill them during the two-year period, the applicants were automatically disqualified. A separate section was devoted to the procedure for the expulsion of a member of the division (Levitt, 1989).

The bylaws draft also listed conjoint efforts with the American Board of Examiners in Psychological Hypnosis (now ABPH), the SCEH, and the ASCH. A special category of fellow would be limited to those who already held an ABPH diploma in either clinical or experimental hypnosis. This proviso created the unusual case of an APA division having two separate categories of fellows. Several members of the interim planning committee noted that the dual fellow provision and references to other organizations would likely not be well received by the APA, and eventually the references to the external organizations were deleted. However, the provisions requiring proof of expertise in hypnosis and for expulsion remained in the bylaws that were subsequently approved by the APA board of directors in May 1968.

Once the APA board of directors had approved the statement of purpose and the bylaws, the establishment of the new division was virtually guaranteed. Mahran, as chair of the interim planning committee, called for a general meeting of the nascent division at the APA annual meeting in San Francisco. Despite fairly late notice, 22 persons attended the first assembly of Division 30 in the Hunt Room of the Fairmont Hotel on September 2, 1968. By general consent, Mahran chaired that meeting. The minutes of the meeting indicate that the interim planning committee was designated as an interim executive committee with Mahran as its chair, until the first set of officers would be elected during the spring of 1968. On October 5, 1968, the APA Council of Representatives voted to approve the establishment of Division 30, which opened the way for the appearance of a Division 30 program at the next APA convention.

The Inaugural Program

Immediately after the creation of Division 30, work began on its scientific program for the 1969 APA convention. Although Shor was elected chair of the division program committee, Mahran wanted to have the primary role in structuring the new division's first convention program. Mahran had begun planning symposia shortly after the September business meeting and apparently had contracted with the APA Program Committee for 15 hours of time, including a workshop. Shor believed that it would not be possible to maintain quality of presentations with that large a program and suggested that the Division 30 program committee should "think small." Shor then suggested a total program of 11 hours, including 3 hours for a business meeting, 6 hours of symposia or papers, a conversation hour, and a social hour (Levitt, 1989).

The committee's correspondence indicated that Mahran objected to Shor's proposal because it did not include the workshop, and believed that he had the right to veto it as interim president. Ill feelings developed, and the program committee disbanded. Mahran then appointed a new program committee consisting of Hilgard, Kline, and Guze, who decided to have three symposia, one organized by each of the committee members. Mahran was unhappy with this development, overruled the committee, and appointed Barber as the new chair together with Edmonston as an additional member. Barber hesitated before accepting, apparently because of the disagreements between the committee members that had already arisen. Edmonston made it clear before accepting that he personally favored a shorter program with no workshop, and he recommended proceeding with the three symposia that had previously been proposed by Guze, Hilgard, and Kline.

As it turned out, the first Division 30 program at the APA annual meeting had four sessions, including two of the symposia suggested by the Guze–Hilgard–Kline team. Barber chaired a paper session with presentations by Frank Vingoe, Spanos and Chaves, Kenneth Schaefler and Perry London, and Lewis Sachs. Another was chaired by Leslie Cooper and included London, Reyher, Edmonston, and Kenneth Bowers, with Levitt as discussant. Barber, Shor, and Josephine Hilgard participated in a symposium on theories of hypnosis chaired by Andre Weitzenhoffer. Another symposium, chaired by Harold Zamansky, included presentations on clinical hypnosis by Kline, Watkins, Harold Lindner, Erika Fromm, Mark Oberlander, Doris Gruenewald, Jacob Conn, and Jerome Schneck. Overall, this was a respectable initial program presented by a number of well-known authorities in the field.

The First Elections

Shor was incensed over his treatment by Mahran when he was program committee chair (Levitt, 1989). As a consequence, Shor, Kline, and Hilgard met at the 1968 SCEH convention to discuss the new division, and this led to a lengthy letter from Shor to Hilgard in January 1969, which was circulated to other members of the interim executive committee. Shor proposed that Hilgard should become the first president of the new division, phrasing the letter in terms of the needs of the division and Hilgard's qualifications but not mentioning Mahran.

Shor's letter mobilized considerable support among the members of the interim executive committee and was followed by memoranda calling for the nomination and election of Hilgard as first elected president of the division. Mahran countered with his own memoranda but could not affect the tide of sentiment. Although Mahran was a candidate for president on the initial Division 30 ballot, Hilgard was elected as the first president. Also elected were Kline as president-elect and Fay Starr as secretary–treasurer. The members-at-large were William Heron, Ronald Shor, George Estabrooks, and Harold Greenwald, and the two representatives to the APA Council were Guze and Gordon. Six of the nine members of this first elective executive committee had previously been members of the interim executive committee.

According to Levitt (1989) there was no doubt that Mahran, who had conceived the idea of a hypnosis division, fervently wished to be its first president. He had signed letters to the interim executive committee as "founding president" as early as December of 1968. Mahran got his wish in part, because after the elections he received a carefully prepared certificate that acknowledged his hard work and officially recognized him as the founding chair of Division 30.

GROWTH AND DEVELOPMENT

We will start our review of the years after the founding of Division 30 by presenting a list of the division presidents to date in Table 6. Regarding theoretical orientation, little apparent favoritism has been shown to traditional and nontraditional approaches. Although the traditionalists have been well-represented, Barber was elected when he was still writing "hypnosis" in quotation marks, and Sarbin was another early president who took an unconventional approach to defining the field. In later years, this diversity in orientation has continued. Neither has there been much indication of a regional bias.

Perhaps the strongest correlates of the presidency have been previous service to the division and academic affiliations. Virtually all the presidents have had academic appointments, and most have been full-time faculty in psychology departments or schools of medicine. Likewise, almost all of the presidents have previously worked for the division in either elected or appointed posts.

TABLE 6
Presidents of Division 30

Years	Presidents	Years	Presidents
1968–1969	Adel M. Mahran	1985–1986	Billie S. Strauss
1969–1970	Ernest R. Hilgard	1986–1987	William C. Coe
1970–1971	Milton V. Kline	1987–1988	Elgan L. Baker
1971–1972	Theodore X. Barber	1988–1989	Donna R. Copeland
1972–1973	Erika Fromm	1989–1990	Steven J. Lynn
1973–1974	M. Erik Wright	1990–1991	Michael R. Nash
1974–1975	William E. Edmonston	1991–1992	Richard P. Horevitz
1975–1976	John G. Watkins	1992–1993	William P. Morgan
1976–1977	Ronald E. Shor	1993–1994	Irving Kirsch
1977–1978	Theodore R. Sarbin	1994–1995	Melvin A. Gravitz
1978–1979	Frederick J. Evans	1995–1996	Ian Wickramasekera
1979–1980	Kenneth R. Graham	1996–1997	James R. Council
1980–1981	Eugene E. Levitt	1997–1998	Stanley Krippner
1981–1982	Shirley Sanders	1998–1999	Edward J. Frischholz
1982–1983	Michael J. Diamond	1999–2000	Cynthia Wickless
1983–1984	John F. Chaves	2000–2001	Etzel Cardena
1984–1985	Helen J. Crawford		

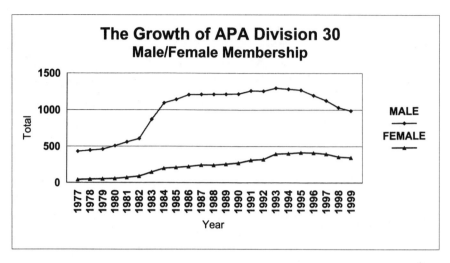

Figure 2. Growth of APA Division 30: Male–Female Membership

The presidency of Division 30 has also been associated with maleness, although women have usually been represented in the division's executive committee. There was only 1 woman among the first 10 presidents, Erika Fromm. In the second decade, this trend showed signs of reversing, with 4 out of 10 presidents being women. As of this writing, however, there has been only one female president since 1989, Cynthia Wickless (term 1999–2000). The weighting toward males could reflect the demographics of the division, which has been predominantly male (see Figure 2), or the bias toward academic backgrounds noted earlier, because there is a similar tilt toward males among hypnosis researchers and theorists. For these reasons, the pool of potential nominees tends to be predominantly male. Nevertheless, better representation of women in division leadership should be a continuing priority.

Organizational Development

The bylaws of the division remained essentially unchanged for the first 13 years, with the exception of the separation of the office of the secretary–treasurer into two offices in 1979. The next major change related to the quasi-certification membership provisions and the expulsion clause mentioned previously. Restricting membership in this way was inconsistent with normal APA practice, which based divisional membership solely on interest by the applicant for membership. Furthermore, there had been no instances in either Division 30 or any other hypnosis society in which membership had been used as a clinical credential (Levitt, 1989). The restrictions on membership prevented psychologists with an interest but no

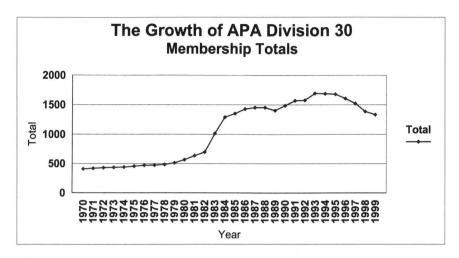

Figure 3. Growth of APA Division 30: Membership Totals

experience in hypnosis from affiliating with like-minded colleagues and also served to keep the division as one of the smallest in the APA—from 1970 to 1980, the division grew only 24 percent, far less than the 65 percent growth of the APA as a whole for the same time frame (Edmonston, 1980; Levitt, 1989). Figure 3 plots the total membership of the division from its founding to the present time.

When Levitt became president-elect in 1980, the membership provisions of the bylaws were rewritten to make Division 30 an outright interest division. When submitted to the division executive committee and then to the membership in 1981, this proposal was overwhelmingly ratified. At that point, as Figure 3 shows, division membership began a period of growth that continued for the next six years.

There was little change in the organization of the division during the 1980s. However, while the APA continued to grow, membership in the division appeared to asymptote around 1500. Not only membership but the division itself seemed to be stagnating. The division's principal—if not sole— activities were to produce a yearly convention program and a quarterly newsletter. Although the division was financially healthy and maintaining its membership, it was losing ground relative to other divisions. As a result, Division 30 came close to losing its one seat on the APA Council of Representatives.

Michael R. Nash (president 1990–1991) and Richard P. Horevitz (president, 1991–1992) deserve credit for recognizing the developing crisis and taking steps to revitalize the division (Horevitz, 1991). In contrast to the previous practice of conducting the division's business in a one-hour executive committee meeting and a general business meeting during the

APA annual convention, Nash arranged for a full-day executive committee meeting prior to the start of the 1991 APA convention. The purpose was to determine the division's current organizational health and to provide future directions. Discussions during this meeting revealed that Division 30 could be doing much more for its members, the APA, and the public than it had been doing. For one thing, most of the members were practitioners, and a survey had shown that they were dissatisfied with the overwhelming emphasis on hypnosis research in divisional activities and programs.

Given the choice of sitting on its assets or investing in the future, in January of 1992 the executive committee of the division authorized three mid-winter meetings of the executive committee to be held in conjunction with the midwinter APA divisional leadership conferences (Horevitz, 1992). As it evolved, the agenda included developing a mission statement, restructuring the operation of the division, developing a needs assessment and growth plan, improving services to the membership, developing relationships with the several APA Directorates, and becoming involved with the National College of Professional Psychology.

Horevitz chaired the first mid-winter meeting in 1992 (described in Horevitz, 1992). The meeting was held in the new APA headquarters building and included sessions with various APA officials, including the APA president, Jack Wiggins. These sessions reinforced the committee's belief that Division 30 could uniquely benefit both the public and the APA, as well as psychologists involved with hypnosis. The renewed purpose of Division 30 is reflected in the mission statement that was developed at that meeting:

> Division 30 brings together psychologists interested in scientific and applied clinical hypnosis. Our mission is to educate the profession and the public, to develop new and innovative clinical interventions and research methods, and to evaluate current treatment approaches. These activities advance our knowledge about basic psychological processes and foster the practices designed to improve human well-being. Division 30 encourages research into the area of hypnosis and develops regional and national continuing education workshops on clinical applications of hypnosis. The Division publishes *Psychological Hypnosis: A Bulletin of Division 30* three times a year. The Division sponsors awards for outstanding contributions to scientific and clinical hypnosis. (APA Division 30, 1999, p. 3)[1]

This mission was to be implemented primarily through standing committees on public information and affairs, scientific affairs, and practice and

---

[1] The Division 30 mission statement is presented in its current form. Only minor changes have occurred since its composition in 1992.

professional affairs (Horevitz, 1992). A major emphasis was service to the practitioners who constitute the majority of the membership. Agreement was unanimous to include more clinically relevant material in the bulletin and convention programs, enhance Division 30's continuing education activities, and promote standards for training and practice in clinical hypnosis.

The day-long mid-winter and preconvention meetings so proved their worth that they continued past the original three. Indeed, the executive committee and invited appointees (e.g., program chair, newsletters editor) attended these meetings every year from 1992 to 1997, largely at their own expense. (The exception was in 1996, when the mid-winter meeting was cancelled because of a severe snow storm in Washington, DC.) Although the mid-winter meetings were finally discontinued for financial reasons, the preconvention meeting has become institutionalized. The agendas of all of these meetings have been so full, and so much has been accomplished in them, that it would be unthinkable to go back to the brief meetings that were the norm beforehand. A major factor underlying the success of these meetings was the division's secretary from 1995–1998, Lynne M Hornyak, whose energy and organizational skills greatly improved the division's efficiency and effectiveness.

Two additional organizational matters should be mentioned as well— the *Policy and Procedures Manual* and the executive committee listserv. The *Policy and Procedures Manual* was first commissioned by the 1991–1992 executive committee as a direct outcome of the first mid-winter meeting in 1992 (APA Division 30, 1999). During that session, it was apparent that the activities of the division, its services to members, and the internal communications of division officers were less than optimal. Organizational memory was defective, in the sense that the functions of officers and committees were not being implemented. Because the division had no permanent executive staff, and those members serving on the executive committee were typically busy and overcommitted professionals, following through on decisions made at executive committee meeting was inconsistent. The *Policies and Procedures Manual* was developed as the division's closest approximation to an executive staff. The manual was intended to function as a living document that not only codifies the minimum responsibilities of each position on the executive committee and its standing and presidential committees but also records the means by which the goals of the division can be consistently realized. The manual has proven to be an invaluable document that is updated yearly and referred to constantly. From 1994 to the present, Roger Page (secretary, 1998–2001) has assumed responsibility for keeping the manual current and deserves great credit for his work.

The other major innovation of recent years was the establishment of an executive committee listserv. The Division 30 listserv was established by James R. Council during his term as president-elect (1995–1996) and as of this writing he continues to maintain it through his position at North Dakota State University. The members of the executive committee, previous presidents, and appointed committee chairs all have their e-mail addresses on the list. Anyone can post news, questions, items for discussion, and so on, to the list, and postings go out to all persons on the list. This procedure not only permits sharing of information and discussion among persons who are geographically separated but also archives all of the messages. Since its inception in 1995, the Division 30 listserv has received at least weekly and frequently daily use.

Initiatives and Achievements

Perhaps the greatest achievement of the division in recent years has been its improvement in organization, communication, and follow-through, all of which bode well for future accomplishments. However, there have been solid achievements in the past, which have improved both the science and practice of hypnosis. We will end this chapter with a review of the highlights.

Defining Hypnosis

Hypnosis researchers and clinicians have been continually handicapped by their inability to agree on the nature of hypnosis. Difficulties in definition have had both theoretical and legal consequences. As a result, the division has initiated two different efforts at definition. The first was known as Project Enlightenment and was directed by Eugene Levitt. About a decade later, while serving his term as divisional president, Irving Kirsch (1993–1994) organized another project to define hypnosis using different methods.

Project Enlightenment stemmed from concerns over lay hypnosis, to be discussed later. According to Levitt (1989), these concerns were prompted by the inclusion of a lay organization in a list of scientific and professional groups that had appeared in the 1973 APA *Membership Directory*. This implicit endorsement of the lay hypnosis organization led to strong protest to the APA by the division, but to no avail at the time. According to Levitt (1989), this failure led to a concerted effort by the division to educate the APA governance about the nature of hypnosis and the need for its regulation.

In 1983–1984, Edmonston and Erika Wick, with Levitt as chair, formed a committee charged with producing a definition of hypnosis. Their product, "A General Definition of Hypnosis and a Statement Concerning Its Efficacy," was based on a survey of the membership, published in the division newsletter (Edmonston, Levitt, & Wick, 1983), and a final opinion was produced by 14 distinguished members.

The Project Enlightenment definition begins,

> Hypnosis is a condition of altered consciousness of the individual which is characterized by: 1) physical relaxation; 2) an apparent inertia, probably related to the relaxation; 3) an enhanced degree of suggestibility; 4) a partial suspension of critical capacities as a consequence of changes in perceptual and memory processes; 5) a narrowing of the focus of attention and thus an increase in the subjective involvement in the experience; 6) increased ability to dissociate consciousness from considerations of reality. . . .

The definition continues, describing such basic parameters of hypnosis as individual differences in hypnotic suggestibility, relations of hypnotizibility with personality, and ability variables, age, gender, and others. It also details representative hypnotic phenomena and induction techniques. Various aspects of the application of hypnosis are also covered in this document. These include questions about hypnotizing a person against his or her will, as well as whether a hypnotized person can be compelled to behave immorally or illegally. Next clinical applications and efficacy were described, as well as the professional and other training deemed necessary for the competent practice of clinical hypnosis. The document ended with a cautionary statement about the ease of both learning and misusing hypnosis, as well as the importance of regulating its practice.

The Project Enlightenment definition was generated primarily for legal and regulatory purposes. However, its premise that hypnosis is an altered state of consciousness generated protests from a number of leaders in the field (Coe, 1992) and encouraged its rejection by prominent researchers and theorists who had differing points of view. Project Enlightenment was to have important consequences within the APA (described later in this chapter) but its impact outside the organization was minimal.

The more successful definition of hypnosis was produced by the working group formed by Kirsch during his presidency. It is a descriptive and theoretically neutral definition generated by a process of building expert consensus (Kirsch, 1994). This definition is theoretically neutral and seeks to present hypnosis in a broad nontechnical way that can be useful for both experts and the public. It is well-suited for explaining clinical hypnosis to clients in therapy, and it may be freely reproduced.

Definition of Hypnosis

> Hypnosis is a procedure during which a health professional or researcher suggests that a client, patient, or research participant experience changes in sensations, perceptions, thoughts, or behavior. The hypnotic context is generally established by an induction procedure. Although there are many different hypnotic inductions, most include suggestions for relaxation, calmness, and well-being. Instructions to

imagine or think about pleasant experiences are also commonly included in hypnotic inductions.

People respond to hypnosis in different ways. Some describe their experience as an altered state of consciousness. Others describe hypnosis as a normal state of focused attention, in which they feel very calm and relaxed. Regardless of how and to what degree they respond, most people describe the experience as very pleasant.

Some people are responsive to hypnotic suggestions and others are less responsive. A person's ability to experience hypnotic suggestions can be inhibited by fears and concerns arising from some common misconceptions. Contrary to some depictions of hypnosis in books, movies, or on television, people who have been hypnotized do not lose control over their behavior. They typically remain aware of who they are and where they are, and unless amnesia has been specifically suggested, they usually remember what transpired during hypnosis. Hypnosis makes it easier for people to experience suggestions, but it does not force them to have these experiences.

Hypnosis is not a type of therapy, like psychoanalysis or behavior therapy. Instead, it is a procedure that can be used to facilitate therapy. Because it is not a treatment in and of itself, training in hypnosis is not sufficient for the conduct of therapy. Clinical hypnosis should be used only by properly trained and credentialed health care professionals (e.g., licensed clinical psychologists), who have also been trained in the clinical use of hypnosis and are working within the areas of their professional expertise.

Hypnosis has been used in the treatment of pain, depression, anxiety, stress, habit disorders, and many other psychological and medical problems. However, it may not be useful for all psychological problems or for all patients or clients. The decision to use hypnosis as an adjunct to treatment can only be made in consultation with a qualified health care provider who has been trained in the use and limitations of clinical hypnosis.

In addition to its use in clinical settings, hypnosis is used in research, with the goal of learning more about the nature of hypnosis itself, as well as its impact on sensation, perception, learning, memory, and physiology. Researchers also study the value of hypnosis in the treatment of physical and psychological problems.[1]

Convention Programming

The division's 1969 APA convention program had been creditable but not complete. In 1970 the program was again chaired by Barber, who

---

[1]This definition and description of hypnosis was prepared by the Executive Committee of the APA, Division of Psychological Hypnosis. Permission to reproduce this document is freely granted, provided its source is appropriately acknowledged.

was then the president-elect (Levitt, 1989). He included not only the customary paper sessions and symposia but a film and a conversation hour led by Orne. Hilgard's presidential address at that meeting, titled "Dissociation Revisited," was the first exposition of his neodissociation theory.

As the division has grown over the years since its inception, so has its APA convention program. The number of hours on the APA program, one of the prime reasons for the establishment of the division, is based heavily on the division size. Thus in its first convention in 1969, Division 30 was allocated 15 program hours. However, in recent years that allocation has typically exceeded 25 program hours. Although a summary of the highlights of past convention programs is beyond the scope of this chapter, it is no exaggeration to say that Division 30 has consistently featured state-of-the-art presentations from internationally recognized hypnosis researchers and clinicians. Furthermore, because of the increased allocation of convention hours, the division has been able to allow many lesser psychologists and students the opportunity to present their work.

Workshops

The controversy between Mahran and the first program committee had been resolved in the latter's favor—there was no workshop in the 1969 convention program. According to Levitt (1989), it was to be four more years before the division had its first true convention workshop. Weitzenhoffer was then chair of the program committee for the 1973 APA meeting in Montreal. That program included a workshop chaired by Wick titled, "Current Trends and Research in Hypnotherapy," with major presentations by John and Helen Watkins, Kline (in absentia), Jack Tracktir, and Weitzenhoffer. Small group discussions on various topics were led by Barber, Edmonston, Fromm, Campbell, Perry, Raginsky, and Erik Wright. It is noteworthy that 90 percent of the participants rated this first division workshop as "good" to "excellent" (Levitt, 1989).

Following this successful debut the division's continuing education effort fell on bad times (Levitt, 1989). An attempted workshop in 1977 did not produce enough participants to make it viable, and no further efforts were made until Norman Katz and Horevitz were designated cochairs for the 1982 workshops. The 1983 APA convention had a two-day workshop titled, "Hypnosis 1983: The State of the Art and Science of Clinical and Experimental Hypnosis," which featured such authorities in the field as Erika Fromm, Bernauer Newton, John Chaves, Clorinda Margolis, and Daniel Arraoz. Obligations compelled Katz to resign his post and he was replaced the following year by Steven Lynn. Under the leadership of Lynn and Horevitz, the successful workshop programs continued until 1988, but thereafter again foundered. Other workshops on aspects of hypnosis appeared intermittently at a number of APA conventions, but these were typically not presented under the auspices of either Division 30 as an organization or its membership.

Fortunately, the on-again and off-again pattern of Division 30 workshops would eventually be reversed. In 1995 the chair of the Education and Training Committee, Manual I. Gerton, undertook the assignment of obtaining APA approval of Division 30 as a continuing education sponsor. This was a significant step forward, because an APA-approved sponsor allows for considerable independence in the presentation of training activities. For example, the division could arrange its own times and places for workshops, and there is much more control over the financial arrangements. Gerton's efforts came to fruition in 1997, when the division received provisional approval as a continuing education sponsor. The division's first "official" workshop under this new authority was an introductory workshop in clinical hypnosis presented by Arreed and Marianne Barabasz at the 1998 APA convention in San Francisco.

Publishing

Fay H. Starr served as interim secretary–treasurer and later as the first elected secretary–treasurer of the division. His contributions included the initiation of the first newsletters beginning in 1969. Newsletters have been published continuously since that time, and they have been one of the principal channels of communication to the membership at large. The newsletters have also been one of the major benefits of membership. Subsequent newsletter editors have included Elgan Baker, J.-R. Laurence, Council, and currently Etzel Cardeña.

Beginning with the fall 1991 issue, the newsletter was upgraded to a more journal-like format. Indeed, it was no longer referred to as a newsletter but as *Psychological Hypnosis: A Bulletin of APA Division 30*. The numbering of volumes and issues commenced with the first issue of the 1992 bulletin. That change permitted articles to be referenced in future publications. The initial numbered issue ran a lead article by John R. Kihlstrom titled, "On the Place of Hypnosis in the APA Publication Structure." *Psychological Hypnosis* took advantage of desktop publishing techniques to acquire a more sophisticated look while retaining a cost-effective tabloid format. Under Council's editorship, research papers, case studies, and even a humorous column supplemented the contemporary notes and news for dissemination to division members. The present bulletin has retained this sophisticated appearance and content under the editorship of Cardeña. One new feature is "Pioneers," a column that has featured recent work by such seminal authorities as Barber, Hilgard, Fromm, David Cheek, and Kenneth Bowers. Periodically, the executive committee has considered converting *Psychologi-*

cal Hypnosis into a true journal, but no action has yet been taken to change the present format because of the expense involved.

Although not directly associated with the division, Lynn's publishing efforts with APA Books should also be acknowledged under this heading. Lynn (president, 1989–1990) has been instrumental in promoting a very significant series of hypnosis publications by the APA. These have almost exclusively featured distinguished members of the division as book or chapter authors, and include the *Handbook of Clinical Hypnosis* (Rhue, Lynn, & Kirsch, 1993), the *Casebook of Clinical Hypnosis* (Lynn, Kirsch, & Rhue, 1996), and *Clinical Hypnosis and Self-Regulation* (Kirsch, Capafons, Cardeña-Buelna, & Amigo, 1999).

Lay Hypnosis

From its inception, Division 30 has tried to ensure that the clinical application of hypnosis is governed by the highest professional standards of training, experience, and conduct. As noted previously, Orne had objected to the formation of the division on the grounds that unqualified persons might present membership as a clinical credential, and for some time the division maintained a training requirement for membership. Fortunately, no cases have developed to support Orne's fears, even after membership requirements were relaxed.

The division's concerns about lay hypnosis crystallized around a survey of psychologists in the United States and Canada that was undertaken in connection with the 1973 APA *Membership Directory* (Levitt, 1989). That survey listed 58 professional or scientific organizations and requested that the respondent indicate to which he or she belonged. The ASCH was included; the SCEH was not. Instead, a lay organization, the Association for the Advancement of Ethical Hypnosis, a predominantly nonprofessional organization, was listed.

At the December 1973 meeting of the APA Council of Representatives, Kline, as Division 30's representative, introduced a motion calling on the Council "to take steps to remedy its unfortunate inclusion of a nonprofessional organization in its recently published Roster of Professional and Scientific Associations, as well as omitting one of the two national professional organizations" (Levitt, 1989). However, that motion was defeated, presumably because of a legal opinion that any remedial action taken against the AAEH could result in legal difficulty. However, the Council did pass a resolution introduced by Kline that directed the APA Board of Professional Affairs (BPA) "to study the issues related to certification or licensure with the intent to draw up standards for the protection of the public in view of recent efforts to license lay hypnotists" (Levitt, 1989). Unfortunately, according to Levitt (1989), the division's resolution died unnoticed. At the APA convention in 1980, the division introduced a resolution stating that it should be considered "unethical to train lay individuals in the use of hypnosis, to collaborate with laymen in the use of hypnosis, or to serve as a consultant for laymen who are utilizing hypnosis" (Levitt, 1989). This resolution was based on similar positions that had already been adopted by the SCEH, the ASCH, and the ISH. That resolution was again referred to the APA Board of Professional Affairs and also to the APA Ethics Committee. In 1981, Joan Scagnelli-Jobsis as the Council representative, with Levitt as immediate past-president of the division, appeared before a meeting of the APA Board of Professional Affairs to speak for the resolution and to ascertain what had happened to the earlier resolution. According to Levitt (1989), they came away with the impression that the BPA would not pursue the resolution because its members seemed unable to deal adequately with the concept of hypnosis itself. The BPA referred the resolution to its Committee on Professional Standards, which in turn concluded that it did not have the resources to develop standards for the practice of hypnosis. This implied that Division 30 should take responsibility for whatever might be lacking to enact the resolution. The division accepted this responsibility and initiated an effort to recast the resolution into a form that would obtain approval from the APA governance.

The primary mechanism for that undertaking was the Project Enlightenment committee, referred to earlier in this chapter, which was composed of Edmonston and Wick, with Levitt as chair. Its task was to develop a comprehensive definition of the term *hypnosis*, which could serve as a basis for legislative action. Their product, noted previously, was titled "A General Definition of Hypnosis and a Statement Concerning Its Application and Efficacy." Levitt became Division 30's APA Council representative in 1985, and he introduced a resolution on the training of lay persons in hypnosis at the following Council meeting. In its final form, the resolution would have put the APA on record as formally opposing "applications of hypnosis by persons who are not fully trained members or advanced students of a health delivery profession," as well as the teaching "of hypnotic induction techniques or applications of hypnosis that involve treatment or assessment with patients or clients to persons who are not fully trained members or advanced students in a health related profession" (Levitt, 1989). The Project Enlightenment report was appended to the resolution.

The resolution was referred to the APA Board of Professional Affairs, which in turn requested that it be reviewed by the APA legal counsel. The board recommended rejection of the resolution, as did the APA Board of Directors. Their reasoning was that the APA Code of Ethics already covered that matter; however, when the resolution came to a vote in the Council of Representatives in 1986, no one on the floor spoke against it. Orne, by special permission of the APA, and Levitt, as a Council member, spoke for it. The resolution passed by a voice vote. The resolution also called for its text to be conveyed to the APA Ethics Committee to consider its incorporation in the overall APA Code of Ethics. Eventually, that effort came to fruition as well. Section 6.04 of the 1992 revision of "Ethical Principles of Psychologists" and "Code of Conduct" (APA, 1992) states that "psychologists do not teach the use of techniques or procedures that require specialized training, licensure, or expertise, including but not *limited to hypnosis*, biofeedback and projective techniques, to individuals who lack the prerequisite training, legal scope of practice, or expertise."

Although Levitt's initiative was successful at the time, the issue of lay hypnosis is far from settled even now. The legal problems associated with the regulation of hypnosis have already been noted, and recent developments in federal antitrust statutes have made the issues even more difficult (J. L. McHugh, personal communication, July 29, 1997). Although lay hypnosis remains an area of considerable concern for all psychologists because of its possible impact on the public's well-being, Division 30 and the APA could be on tenuous legal grounds if an attempt were made to discourage the use of hypnosis by nonprofessionals. Essentially, because of the developments of antitrust law that have occurred since they were adopted by the APA, the resolutions stemming from Project Enlightenment are no longer valid or binding. Yet the issue of lay hypnosis cannot be ignored, especially because lay organizations have been pursuing their own aggressive legislative agenda. During his term as president-elect, in 1995 Council worked with the division, the APA Practice Directorate, and representatives of the lay hypnosis community to consider solutions to the problems presented by lay hypnosis (Council, 1997a, 1997b). At the 1997 APA convention, Melvin Gravitz and Council presented papers on the impact of lay hypnotists on professional psychology, which generated considerable discussion (Council, 1997a; Gravitz, 1997b). At present, Division 30's position on lay hypnosis emphasizes information gathering and dissemination, education of the public and other professional groups about hypnosis, and communication with lay hypnosis organizations.

THE FUTURE OF PSYCHOLOGICAL HYPNOSIS

At the time of this writing, virtually none of the founding members and early leaders of the division who had dominated the division for the first dozen years of its existence are still active in its governance. Gravitz, who served his term as division president from 1994 to 1995, was the last division president who was a founding member. Some, including Sarbin, Watkins, Fromm, and Barber, are still active contributors to psychology and hypnosis, and their work appears in convention programs and the division bulletin. Unhappily, a number of the Old Guard are deceased, including Estabrooks, Guze, Levitt, London, Starr, Shor, and Wright. In fact, even the second generation of division leaders, as represented by the presidents of the 1980s and listed in Table 6, has mostly phased out of active roles in the division and its affairs. The mantle has been passed to a third generation of leadership as represented by the presidents of the 1990s and of the 21st century.

Many challenges remain as the division enters its fourth decade. Recent presidents of Division 30 have addressed a variety of challenging issues through special initiatives during their terms, and most of these initiatives have remained active. Council's work on lay hypnotherapy has already been described. Division 30 can benefit psychology in general through its continued involvement in this arena because of the implications of "lay therapists" for the profession. Ian Wickramasekera (1995–1996) has been particularly active in promoting the importance of hypnosis for primary health care. He has used convention programming, outreach, and political activism to ensure that the contributions of psychological hypnosis are not overlooked by other professions. Other current presidential initiatives include Stanley Krippner's (1997–1998) attention to educational, cross-cultural, and ethnic issues, and Edward J. Frischholz's (1998–1999) work on legal and regulatory issues. Frischholz has worked particularly hard to promote linkages between Division 30 and Division 41 (American Psychology-Law Society). Cynthia Wickless (1999–2000) focused on facilitating the use of hypnosis in clinical practice. Still another critical issue concerns the place of hypnosis in the new APA College of Professional Psychology (CPP), and this has been a concern of presidents through the 1990s. In reference to the latter, the division is presently studying the question of whether clinical hypnosis may be considered either a specialty or a proficiency, and the implications of this decision. The conclusion is that it *is* a proficiency and certification at that level should be included in the agenda of the college. The final and ultimate challenge is the continuing decline in divisional membership (see Figure 3). This problem is likely multiply determined, ranging from problems in reimbursing hypnosis under managed care to a general tightening of purse strings that has also led to a general decline in APA membership. This threat has been recognized for years, and a number of initiatives have been undertaken to reverse the trend. Most recently, based on an initiative by the 1998–1999 executive committee, the membership has voted to open up membership to psychologists and other health professionals who are not members of the APA (APA Division 30, 1999).

In addition to recognizing and managing current challenges, Division 30 also undertook a more formalized approach to the prediction of trends in the field by means of a "Delphi Poll" conducted by Lynn (president,

1989–1990). This project involved polling a large number of experts in hypnosis to delineate significant future trends in the field. Results indicate that important research areas in the years to come will include hypnosis and pain management, eyewitness memory, pseudomemories, information processing, individual differences, and psychophysiological processes–mechanisms. Important areas for clinical applicaitons by hypnosis are also apt to involve, among others, mind–body behaviors, including pain, cancer, and psychoneurimmunology, as well as a variety of dissociated and anxiety disorders.

CONCLUSION

It is apparent that during its three decades of existence, Division 30 has successfully faced a wide variety of challenges. These have included its own initial and continuing organizational changes, broad scientific and professional issues, and a host of other matters that are important to the larger field of psychology as well as to psychological hypnosis. As it has grown to meet these challenges, the division has become a vital, active, and significant force within the APA. The membership of the division continues to play an important role in firmly establishing hypnosis within scientific and professional psychology. There will be difficulties in the future, of course, but the division's past achievements afford every hope and anticipation that Division 30 will be in the vanguard of positive developments in the field.

REFERENCES

APA Division 30. (1999). *Policy and procedures manual.* Washington, DC: Author.

American Psychological Association. (1992). Ethical principles of psychologists and code of conduct. *American Psychologist, 47,* 1597–1611.

Barber, T. X. (1969). *Hypnosis: A scientific approach.* New York: Van Nostrand Reinhold.

Brenman, M., & Gill M. M. (1947). *Hypnotherapy: A survey of the literature.* New York: International Universities Press.

Breuer, J., & Freud, S. (1955). Studies in hysteria. In J. Strachey (Ed. and Trans.), *The standard edition of the complete psychological works of Sigmund Freud* (Vol. 2). London: Hogarth Press. (Original work published 1895.)

Clemens, S. L. (1959). *The autobiography of Mark Twain.* New York: Harper & Row.

Coe, W. C. (1992). Hypnosis: Wherefore art thou? *International Journal of Clinical and Experimental Hypnosis, 40,* 219–237.

Council, J. R. (1997a, August). *Presidential address: The challenge of lay hypnosis for professional psychology*. Paper presented at the annual meeting of the American Psychological Association, Chicago.

Council, J. R. (1997b). Response to Division 30 proposed policy on lay hypnosis: Toward a position on lay hypnotherapy. *Psychological Hypnosis, 6,1,3,* 11–13.

Crabtree A. (1988). *Animal magnetism, early hypnotism and psychical research, 1766–1925: An annotated bibliography*. White Plains, NY: Kraus International.

Edmonston, W. E. (1980, Summer). Letter to the editor. *Division 30 Newsletter.*

Edmonston, W. E., Levitt, E. E., & Wick, E. (1983, December). Project Enlightenment, *Division 30 Newsletter,* 3–4.

Gravitz, M. A. (1997a). First uses of hypnotism nomenclature: Clarifying the historical record. *Hypnos, 24,* 42–46.

Gravitz, M. A. (1997b, August). *Lay therapists and professional psychologists*. Paper presented at the annual meeting of the American Psychological Association, Chicago.

Hilgard, E. R. (1965). *Hypnotic susceptibility*. New York: Harcourt Brace & World.

Hilgard, E. R. (1977). *Divided consciousness: Multiple controls in human thought and action*. New York: Wiley.

Hilgard, E. R. (1993). History of research centers and professional hypnosis societies in the United States. *International Journal of Clinical and Experimental Hypnosis, 41,* 173–190.

Hilgard, E. R., & Hilgard, J. R. (1975). *Hypnosis in the relief of pain*. Los Altos, CA: William Kaufmann.

Horevitz, R. P. (1991). A message from the president. *Psychological Hypnosis (Fall),* 2–3.

Horevitz, R. P. (1992). President's message. *Psychological Hypnosis, 1,2* (1), 12–14.

Hull, C. L. (1933). Hypnosis and suggestibility: An experimental approach. New York: Appleton Century Crofts.

James, W. (1890). *Principles of psychology*. (Vols. I and II). New York: Holt.

Kardiner, A. (1947). *War stress and neurotic illness*. New York: Hoeber.

Kirsch, I. (1990). *Changing expectations: A key to effective psychotherapy*. Pacific Grove, CA: Brooks/Cole.

Kirsch, I. (1994). APA definition and description of hypnosis: Defining hypnosis for the public. *Contemporary Hypnosis, 11,* 142–143.

Kirsch, I., Capafons, A., Cardeña-Buelna, E., & Amigo, S. (1999). *Clinical hypnosis and self-regulation*. Washington, DC: American Psychological Association.

Levitt, E. E. (1989, August). *Twenty years of trances: A history of the Division of Psychological Hypnosis*. Paper presented at the annual meeting of the American Psychological Association, New Orleans.

Lynn, S. J., Kirsch, I., & Rhue, J. W. (Eds.). (1996). *Casebook of clinical hypnosis*. Washington, DC: American Psychological Association.

Miller, G. A., Galanter, E., & Pribram, K. H. (1960). *Plans and the structure of behavior*. New York: Henry Holt.

Prince, M. (1905). *The dissociation of a personality: A biographical study in abnormal psychology*. New York: Longmans, Green.

Rhue, J. W., Lynn, S. J., & Kirsch, I. (1993). *Handbook of clinical hypnosis*. Washington, DC: American Psychological Association.

Sarbin, T. R. (1950). Contributions to role-taking theory: I. Hypnotic behavior. *Psychological Review, 57*, 255–270.

Sarbin, T. R., & Coe, W. C. (1972). *Hypnosis: A social psychological analysis of influence communication*. New York: Holt Reinhart & Winston.

Spanos, N. P., & Chaves, J. F. (Eds.). (1989). *Hypnosis: The cognitive–behavioral perspective*. Buffalo, NY: Prometheus.

Watkins, J. G. (1949). *Hypnotherapy of war neuroses: A clinical psychologist's handbook*. New York: Ronald Press.

Watkins, J. G. (1995). Organization and functioning of ISCEH, the International Society for Clinical and Experimental Hypnosis. *International Journal of Clinical and Experimental Hypnosis, 43*, 332–341.

Weitzenhoffer, A. M., & Hilgard, E. R. (1959). *Stanford Hypnotic Susceptibility Scale: Forms A and B*. Palo Alto, CA: Consulting Psychologists Press.

Weitzenhoffer, A. M., & Hilgard, E. R. (1962). *Stanford Hypnotic Susceptibility Scale: Form C*. Palo Alto, CA: Consulting Psychologists Press.

White, R. W. (1941). A preface to a theory of hypnotism. *Journal of Abnormal and Social Psychology, 36*, 477–505.

4

A HISTORY OF DIVISION 32 (HUMANISTIC PSYCHOLOGY)

CHRISTOPHER M. AANSTOOS, ILENE SERLIN,
and THOMAS GREENING[1]

As with most complex human endeavors, the history of APA Division 32 (Humanistic Psychology) has many facets and lends itself to many narratives and interpretations. Presented here is one version, resulting from the input of three authors and many other people. Our audience may wish to read between the lines or project onto the text other versions. In humanistic psychology, in writing the division's history, and indeed in psychology itself, there are always texts and subtexts and multiple "stories" and interpretations. Right and left brains play their parts in the making of history and in the recording and interpretation of it. Other fascinating chapters besides this one could be written about the people involved in this division, the intellectual and interpersonal currents, and the creative, socially responsible, and sometimes spontaneous and chaotic events that underlay this history.

---

[1]Serlin and Aanstoos are primary coauthors.

The authors thank Carmi Harari, Myron Arons, Gloria Gottsegen, Mark Stern, Amedeo Giorgi, Stanley Krippner, and Alvin Mahrer, all early leaders in Division 32 history. Their willingness to be interviewed greatly assisted in the research that led to this chapter. Harari's own written correspondence and other archival materials, which he kindly shared, were also indispensable. Further thanks are owed to Eleanor Criswell, David Elkins, Kirk Schneider, and Myron Arons, without whose support the chapter could not have been completed. We also thank Donald Dewsbury, without whose patience and perseverance this chapter would not have reached a final publishable form.

PRIOR HISTORY: AN EMERGENT CULTURAL ZEITGEIST

Humanistic psychology is sometimes known as the Third Force in contrast to two major orientations in American psychology, behaviorism and psychoanalysis, which along with the biomedical model are considered by humanistic psychologists to be reductionistic, mechanistic, and dehumanizing in regard to human beings as whole persons. As one critic of behaviorism put it, "American psychology first lost its soul, then its mind, and finally its consciousness, but it still behaved" (Waters, 1958, p. 278). In regard to psychoanalysis, Freud's own words present the challenge to which humanistic psychology responded.

> The moment a man questions the meaning and value of life he is sick, since objectively neither has any existence; by asking this question one is merely admitting to a store of unsatisfied libido to which something else must have happened, a kind of fermentation leading to sadness and depression. (Freud, 1960, p. 436)

Many psychologists were crucial in preparing the ground for what emerged as humanistic psychology's alternative, but three stand out: Abraham Maslow, Carl Rogers, and Rollo May. Maslow founded the psychology department at Brandeis University in 1951 with a strong humanistic orientation even before the movement was thus named. Originally working within experimental psychology, Maslow (1954) developed a research program and subsequent humanistic theory of motivation. He argued that people are motivated not only reactively by the "deficiency needs" with which psychology had hitherto been concerned, but also proactively by "being needs," ultimately including such motives as self-actualization.

Rogers (1951) sought ways to facilitate clients' yearning for self-actualization and fully functioning living, especially via person-centered therapy and group work. He was one of the first researchers to study psychotherapy process using tape-recordings and transcripts, and he and his students also made extensive use of Q-sorts to study self-concept and change. He explored the necessary conditions for therapeutic progress and emphasized congruence, presence, and acceptance on the part of the therapist. May (1953; May, Angel, & Ellenberger, 1958) built a bridge from interpersonal psychoanalysis and European existentialism and phenomenology, having been influenced by Harry Stack Sullivan, Ludwig Binswanger, and Medard Boss. May's books integrated creativity, the arts, mythology, and the humanities with psychology, and encompassed the tragic view of life and the demoniac forces. Charlotte Bühler, Erich Fromm, and Viktor Frankl also contributed European perspectives to this stream, including a concern for values in psychotherapy, human development over the whole course of human life, humanistic psychoanalysis, social issues, love, transcendence of evil, and the search for meaning.

In the 1960s many isolated voices began to gather momentum and form a critique of American culture and consciousness and to form the basis of a new approach to psychology. Massive cultural changes were sweeping through America. That larger movement was an expression of a society eager to move beyond the alienating, bland conformity, embedded presuppositions, and prejudices that had characterized the 1950s return to "normalcy" after World War II. In psychology, adjustment models were challenged by visions of growth, and the human potential movement emerged. T-groups, sensitivity training, human relations training, and encounter groups became popular. The goal was greater awareness of one's own actual experience in the moment and authentic engagement with others, goals not well-served by academic psychology, clinical psychology, or the culture in general. Growth centers sprang up across the country, offering a profusion of workshops and techniques, such as transactional analysis, sensory awareness, gestalt encounter, body work, meditation, yoga, massage therapy, and psychosynthesis. The best known of these was Esalen Institute, founded in Big Sur, California, in 1964, which is in operation to this day. Begun as a site for seminars, it featured psychologists such as May, Maslow, and Rogers and also scholars from other disciplines such as Arnold Toynbee, Paul Tillich, Gregory Bateson, and Alan Watts.

These developments in the culture and in "pop psychology" paralleled changes in clinical and academic domains. Existential and phenomenological trends in continental psychiatry affected the Anglo American sphere through the work of R. D. Laing and his British colleagues. His trenchant critique of the prevailing medical model's reductionistic and pathological view of schizophrenic patients began a revisioning of even psychotic processes as meaningful, growth-seeking experiencing. Various American psychiatrists also contributed to the elaboration of this alternative, most notably John Perry and Thomas Szasz. At the same time, gestalt therapy was developed and popularized, especially by Perls.

Meanwhile, from the academic side a rising tide of theory and research focused attention on this nonreductive, holistic view of the person. As the 1960s unfolded, new books by Rogers (1961, 1969), Maslow (1962, 1964, 1965a, 1966), and May (1967, 1969) were enormously influential in this more receptive era. May pointed out that if psychologists are to study and understand human beings, we need a human model. He advocated a science of persons, by which he meant a theory that would enable psychologists to understand and clarify the specific, distinguishing characteristics of human beings. Many new voices also began to be raised. Amedeo Giorgi (Division 32 president in 1987–1988) criticized experimental psychology's reductionism, and argued for a phenomenologically based methodology that could support a more authentically human science of psychology (Giorgi, 1965, 1966, 1970). Giorgi argued that psychology has the responsibility to investigate the full range of behavior and experience of people in such a way that the aims of rigorous science are fulfilled, but that these aims should not be implemented primarily in terms of the criteria of the natural sciences.

As an organized movement, humanistic psychology grew out of a series of meetings in the late 1950s initiated by Maslow and Clark Moustakas and including Rogers, all APA members. They explored themes such as the nature of the self, self-actualization, health, creativity, being, becoming, individuation, and meaning. Building on these meetings, in 1961 an organizing committee including Anthony Sutich launched the Journal of Humanistic Psychology. Its early editorial board included many well-known scholars such as Andras Angyal, Fromm, Kurt Goldstein, May, Moustakas, and Lewis Mumford. Maslow had compiled a mailing list of colleagues to whom he sent his papers that conventional journals would not publish, and this was used to begin the promotion of the journal (deCarvalho, 1990).

The new journal's success in coalescing a responsive subscriber base quickly convinced its founders that a professional association could also meet a need. With the assistance of James Bugental, who served as its first president pro tem, and a grant arranged by Gordon Allport, the inaugural meeting of the Association for Humanistic Psychology (AHP) was held in Philadelphia in 1963. Among the 75 attendees were many who would later play prominent leadership roles in this movement. (For a summary of this meeting see deCarvahlo, 1991, pp. 10–11.)

In 1963 Bugental published a foundational article, "Humanistic Psychology: A New Breakthrough," in the *American Psychologist*, which was adopted by the AHP as a basic statement of its own orientation. This statement was amplified in Bugental's 1964 article, "The Third Force in Psychology" in the *Journal of Humanistic Psychology* and appears, in the following slightly amplified version, in each issue of the journal.

Five Basic Postulates of Humanistic Psychology

1. Human beings, as human, are more than merely the sum of their parts. They cannot be reduced to component parts or functions.
2. Human beings exist in a uniquely human context, as well as in a cosmic ecology.
3. Human beings are aware and aware of being aware—i.e., they are conscious. Human consciousness potentially includes an awareness of oneself in the context of other people and the cosmos.

4. Human beings have some choice, and with that, responsibility.
5. Human beings are intentional, aim at goals, are aware that they cause future events, and seek meaning, value and creativity. (Bugental, 1964, pp. 19–25)

The second AHP meeting took place in Los Angeles in September 1964, with about 200 attendees. As Bugental observed, this group already included the four major subgroups that have characterized and sometimes strained the association since then: therapists, social–political activists, academic theorists and researchers, and "touchy feely" personal growth seekers (deCarvalho, 1991, 1992).

To develop the philosophy, themes, and direction of the AHP and humanistic psychology theory, The Old Saybrook Conference was convened in 1964 at a Connecticut country inn. It was an invitational conference sponsored by AHP, financed by the Hazen Foundation, and hosted by Wesleyan University under the direction of Robert Knapp. Leading figures in the psychology of personality and in the humanistic disciplines participated: Allport, George Kelly, Moustakas, Gardner Murphy, Henry Murray, and Robert White of the founding generation; Charlotte Bühler, representing a European tradition of research labeled "life-span development," Jacques Barzun and Rene Dubos as humanists from literature and biological science, and Bugental, Maslow, May, and Rogers, who became the intellectual leaders of the movement. These founders did not intend to neglect scientific aspirations; rather, they sought to influence and correct the positivistic bias of psychological science as it then stood. The titles of some of the papers indicate the focus of the conference: "Some Thoughts Regarding the Current Philosophy of the Behavioral Sciences" by Rogers, "Intentionality, the Heart of Human Will" by May, "Psychology: Natural Science or Humanistic Discipline?" by Edward Joseph Shoben, and "Humanistic Science and Transcendent Experiences" by Maslow.

In addition to the *Journal of Humanistic Psychology*, the AHP, and the Old Saybrook Conference, the subsequent years also saw the founding of graduate programs in humanistic psychology. Masters' programs in humanistic psychology were begun in 1966 at Sonoma State University (then Sonoma State College), and in 1969 at the State University of West Georgia (then West Georgia College). An MA program in existential–phenomenological psychology was created at Duquesne University in 1959, and a PhD program was added in 1962. Several free-standing institutes also initiated humanistic graduate programs. John F. Kennedy University and the Union Institute, both begun in 1964, and the California Institute of Integral Studies in 1968 were among the first. In 1971 the AHP created the Humanistic Psychology Institute (now known as Saybrook Graduate School, named after the famous conference). These early programs, still in operation, have since been joined by many others. Thirty-seven are listed in the current *Directory of Graduate Programs in Humanistic–Transpersonal Psychology in North America* (Arons, 1996). Some of these have focused on synthesizing humanistic scholarship with eastern philosophies such as Hinduism and Buddhism (the best-known of these are the California Institute for Integral Studies, John F. Kennedy University, the Institute for Transpersonal Psychology, and Naropa Institute). Faculty members from these graduate programs have been active in Division 32 and many, especially from State University of West Georgia and Saybrook Graduate School, have served as its president.

FOUNDING: AMBIVALENCE AND COLLABORATION

During the 1960s the primary organizational forum for the burgeoning humanistic movement was theAHP, which had become an organization of 6000 members. As a protest movement against the mainstream approaches in psychology, this alternative venue outside of the APA seemed most appropriate. However, as the momentum of change during the 1960s continued, the mainstream also began to open up to much of this new thinking. Abraham Maslow was elected president of the APA in 1968. (Rogers had been president in 1947, and later Stanley Graham and Brewster Smith, two Division 32 presidents, also served as APA presidents.) Eventually, a group of psychologists within the APA decided to pursue the organization of an APA division devoted to humanistic psychology.

This effort was spearheaded by Don Gibbons, then a faculty member at West Georgia College. To propose a new division, the signatures on a petition to the APA of 1% of APA's existing membership were required (approximately 275 at that time). In January 1971 Gibbons wrote to Levy, the executive director of the AHP, seeking his support in soliciting these signatories from APA members who belonged to the AHP. Many members of the AHP were also members of the APA, so it was evident that the two groups would have a significant overlapping membership. As Gibbons wrote in that January 12, 1971 letter:

> We would like to see it set up in such a way as to facilitate communication between the A.P.A. and all areas of the humanistic movement. In particular, we would like to see the new division maintain the closest possible degree of collaboration with A.H.P.

In the end, 374 members of the APA petitioned for the proposed division. As a result, the APA Council of Representatives, after receiving affirmation from the existing divisions of the APA, confirmed and made official the new Division of Humanistic Psychology.

This prospect of another humanistic organization raised concern on the part of some that it would dilute the movement (M. Arons, personal communication, June 6, 1998). The proponents of the proposed division, however, were in any case determined to proceed, and viewed the eventual formation of a Division of Humanistic Psychology within the APA as inevitable, given the continuing rapid growth of humanistic psychology at that time. Though still wary, previously opposed members of the AHP who also belonged to the APA chose to help make the proposed division the best it could be, and gathered at the official organizational meeting scheduled by Gibbons during the 1971 APA convention (C. Harari, personal communication, June 26, 1998). For unknown reasons, Gibbons himself did not attend the meeting, though he was scheduled to. Spontaneously, a group of individuals occupied the dais and took charge of the meeting.

Several people presented the case for a new division. Albert Ellis spoke eloquently for its value in giving a voice within the APA to humanistic psychology. Fred Massarik indicated that originally he had been opposed to the proposed division but now supported it. It was proposed that a steering committee of 11 be elected who would constitute an acting executive board during the coming year, to establish bylaws and a statement of purpose.

As Harari described this first meeting in his letter to the new division's members:

> On Saturday, September 4, 1971, an organizing meeting was held for the Division of Humanistic Psychology of APA during the recent APA meetings held in Washington, DC. Fifty-seven persons attended the organizing meeting and together with original petitioners for the formation of the new Division, as well as other interested members and fellows, became the charter members of the new Division. In the absence of the originally scheduled chairperson, Don Gibbons of West Georgia College, Albert Ellis was appointed Chairman of the meeting and Carmi Harari was appointed Recording Secretary. . . . Several signers of the original petition were present in the room and assisted in the conduct of the meeting, together with the expert consulting assistance of Jane Hildreth, representing APA Central Office. . . . Serving as Presiding Officers for the organizing meeting were Albert Ellis, Stanley Graham, Carmi Harari, Fred Massarik, Denis O'Donovan and Everett Shostrom. (Harari, 1971)

The first meeting of the acting executive board took place immediately following the organizational meeting of the new division. Officers were elected, with Harari chosen as acting president, Graham as acting treasurer, Ellis as acting council representative, and Shostrom and Massarik as cochairs of the next convention's program. Three other decisions were made, all of which would be subsequently challenged and changed: the first program would be on an invitational basis; dues were set at $3; and fellows, members, and associates of the APA would be eligible for division membership on an equal basis, with no classes of membership in the division.

THE EARLY YEARS: GROWTH AND INNOVATION

The following year, 1972, saw the usual development and application of those processes by which a new organization becomes normalized, including membership, governance, programs, and publications. What was reflective of the spirit of Division 32, however, was the open, explorative approach to these features, which were handled in innovative ways.

Membership

A highly successful recruitment of new members, by Barton Knapp as acting membership chair, brought in about 300 new applications during the division's first year, almost doubling the membership total. By January 1, 1973, the total was 647; in 1974 it was 784. By 1975 it topped 900, and by 1976 it was more than 1000. In 1977 it reached 1150, the highest level of membership, where it then stabilized for the next few years.

During the 1973–1974 year, the membership chair, Nora Weckler, conducted a survey of members and itemized their major fields of involvement. Most heavily represented was counseling psychology. Clinical and educational psychologists were also strongly represented, followed by psychotherapy, experimental, social, industrial, and developmental psychologists. Smaller numbers included engineering, environmental, perception, rehabilitation, and philosophical psychologists. Weckler noted that the division's first international members came from Venezuela, Japan, and India. She also itemized reasons given for joining the division. These included

> to have closer contact with others of similar interests; to learn more about the humanistic approach . . . a desire for personal and professional growth and training . . . to learn how psychology can help people lead a more fulfilling life . . . to support the philosophy of Division 32 . . . because of dissatisfaction with AHP's anti-intellectual and anti-scientific attitude . . . an appreciation of the blending of both art and science . . . a desire to learn more of what the Division was doing . . . an interest in the unresolved theoretical and philosophical problems of humanistic psychology . . . with the hope that the Division will further develop theory and research following an existential-phenomenological approach. (Weckler, 1971)

In the following year's membership survey (1974–1975), Weckler turned up mostly continuations of these trends. Members now also came from Great Britain, Canada, Guam, and Puerto Rico. Interest areas covered almost every subfield of psychology, with clinical psychology being the most heavily represented, counseling a close second, and educational psychology third. Social psychology, developmental psychology, rehabilitation psychology, speech and communication psychology, and pastoral psychology were also prominently mentioned.

At that point in its history, Division 32 defined its mission as follows in an undated statement:

> Humanistic psychology aims to be faithful to the full range of human experience. Its foundations include philosophical humanism, existentialism, and phenomenology. In the science and profession of psychology, humanistic psychology seeks to develop systematic and rigorous methods of studying human beings, and to heal the fragmentary character of contemporary psychology through an ever more comprehensive and integrative approach. Humanistic psychologists are particularly sensitive to uniquely human dimensions, such as experiences of creativity and transcendence, and to the quality of human welfare. Accordingly, humanistic psychology aims especially at contributing to psychotherapy, education, theory, philosophy of psychology, research methodology, organization and management and social responsibility and change.

Governance

In early 1972 drafts of the new division's bylaws were circulated to Levy, the executive director of the AHP, to Jane Hildreth at the APA Central Office, and to the Division 32 members for their comments. The purpose of the division, as stated in these first bylaws, was to apply the concepts, theories, and philosophy of humanistic psychology to research, education, and professional applications of scientific psychology.

Only two aspects of the draft bylaws were seen as problematic. Levy pointed out that requiring decisions to be approved at the annual business meeting might result in a small turnout producing unrepresentative results. Mail-in balloting was then also included as a decision-making tool. Levy also questioned the unwieldy large size of the executive board, which included nine at-large members. (This number was later reduced to six.) Hildreth noted (in her letter to Gloria Gottsegen, March 7, 1972) that the division's desire to have only one class of members, although laudable, conflicted with the APA bylaws that prohibit a person from holding higher member status in a division than he or she does in the APA. In the case of the APA's three classes of membership (fellow, member, and associate), it would be no problem to consider APA fellows to be members of Division 32, but associates in the APA could not be "promoted" to member status in the division. This dilemma was resolved, however, by allowing APA associates to enjoy full membership status in the division as members who could vote and hold office on an equal basis, with the sole exception that they could not vote for the Council Representative position (as that voting eligibility is part of APA's own bylaws). Division elections would henceforth require the division secretary to count the ballots of division members who, as associates in the APA, were not eligible to vote in the APA elections and whose ballots would therefore not be sent to the APA. This added complication was seen as well worthwhile, to be able to establish a more egalitarian collegium of members, of whom about 20% were associate members of the APA.

As a result of the initial rapid growth in membership, along with a very positive response to Harari's first appeal of support in the APA apportionment balloting, the new division was awarded two seats on the APA's Council of Representatives. Following a call for nominations, the division's first election was held, in 1972, to select its first actual (rather than acting) officers. Harari was elected president, Everett Shostrom president-elect, Gloria Gottsegen secretary, Barry Crown treasurer, Fred Massarik and Albert Ellis Council representatives. Members-at-large of the executive board were also elected, to serve staggered terms. These included David Bakan, Elizabeth Mintz, Joen Fagen, Robert Strom, Leonard Blank, Lawrence LeShan, James Klee, Janette Rainwater, and Barton Knapp.

When Shostrom became president he presented the executive board with a silver oil can engraved with the inscription, "APA Division 32 President's Actualizing Oil Can," on which he had inscribed the names of the first two division presidents (Harari and Shostrom). He recounted the story of the Wizard of Oz. The straw man, the tin man, and the cowardly lion were seeking from an outside authority qualities they already possessed within themselves. Opening to these inner qualities is a prime message of humanistic psychology. The oil can used by the tin man to lubricate his joints became a ritual reminder of this message as it passes, each name added, from outgoing to incoming presidents.

Beginning with the first elected executive board meeting in 1972 during the APA convention in Honolulu, innovations and changes were typical. Convention programming was changed from being exclusively invitational. It was decided to allot only 50% to invited symposia and 50% to proposals solicited from members. A newsletter was inaugurated, with Alvin Manaster appointed as its first editor, and the Social Responsibility Committee was formed with Klee as its first chair. A proposal by Robert Strom to hold a mid-year executive board meeting was also accepted. It was also decided to include a regular column about Division 32 in the AHP's newsletter to continue the hoped-for collaboration between the two groups.

The election of 1974 featured a problem and creative resolution. The balloting for the position of president-elect resulted in a tie vote between Arons and Graham. With the concurrence of the two candidates, President Shostrom flipped a coin to determine the results. It was agreed that, because Graham won the toss, he would function as president-elect for the 1974–1975 term and that he would function as president from September 1, 1975, until March 1, 1976, at which time he would resign that office and Arons would complete the term of president from March 1, 1976, and continue as past-president from September 1, 1976, to September 1, 1977. In effect, both individuals functioned as copresidents and were so listed in divisional correspondence (Division 32, 1974).

One issue that came up early for Division 32 concerned the growing split within psychology between the professional guild interests and those of academia. Division 32 sought, and has largely succeeded, in housing both within a unity drawn together by a common approach. Nevertheless, this collaborative prospect between clinicians and researchers has not been easy to maintain. The split was first evidenced when the March 1975 midwinter executive board meeting was scheduled to take place during the meeting of Division 29 (Psychotherapy) on Marco Island, Florida. For clinicians, a meeting at a relatively expensive tourist resort seemed agreeable, but academic members of the executive board protested that only those in the clinical end of the profession could afford such locales for meetings (M. Arons, 1974). A committee was appointed at that meeting to examine more mutually agreeable possibilities for future executive board meetings (Gottsegen, 1976, p. 6). Compared to the tensions emerging between clinicians and academicians in the APA at large, this was a minor dispute. However, it did reveal that differences recur between academicians and practitioners, even where larger visions align. A resolution of this conflict came when the next year's midwinter executive board meeting was hosted by Arons at a lodge in the woods of a state park. Despite its very minimal expense, it was fondly remembered later as having been one of the best (G. Gottsegen, personal communication, June 9, 1998).

Convention Programming

The 1972 program also included a collaborative effort with the AHP, which at that time was still scheduling its annual meeting in the same place as the APA's, during the week immediately preceding or following it. The AHP and Division 32 created and cosponsored a joint hospitality suite at the APA meeting. The idea was to parallel the regular program with a center and meeting place for friends and colleagues where they can learn of the differences, similarities, and uniqueness of both the AHP and the division (Harari, 1973b, p. 2). This arrangement was such a success that it quickly became a staple, continued to this day. Indeed, by the following year's APA meeting in 1973 in Montreal, the suite had become an informal division headquarters and provided a meeting place for many humanistic people, especially members and their guests (Harari, 1973a, p. 2). Many outstanding presentations and workshops were given in the hospitality suite, with titles such as "Creative Marital Fighting"; "Existential Psychodrama"; "The Yin and Yang of Chinese Psychology"; "Etiology and Cure of Normality"; and "Humanistic Parenting." Many prominent humanistic psychologists, such as Perls, May, Albert Ellis, Krippner, William Schutz, Nathaniel Branden, and Sidney Jourard, gave presentations or workshops, and were available for spontaneous conversation. These sessions often attracted such overflow audiences that it became necessary to move into larger nearby unoccupied meeting rooms.

The hospitality suite, a major expense for the new division, sometimes left the budget quite strained, but it was always supported as a worthwhile endeavor. Opportunities to simply sit and talk with leaders in the field are among the most fondly recalled events of these early years (G. Gottsegen, personal communication, June 9, 1998; S. Krippner, personal communication, June 30, 1998; A. Mahrer, personal communication, April 22, 1998; E. M. Stern, personal communication, April 24, 1998). This innovation of having a parallel program in a hotel suite during the APA convention has since been adopted by many other divisions.

Regular Division 32 programming at APA conventions also was broad-based and emphasized collaboration with other divisions, including informal conversation hours and workshops. First under Shostrom in 1972, then Alvin Mahrer in 1973, Division 32 cosponsored events with the Divisions of General Psychology (1), Society for the Teaching of Psychology (2), Evaluation, Measurement, and Statistics (5), Developmental Psychology (7), Society for Personality and Social Psychology (8), Psychology and the Arts (10), Society of Clinical Psychology (12), Consulting Psychology (13), Society for Industrial and Organizational Psychology (14), Educational Psychology (15), School Psychology (16), Counseling Psychology (17), Adult Development and Aging (20), Theoretical and Philosophical Psychology (24), Society for Community Research and Action: Division of Community Psychology (27), and Psychotherapy (29; Shostrom, 1973, p. 1). These programs fulfilled the executive board's aim, well-expressed by the 1973 program chair, that the program achieve a good integrative balance among an exciting broad spectrum of what the division represents—humanistic psychology theory, humanistic research, humanistic educational changes, professional applications, humanistic social philosophy, and a chance to speak directly to the APA and the public at large about these issues (Mahrer, 1973, p. 3).

By the 1974 APA meeting in New Orleans, a new programmatic feature was developed: the division sponsored all-day preconvention workshops. One on humanistic psychology was chaired by Robert Hilton and directed by Harari, and one on actualizing therapy was conducted by Shostrom. The following year saw another all-day preconvention workshop success, this one led by Barton Knapp and Marta Vargo titled, "Self-Actualization Through Transactional Analysis."

Beyond convention programming, several members of the Division 32 executive board, particularly Harari, were instrumental in London, Würzburg, Amsterdam, Paris, and Tokyo, and even an around-the-world humanistic psychology study tour with stops in France, Iran, Soviet Union, India, Nepal, Thailand, Hong Kong, Japan, and Hawaii (for the APA meeting). Harari and Krippner were particularly central to these early activities, which were also sponsored by the AHP. Graham joined Harari in a number of subsequent efforts, and Arons, Jourard, Gottsegen and others also became active.

Publications

The first Division 32 *Newsletter* was issued from President Harari's office November 1, 1971, with news about the formation of the division. A second issue was dated May 29, 1972, and carried news of the division taking seats in the APA Council of Representatives.

Between APA conventions, communication among members was also nourished with the establishment of a division newsletter. *The Bulletin: Division of Humanistic Psychology*, the first formal division publication, appeared in 1973, edited by Alvin Manaster. It began as four pages of news items about the division's business, then expanded (by the third issue) to eight pages, with the intention to serve also as a scholarly exchange network for members to become aware of each other's research and writing projects. One early problem, often recurring, was of getting issues out on time, given the deadlines with regard to apportionment balloting, elections, calls for nominations, and programming. In March 1974 Zaraleya Harari was named newsletter editor. She brought to the task a personal and informal style. After a few years, however, Manaster resumed editorship and continued until 1985.

Another publication possibility was proposed in August 1973 by Fred Massarik, who suggested that the division adopt as its official journal *Interpersonal Development*, a journal founded in 1970 for which he had been serving as editor. Under the proposed arrangement, all division members would receive a subscription at a reduced rate as part of their membership benefits. To cover the cost of these subscriptions, dues would have to be increased to $10. Instead of adopting a journal, the division executive board, at its

September 1974 meeting, chose to begin a policy by which journals that chose to affiliate with the division would offer subscriptions at reduced rates to division members and offer space in their pages for division news. In November 1974 both *Interpersonal Development* and the AHP's *Journal of Humanistic Psychology* became affiliated journals.

THE MIDDLE YEARS: BUILDING UP AND SETTLING DOWN

When B. F. Skinner, nearing the end of his long career, contemplated the question of why psychology had not become a science of behavior, as he phrased it, he posited three formidable obstacles on that path (Skinner, 1987). He proclaimed the number one obstacle had been humanistic psychology; the other two were cognitivism and psychotherapy. Although the relative order of these three impediments is open to question, it certainly indicated a significant recognition for humanistic psychology that it should be seen as such a decisive foe to the behaviorist paradigm that had seemed so hegemonic before the humanistic approach emerged.

However, the popularity of humanistic psychology began to wane as the 1970s turned into the 1980s. The Reagan years brought a new sociocultural conservatism for which the very term "humanistic" meant something sinister. Usually dubbed "secular humanism" by conservative opponents, many strange bedfellows soon arose. Perhaps the most peculiar irony was Skinner himself supporting an association of secular humanists (the American Humanist Association), while blaming humanistic psychology for the failure of his own project—at one point even comparing humanistic psychology to the creationists he and his "secular humanists" were battling (Skinner, 1987). Religious fundamentalists also condemned humanistic psychology—and continue to do so. For example, religious, conservative radio broadcaster James Dobson (head of Focus on the Family) often depicts a basic struggle between fundamentalist Christianity and secular humanism. A letter from him to his supporters asserted that secular humanism, the sexual revolution, and the New Age movement "have taken a heavy toll on America" (Boston, 1998, p. 13).

This new conservatism reduced humanistic psychology's previously wide base of support among lay people. Even within humanistic organizations, it became clear that the very word "humanistic" was seen by some as a distinct handicap. The Humanistic Psychology Institute, begun in 1970 by the AHP, even changed its name to Saybrook Institute, primarily to give itself and its graduates a more mainstream image (Saybrook, the name of the 1964 conference on humanistic psychology, was a meaningful signifier within humanistic circles, but neutral to outsiders.) The Association of

Humanistic Education likewise debated changing its name in the mid-1980s, and barely decided not to. The Division of Humanistic Psychology did not waver but did experience membership declines during this time, from a peak of about 1150 down to about 700.

The question of self-identity, however, became a thematic issue for the division during the 1980s. The division had always been home to both secular and spiritual humanists (Smith, 1986) and many others an observer would be hard-pressed to classify. Those on the secular side tended to see the impact of the countercultural trends in the 1960s as having given humanistic psychology a reputation of too much irrational mysticism and antiintellectual preference for raw experience. But another wing saw within humanistic psychology a psychospiritual paradigm, able finally to restore questions of ultimate value and meaning to a discipline that had needlessly forfeited them in its misguided quest for scientific legitimacy. During the 1970s this perspective had coalesced under the banner of transpersonal psychology, with an association (Association for Transpersonal Psychology), a journal (*Journal of Transpersonal Psychology*), and a graduate training center (the Institute of Transpersonal Psychology). In relation to humanistic psychology's sense of itself as the third force, tranpersonalists called their movement the fourth force, after Maslow's introduction of that term.

By the early 1980s this movement had grown sufficiently to seek to have its voice become a part of the conversation within the APA. The transpersonal group hosted its own hospitality suite at annual APA conventions and became a proposed division. The group presented a petition to the APA for the establishment of a Division of Transpersonal Psychology containing the requisite number of signatures from APA members pledged to join such a division. The leadership included several leaders of Division 32, although the principal protagonist was Mary Jo Meadow, active in Division 36 (Psychology of Religion). The question was whether or not Division 32 should support the proposed new division. Significant arguments for both sides divided the division's executive board. First, there was the question of whether or not transpersonal psychology was something other than humanistic psychology or was in fact a branch of a broader humanistic vision. Although most humanistic psychologists were convinced of the latter, transpersonal theorists argued not only for distinct conceptual foundations but even that the transpersonal view was the more encompassing one, within which the humanistic orientation could be seen to be a subset. Others saw humanistic and transpersonal psychology as two approaches to plowing the same field, just starting at opposite ends. In addition to strictly conceptual issues, of course, there were also concerns about the impact of splitting an already small division into two even smaller ones. Would it be more pragmatic to support one stronger division or two weaker ones?

The Division 32 executive board voted to support the proposed Division of Transpersonal Psychology. The petition for divisional status first came before the APA Council in 1984. Harari, Division 32 Council representative, spoke for the motion to approve the division. However, it did not receive the needed two thirds votes in the APA Council, and so was turned down there. Concern was raised that transpersonal psychology had too religious a basis. The following year, the request was renewed. Once again, it was narrowly supported by Division 32 but failed to win the requisite two thirds of the Council of Representatives.

In 1986 the petition was brought forward for a third and final vote (such proposals have a three-year limit). Prior to the convention, May (1986) disputed the conceptual foundations of transpersonal psychology in pieces published both in the APA *Monitor* and the Division 32 newsletter. May's arguments were vigorously rebutted in the following issue of the newsletter (Hendlin, 1986; Valle, 1986). This time, the vote in the Division 32 executive board meeting was a tie. As a result, the board instructed Harari, its council representative, to vote his conscience. Harari, sensing the potential defeat, withdrew the petition.

Following this final defeat, the group could no longer be identified as a proposed division. Instead it re-formed as the Transpersonal Psychology Interest Group (TPIG), and for a while continued to sponsor its own hospitality suites and then did so in collaboration with Division 32. Division 32 included transpersonal themes and presenters in its programs and changed its stated purpose in the bylaws to include fostering transpersonal psychology (as well as the other recently emergent trend, human science research):

> The purpose of this organization shall be to foster, develop, and create concepts, theories, and philosophies of the humanistic and transpersonal psychologies and human science research for education, practice, and other areas of human endeavor. (Division 32 By-Laws)

In 1998 the TPIG board voted to conclude its independent existence and to donate its remaining funds (about $4000) to Division 32, which it recognized as being the most harmonious platform for its goal of maintaining a presence within the APA. Division 32 programming continues to include a variety of transpersonal themes. A representative of the group was given a place on the division executive board. It is also an ongoing question as to whether to change the division name to Humanistic and Transpersonal Psychology. (Curiously, for such a name change to gain routine approval by the APA it would have to be shown that it does not involve any extension of the scope identified by the name, *Humanistic.)*

Even as the division wrestled with identity issues, it also developed a variety of new projects to deepen its presence and facilitate more cohesive networking. The four most significant of these were preparing a brochure describing the division, launching an oral history project, publishing a directory of graduate programs, and establishing a division journal.

To have a short handout to offer potential new members and others interested in the division, the executive board prepared a short brochure about Division 32. Most of all, this entailed developing a brief statement describing humanistic psychology. The board approved the following statement in 1985:

> Humanistic psychology aims to be faithful to the full richness of human experience. Its foundations include philosophical humanism, existentialism, and phenomenology. Its approach to the science and profession of psychology accepts the challenge to develop a systematic and rigorous understanding of human beings. Humanistic psychologists are particularly sensitive to uniquely human dimensions, such as experiences of actualization and transcendence, and with the quality of human welfare. Accordingly, humanistic psychology is especially concerned with contributing to psychotherapy, education, theory and philosophy of psychology, research, organization and management, and social responsibility and change.

Next the executive board appointed Arons and Harari, two of the division's founding members and longtime leaders, as archivists for the division's history. They have since launched an ongoing oral history project involving videotaping interviews with prominent scholars in the field. Already concluded are interviews with May, Moustakas, Paul Ricouer, Bugental, and Krippner.

A second project was the development of a list of graduate programs in humanistic psychology, a project long advocated by one of the division's earliest executive board members, Weckler. This booklet, titled *Directory: Graduate Programs in Humanistic-Transpersonal Psychology in North America* (Arons, 1996), has now gone through five editions, first appearing in 1981, with revised editions in 1985, 1988, 1992 and 1996, all under the editorship of Arons and assisted by the psychology department at the State University of West Georgia. The first edition was sponsored solely by Division 32; the subsequent ones have been cosponsored by the AHP. The current edition lists 37 programs, with masters or doctoral programs. These programs are centered around a humanistic orientation rather than simply including some humanistic coursework. As the *Directory* further reminds readers, there are many programs not listed in the directory that have on their faculties individuals who are interested in questions raised by humanistic psychology or who take a humanistic approach to instruction, research, and practice.

The other major initiative undertaken by the division in the 1980s involved establishing a journal, *The Humanistic Psychologist*. This development emerged in phases, beginning in 1985, with the appointment of Christopher Aanstoos as the division's newsletter editor. With the support of the executive board, Aanstoos revised the format from its former layout of folded pages of news items to a 44-page bound format, containing articles and reviews. By the second issue, it expanded to 64 pages, a productivity gain made possible because it was self-published by the division.

With this increase, several thematic series were established. For example, one article in each issue was devoted to the humanistic foundations of allied disciplines. These came to include sociology, geography, ecology, international relations, environmental design, health care, and communicology. Another continuing series of articles was invited from psychotherapists as replies to the question: What is the essence of your contribution, as therapist, to your client's growth toward greater psychological well-being? Another series reported on various graduate programs in humanistic psychology, providing a history and orientation of each program.

In addition, a wide variety of other articles, including philosophical and literary pieces, began to appear. Clinical topics included were family therapy, depth therapy, and gestalt therapy. Research themes included qualitative methodology, alongside philosophical themes such as mythology, phenomenology, and constructionism. Also, social commentaries on television, the nuclear arms race, and the war on drugs expanded the range of topics covered. An editorial board was assembled, supported by the willingness of prominent humanistic psychologists to serve, including Rogers, Medard Boss, R. D. Laing, Bugental, May, Moustakas, Virginia Sexton, Thomas Szasz, Giorgi, Smith, Howard Pollio, Mahrer, Eugene Gendlin, and Jean Houston.

Under this new format, the publication continued to expand, as subscriptions from nonmembers and libraries enabled it to operate on a larger budget. By 1987 the autumn issue contained 86 pages, and in 1988 it undertook a new project: a large special edition. Titled *Psychotherapy for Freedom: The Daseinsanalytic Way in Psychology and Psychoanalysis*, the spring 1988 issue was almost 300 pages. It was guest edited by Erik Craig, who made several trips to Zurich and enlisted the support of prominent *daseinsanalysts* in Europe, especially Medard Boss, to provide an exceptional presentation of this tradition of existential psychotherapy that had first arisen in the 1940s as a blending of Freudian psychoanalysis with Heideggerian existential phenomenology. A larger print run of this issue was produced, and it was sold for several years thereafter as a textbook for many university courses.

As a result of this successful expansion of scope, in 1989 Aanstoos proposed that the division request permission from the APA to upgrade the publication's status. Officially still known as the division's newsletter (and continuing to carry newsletter items as well), it was by then identifying itself on the cover as the *Bulletin: Division of Humanistic Psychology*. Aanstoos proposed the division seek for it the status of an APA division journal, an idea approved by the executive board. APA's Publications and Communications Board supported the proposal, and it was approved by the Council of Representatives in August 1989. Its first issue as a journal was in autumn 1989; for the sake of continuity, however, volume numbers were counted as a continuation from those while it was a newsletter (hence 1989 was volume 17).

Once the division's newsletter had become a journal, the executive board then voted to support the creation of another regular publication in newsletter format to carry the usual news items for division members. Published twice a year under the editorship of Mary Anne Siderits, this newsletter has developed in such a way that it is recognized not only for the quality of its writing but also for its aesthetic appearance.

As a journal *The Humanistic Psychologist* continued to expand, to average 134 pages per issue (still published in three issues per annual volume). Five-year cumulative indexes appeared in 1989 and again in 1994. The number of submissions also expanded rapidly, resulting in a discriminating peer review process, with rejection rates at about 75%. Special issues were published in 1990 on *Psychology and Postmodernity and on Personal Mythology* (the former subsequently published as a book by Sage Publications). In 1992 a special double issue of more than 350 pages appeared, guest edited by Fred Wertz, titled *The Humanistic Movement in Psychology: History, Celebration, and Prospectus*. It was later published as a book by Gardner Press. More recent special issues have included *Psychotherapy* (Summer 1995); *Foundations of Humanistic Psychology* guest edited by Arthur Lyons (Autumn 1995); *Social Action as Compassionate Heartwork* (Autumn 1996); and *Holistic Alternatives in Psychological Healing* guest edited by Gregory Kuschwara (Summer 1997). Currently in preparation is a special issue on ecopsychology guest edited by Elizabeth Roberts.

The viability of such an expanded journal has depended on its being self-published. But this arrangement has imposed daunting workloads on those involved. The impracticality of depending on such workloads being continued, or of finding successors able to do likewise, has often led to questions of turning the journal over to an outside publisher, as is more typical of the APA's division journals. Almost annually for the past few years, the executive board has considered proposals by publishers who have offered their services. However, the rate that would then be charged to the division for the copies sent to members has exceeded the amount budgeted for the journal by such an extent that these proposals have always been rejected. Nevertheless, the question remains open about the wisest course of action to take in this regard.

As this chapter goes to press, a plan by Aanstoos, editor of *The Humanistic Psychologist*, and Thomas Greening, editor of the *Journal of Humanistic*

Psychology, to merge these two journals is being developed by Sage Publications. The combined journal would be published six times a year, combine the two editorial boards, and become the preeminent international journal in the field, combining the subscription bases of Division 32 and the Association for Humanistic Psychology.

RECENT HISTORY: CHALLENGES AND CHANGES

As the 1980s turned into the 1990s, the membership decline begun by the conservative tide of both psychology and the culture at large continued. From its highest point in 1977 of 1150, total membership declined to 673 by 1998. A new challenge also emerged. The bulk of the division's members had joined during the heady early 1970s. By the 1990s these supporters were aging and retiring from the field. Many others, by virtue of seniority, had become dues-exempt members. The most prominent leaders and inspirers of the movement in the 1960s and 1970s died, including Roberto Assagioli, Medard Boss, Charlotte Bühler, Aldous Huxley, Sidney Jourard, R. D. Laing, Maslow, May, Perls, Rogers, and Anthony Sutich. The question of whether the humanistic presence in the APA was to be a one-generation phenomenon was a pressing one. Fortunately, a new generation of Division 32 members emerged whose numbers have just about replaced the older generation. The result appears as a stagnant division membership total, but this has masked a considerable turnover and replacement rate during the 1990s, changing the face of humanistic psychology and the division.

It is still too early to tell precisely how this generational shift will affect the direction of the field, but some trends are already discernible. Throughout the 1990s there was a clear shift with respect to a deeper and more sophisticated understanding of two important bases of humanistic psychology: contemporary continental philosophy and eastern thought. The philosophical expertise contrasts with some of the early pioneers, such as Maslow and Rogers, whose home-bred versions of humanistic psychology remained somewhat detached from European sources such as existentialism and phenomenology. Such scholars as May, Laing, Giorgi, and Boss appreciated and used these sources as an important enriching influence.

The integration of Eastern sources, especially from Hinduism and Buddhism, has also become much more sophisticated. In the 1960s Zen had made a beachhead in this country, popularized for humanistic thinkers, especially by Alan Watts. But a generation later it is more than a mere novelty. It has become a daily practice for many, and a deep inspiration for many more. The infusion of Tibetan Buddhism in the 1970s and 1980s has likely been a great contribution to that development, so that in this respect, the disaster for the Tibetans of the loss of their homeland and their subsequent Diaspora ironically has resulted in the spread of their wisdom to the rest of the world. Infusion of these sources has enriched humanistic thought with new insights into the meaning of consciousness, personal growth and freedom, and how practices of mindfulness and self-awareness can be cultivated to enhance our development.

Beyond these shifts in scholarly and experiential sources, the newer group of division members has also changed some older governing practices. Originally the division was founded on the basis of a very strong commitment to a classless egalitarian organization. Only one class of members was designated—no fellow or associate status. Also, no awards were sponsored by the division. This stance flowed from the conviction that people acted best from intrinsic rather than extrinsic motivation. Indeed, an early proponent of this policy, Arons, was given a tongue-in-cheek award from the division executive board for his efforts: a plaque with an inscription honoring him for his undying devotion and ceaseless energy toward the creation of a plaqueless society.

But by the 1990s some humanistic psychologists had come to find themselves so marginalized in their employment settings that they raised an alternative argument. They pointed out the usefulness of such awards for vitas and careers, especially for humanistic psychologists branded as mavericks by employers. Of all divisions, it seemed most important that this one support its members by honoring achievements and contributions that might otherwise go unrecognized. A subcommittee, chaired by Constance Fischer, examined the question and proposed the division award fellow status to deserving members, as did every other division except one. A lively debate ensued, and the proposal was accepted by a narrow majority. Only one or two members each year have subsequently been nominated to the APA for initial fellow status by the division to ensure that its nominees are deserving of this honor.

In the 1990s the executive board also began to establish awards (actual plaques) presented to outstanding humanistic psychologists in recognition of a lifetime of distinguished contribution to the field. Named after famous humanistic psychologists, they are The Charlotte and Karl Bühler Award, The Rollo May Award, The Abraham H. Maslow Award, and The Carl Rogers Award.

The Charlotte and Karl Bühler Award goes to an institution, and an individual associated with that institution, that have made an outstanding and lasting contribution to humanistic psychology. The following is a list of recipients.

1991   *Journal of Humanistic Psychology*, Thomas Greening, editor
1992   Saybrook Graduate School, Stanley Krippner
1993   Psychology Department at West Georgia State College, Myron Arons
1994   Sonoma State University Psychology Department, Arthur Warmoth
1995   Department of Psychology, Duquesne University. (No one individual was named in the award; Fr. David Smith, former chair, accepted on behalf of the faculty as a whole.)
1997   *Journal of Phenomenological Psychology*, Amedeo Giorgi
1998   College of Education, University of Florida, Arthur W. Combs, Jr.

The Rollo May Award goes to a person unaffiliated with an institution who has made an inspiring contribution to a more humanistic vision of human suffering and growth. See the following for a list of recipients.

1996   James Bugental
1997   Carmi Harari
1998   Thomas Szasz

The Abraham H. Maslow Award is given to an individual for an outstanding and lasting contribution to the exploration of the farther reaches of human nature. This was first awarded in 1999 to Myron Milford Arons.

The Carl Rogers Award is given to an individual for an outstanding contribution to the profession and practice of humanistic psychology. This was first awarded in 1999 to E. Mark Stern.

In addition, the division established the Sidney Jourard Award, which is given for the best paper submitted by a graduate student. The finalists are invited to present their work at APA's annual convention.

New Projects for New Times

Two division projects developed during the 1990s also exemplify these changing times. The first arose as a response to the crisis in psychotherapy generated by the APA's support of manualized, outcome-based, empirically validated practice. This was itself a symptom of the larger crisis brought on by the managed care industry's cost control and regulation of psychotherapy. Concerned that humanistic approaches to psychotherapy were being excluded in the preliminary versions of the APA guidelines, the division executive board in 1996 authorized a task force to draft guidelines to provide humanistic psychotherapy. Arthur Bohart chaired this committee, which also included Maureen O'Hara, Frederick Wertz, Mark Stern, Kirk Schneider, Ilene Serlin, Larry Leitner, and Tom Greening. Their preliminary report was published in the division journal in 1997 (Task Force, 1997). Feedback was solicited from members preliminary to a vote to adopt these guidelines by the executive board. It is hoped this will allow practitioners a choice of therapies, each supported by its own set of appropriate guidelines for proper care.

A second project exemplary of this new era was the development of a *Directory* of division members. Edited by Criswell, it was produced in 1998 and given to all members.

This more feasible, and more urgent, prospect of linking up is also the motif of another new project sponsored by the division. In cooperation with the Consortium for Diversified Psychology Programs (CDPP), the Association for Humanistic Psychology, the AHP Midwest Conference Committee, the National Psychology Advisory Association (NPAA), Saybrook Graduate School, Sonoma State University, and State University of West Georgia, the division is currently supporting the development of a special conference, scheduled for May 2000 and hosted by the State University of West Georgia. It will bring together the leading voices in humanistic psychology in a double forum of conversation: both to a live audience meeting in Georgia and to an electronically connected worldwide audience meeting over the Internet. Conceived as the sequel to the foundational 1963 conference at Old Saybrook, Connecticut, that galvanized the humanistic movement, this one will seek to foster the next phase in the development of the field, embracing and extending its legacy.

CONCLUSION

Three long-standing trajectories seem relevantly predictive of what will come for the division in the 21st century: the dynamic of its providing leadership of an alternative approach within psychology; its role as a bridge between psychology's clinical and research wings; and its place in elucidating new content areas for psychological exploration.

Division 32 has an illustrious history of providing leadership in the development of a human science approach to psychology, an approach emphasizing qualitative research focused on the actual lived experience of persons. One may say that its role has been to bring psychology to the uniquely psychological (A. Giorgi, personal communication, July 3, 1998). In some ways, this approach is as old as William James (Taylor, 1991). Yet it has only rarely been evidenced in mainstream psychology since James. Instead, the field adopted a reductionistic approach by which the psychological was reduced to the physiological, the neurological, or other substrates presumed to underlie causally the psychological level. Rogers, May, Maslow, Giorgi, Moustakas, Laing, and other humanistic pioneers thus reintroduced psychology to its Jamesian roots, and in the process articulated new methodologies for its becoming a science of human experience. But this phase of its history is now drawing to a close on two accounts. First, most of its early leaders are now passing from the scene. Buoyed as they were by the larger cultural zeitgeist then in place, their stature was easily recognizable and had great currency. Now, however, there may be emerging a more critical phase in which a leadership vacuum is waiting to be filled. Until that happens, a certain kind of treading water may be evident. Second, the field of psychology has itself now incorporated many of these humanistic innovations.

Cognitive psychology, in spite of its original tendency to favor dehumanizing artificial intelligence perspectives, is no longer as reductionistic as it was when humanistic psychology first arose in the 1960s. In fact, in spite of the proclivity of information-processing theorists to portray computer programs as simulations of human experience, cognitive psychology has helped open up the field more widely to issues of consciousness and experience.

Partly because of lack of funding, psychology has tended to abandon community psychology as a means of being relevant to society at large, and faces the disturbing prospect of future marginalization, or losing its identity by embracing the medical model and merging with psychiatry and pharmacology. Despite a generation of calls to "give psychology away," academic psychology remains split off from clinical and popular psychology, to which the public mostly attends. As psychology increasingly realizes this need to pursue more adequately this goal of offering a meaningful and useful understanding of human experience, humanistic psychology's historical role will position it well for contributing to this overarching project.

A second long-standing trend that may offer opportunities to Division 32 concerns the way that it has brought together the clinical and research wings of the discipline, during a period when these had become increasingly antagonistic in psychology at large as well as within the APA. The division was founded largely by clinicians, who also dominated its early membership. Typically, these were therapists whose own professional practices were opening up to new techniques then being formulated by humanistic psychologists: Gestalt, body work, psychosynthesis, encounter groups, sensitivity training, person-centered counseling, marital and family therapies. Often, the legitimacy of these new practices was questioned by more mainstream approaches. Hence an important reason for collaborating as an APA division was to establish respectability for these less conventional innovations. Meanwhile academic rebels from the natural scientific foundations of research psychology, such as Giorgi, also saw in humanistic psychology a viable alternative: a way to develop a science of experience qua experience—nonreductively. From both the clinical and research wings, then, came a vision of psychology that could embrace each side of that divide. Because clinical practice was not reduced to a medical model it could align with a view of persons as experiencing and creating meanings. And because researchers did not cut the person apart from their meaningful involvement in their experienced world, their findings could more readily be related to the concerns of clinicians.

As the division evolved within the APA, it played an early part in the coming together of the clinical interests. Division 29 (Psychotherapy) invited representatives of APA divisions related to professional psychology and APA's Board of Professional Affairs to meet on June 1–2, 1973, in New York to discuss the need for such divisions to stimulate interest and action on the part of the APA concerning clinical issues. Graham and Harari attended as representatives of Division 32. The conflict between the clinical and academic areas received considerable airing at this meeting, and the participants reached a consensus regarding the need to heal the rifts. A subcommittee was appointed to meet with various divisions to work through means of resolving existing conflicts. Harari and Graham were both named to this committee, along with Logan Wright, Florence Halpern, and Tamara Dembo (Krasner, 1973).

Despite this early important collaboration, the major clinical divisions did not embrace Division 32. The APA Convention Affairs Office assigned the division meeting rooms not in the hotel with clinical divisions but in the hotel with such nonclinical divisions as Division 10 (Psychology and the Arts); Division 24 (Theoretical and Philosophical Psychology); Division 26 (History of Psychology); Division 36 (Psychology of Religion); and Division 48 (Society for the Study of Peace, Conflict & Violence). Thus its early promise of serving as a bridge to reconcile clinical and academic interests remains a potential but not fully actualized capacity. Humanistic psychologists face the challenge of reaching out more creatively to others in the APA who share similar values and goals, rather than maintaining adversarial boundaries.

The third trend that may be projected from Division 32's history to its future concerns its role in the inculcation of new sociocultural developments into psychology. Having helped bring psychology into contact with such earlier social developments as the women's movement, the peace movement, and global dialogue, it may be wise to discern what new topic areas are now emerging. In that respect, two may already reliably be noted: the attention being given by the division to holistic health and to ecology (Metzner, 1999). In both cases, it is the experiential dimension that is only now being understood as the crucial, previously overlooked, factor.

Holistic health has already been the focus of a special issue of the division's journal, and ecology is the theme for a forthcoming issue. Both were featured in the division's program theme for the 1998 convention, and the division helped cosponsor a miniconvention at the APA meeting related to holistic health issues. Ilene Serlin of Division 32 and Marie DiCowan of Division 22 (Rehabilitation Psychology) were cochairs. These topics are not only being advanced by Division 32 but it may well be Division 32 that most ardently brings these themes into psychology. Such a development will come as no surprise to veteran humanistic psychologists, who would easily recognize the essential holism that has always been the hallmark of humanistic thought.

Martin Seligman (1998), while president of the APA, began advocating the development of what he calls "positive psychology" as an alternative to much of psychology's focus on DSM-categorized psychopathology, "mental illness," and what a generation earlier Maslow called "deficiency motivation." Although Seligman's 1998 article made no reference to humanistic psychology, the agenda presented in it is essentially the same and uses many of the field's concepts. He called for studies of "self-actualization," "positive traits," "the human strengths and civic virtues," and "best exemplars" just as Maslow and others have done for decades. Seligman subsequently stated in his 1999 APA address that "positive psychology" intends to remedy humanistic psychology's lack of validating empirical research and its emphasis on narcissistic forms of individualized self-actualization. Such critiques of humanistic psychology have long been addressed in Division 32's *The Humanistic Psychologist*, in the *Journal of Humanistic Psychology*, and in books and articles by Division 32 members, and they still sometimes appear. Often, humanistic psychology has been ahead of its time and has not connected well with mainstream psychology. Members must take on the continued challenge of communicating better the theory, research, and practice of the field to the wider community of psychology. Especially now when there are many antihumanistic forces at work in psychology and the United States, let us hope that Division 32 will continue to play an active role in the furtherance of its mission within the APA and in the larger society.

REFERENCES

Arons, M. (1974). Letter to Division 32 Executive Board. Division 32 Archives.

Arons, M. (Ed.). (1996). *Directory of graduate programs in humanistic and transpersonal psychology in North America*. Carrollton. Georgia: Psychology Department, State University of West Georgia.

Boston, R. (1998). Family feud. *Church & State*, 51(5), 9–14.

Bugental, J. (1963). Humanistic psychology : A new breakthrough. *American Psychologist*, 18, 563–567.

Bugental, J. (1964). The third force in psychology. *Journal of Humanistic Psychology*, 4(1), 19–25.

deCarvalho, R. J. (1990). A history of the "Third Force" in psychology. *Journal of Humanistic Psychology, 30*(4), 22–44.

deCarvalho, R. J. (1991). *The founders of humanistic psychology.* New York: Praeger.

deCarvalho, R. J. (1992). The institutionalization of humanistic psychology. *The Humanistic Psychologist, 20,* 124–135.

Division 32. (1974). Executive board minutes.

Division 32. (1985). *Division of Humanistic Psychology (brochure).* Division 32 archives.

Division 32. (1986). Bylaws. Division 32 archives.

Freud, S. (1960). Letter to Marie Bonaparte, 13 August 1937. In E. L. Freud (Ed.), *Letters of Sigmund Freud* (Tania and James Stern, Trans.). New York: Basic Books.

Giorgi, A. (1965). Phenomenology and experimental psychology: I. *Review of Existential Psychology and Psychiatry, 5,* 228–238.

Giorgi, A. (1966). Phenomenology and experimental psychology: II. *Review of Existential Psychology and Psychiatry, 6.* 37–50.

Giorgi, A. (1970). *Psychology as a human science.* New York: Harper & Row.

Gottsegen, G. (1976). Executive board minutes. *Newsletter: Division of Humanistic Psychology, 3*(1), 5–6.

Harari, C. (1971, November). Letter to Division 32. Harari, C. (1973a). Past president's report. *Bulletin: Division of Humanistic Psychology, 1*(3), 1–2.

Harari, C. (1973b). President's report. *Bulletin: Division of Humanistic Psychology, 1*(1), 1–2.

Hendlin, S. J. (1986). The personal in the transpersonal: A reply to Rollo May. *The Humanistic Psychologist, 14,* 214–215.

Hildreth, J. (1972). Letter to Gottsegen. Division 32 archives.

Krasner, J. D. (1973). Inter-divisional committee for professional and applied psychology. *Bulletin: Division of Humanistic Psychology, 1*(3), 4–5.

Mahrer, A. (1973). Program comments. *Bulletin: Division of Humanistic Psychology, 1*(3), 3.

Maslow, A. H. (1954). *Motivation and personality.* New York: Harper.

Maslow, A. H. (1962). *Toward a psychology of being.* New York: Nostrand.

Maslow, A. H. (1964). *Religion, values and peak-experiences.* Columbus: Ohio State University Press.

Maslow, A. H. (1965). *Eupsychian management.* Homewood, IL: Dorsey.

Maslow, A. H. (1966). *The psychology of science.* New York: Harper & Row.

May, R. (1953). *Man's search for himself.* New York: Norton.

May, R. (1965). Intentionality, the heart of human will. *Journal of Humanistic Psychology, 5*(2), 202–209.

May, R. (1967). *Psychology and the human dilemma.* Princeton, NJ: Van Nostrand.

May, R. (1969). *Love and will.* New York: Norton.

May, R. (1986). Transpersonal or transcendental? *The Humanistic Psychologist, 14,* 87–90.

May, R., Angel, E., & Ellenberger, H. F. (Eds.). (1958). *Existence.* New York: Basic.

Metzner, R. (1999). *Green psychology: Transforming our relationship to the earth.* Rochester, NY: Park Street Press.

Rogers, C. (1951). *Client-centered therapy.* Boston: Houghton-Mifflin.

Rogers, C. (1961). *On becoming a person: A therapist's view of psychotherapy.* Boston: Houghton-Mifflin.

Rogers, C. (1969). *Freedom to learn.* Columbus, OH: Merrill.

Seligman, M. (1998). President's column: What is the "good life"? *Monitor.*

Shostrom, E. (1973). President's report. *Bulletin: Division of Humanistic Psychology, 1*(3), 1–2.

Skinner, B. F. (1987). Whatever happened to psychology as the science of behavior? *American Psychologist, 42,* 780–786.

Smith, M. B. (1986). Toward a secular humanistic psychology. *Journal of Humanistic Psychology, 26*(1), 7–26.

Taylor, E. (1991). William James and the humanistic tradition. *Journal of Humanistic Psychology, 31*(1), 56–74.

Task Force. (1997). Guidelines for the provision of humanistic psychosocial services. *The Humanistic Psychologist, 25,* 64–107.

Valle, R. S. (1986). Transpersonal psychology: A reply to Rollo May. *The Humanistic Psychologist, 14,* 210–213.

Waters, R. H. (1958). Behavior: Datum or abstraction? *American Psychologist 13,* 278–282.

Weckler, N. (1971). Membership chair report. Division 32 Board of Director's Minutes. Division 32 archives.

5

A HISTORY OF DIVISION 34 (POPULATION AND ENVIRONMENTAL PSYCHOLOGY)

JAMES M. RICHARDS, JR.

Division 34 (Population and Environmental Psychology) is a product of the 1960s and was strongly influenced by two social issues that were of concern in that decade: population growth and environmental degradation (both in an aesthetic sense and in the sense of ability to sustain human life). These concerns were reflected in the establishment of two task forces by the APA during the 1960s: the Task Force on Psychology, Family Planning, and Population Policy and the Task Force on Environment and Behavior. The activities of these two task forces are important in the history of Division 34. The description of activities of task forces will rely heavily on the accounts by Henry P. David (1998) for the Task Force on Psychology, Family Planning, and Population Policy and by Willo P. White (1979) for the Task Force on Environment and Behavior. Records of the activities of these two task forces also are preserved in the APA Archives at the National Library of Congress.

Both then and now the concerns of population and environmental psychologists have included issues besides population growth and environmental degradation. This history will attempt to give appropriate recognition to these other issues. These two concerns, however, do represent the main conceptual framework that unifies population and environment, the ecological perspective (e.g., Hardin, 1993). This perspective holds that populations and their environments must be viewed as integrated wholes (Severy, 1975) and provides one answer to the question sometimes posed by Division 34 members (perhaps especially new members), "Why population and environmental psychology?" Concern with population growth and environmental degradation seems to have become less stylish in the general society than such concern was in the 1960s, but both issues continue to be critically important for human survival and the opportunity for a decent life for all (Hardin, 1993). Therefore, they continue to be major concerns for many members of Division 34 and the ecological perspective continues to receive explicit recognition in the work of the members (Howard, 1997; Winter, 1996). The ecological perspective is, of course, directly opposed to the view that there are no inherent limits on human activities, and especially no inherent limits on economic growth.

A serious problem for all efforts to describe the history of an APA division is the large number of individuals who have played a role in its development and the large literature that is relevant. This history cannot give full recognition to all individuals who have played a role, and certainly cannot cite all of the relevant literature. Therefore, it necessarily must deal with a sample of individuals and literature. The best that can be hoped for is that these samples be representative, and my goal in selecting these samples has been to be representative. Inevitably the sampling will involve injustices, and such injustices are especially problematic when citation counts have become highly important in evaluating specific contributions, the overall work of individuals, and even total fields of endeavor. Although I cannot avoid these injustices, I still apologize for them.

Another problem is that some trends and events in the history of the division are not formally recorded in any archival record, or at best have been recorded in some fugitive source. Whenever assertions in this history can be documented, I have attempted to cite the source. Assertions without citation are based on my informal recollections or the informal recollections of other members of Division 34.

TASK FORCE ON PSYCHOLOGY, FAMILY PLANNING, AND POPULATION POLICY

The Task Force on Psychology, Family Planning, and Population Policy emerged from the small number of psychologists who were at that time concerned with population issues. Three concerns seem especially important both in the establishment and work of the task force and in the subsequent history of population issues in Division 34. The first was a neo-Malthusian conviction that population growth could not be sustained indefinitely (Ehrlich, 1968; Malthus, 1798). This concern probably was the major factor in recruiting members to Division 34 immediately after it was established. An important event in the history of this concern occurred in 1969 when the book *The Psychology of Birth Planning* (Pohlman, 1969) was published. This appears to be the first substantial work that explicitly involved population psychology.

The second was that some psychologists were concerned with convincing population scientists from other disciplines, especially demographers, of the relevance of psychological concepts and methodologies for population research. Scientists from other disciplines were highly skeptical, largely because the yields from psychological analyses in the germinal Indianapolis and Princeton demographic studies (Westoff, Potter, Sagi, & Mishler, 1961) had been scanty. This concern played a major role in the writing of James Fawcett's (1970) book *Psychology and Population*. Efforts to persuade other scientists of the importance of psychology in the field have met with mixed success. For example, members of the task force, in cooperation with some members of the Population Association of America (PAA), organized the Workshop on Psychosocial Factors Population Research (now called the Psychosocial Workshop). Since 1972 the workshop has been held the two days before the PAA convention, meeting in the convention hotel. It has become an important venue for some Division 34 members and has succeeded in attracting population researchers from other disciplines. It is listed in the PAA convention program (as a related organization) and has organized or cosponsored convention sessions. However, it still has no formal connection with the PAA (or with Division 34).

The third was a concern with abortion issues, and this continues to be a major area of research by division members (Beckman & Harvey, 1998; David, 1992). Overall, this research has been broadly supportive of the prochoice position, indicating that abortion has no negative consequences for most women (Beckman & Harvey, 1998) and that denial of abortion produces a strong negative impact on the children who are born unwanted (David, 1992).

The October 1969 meeting of the APA's Council of Representatives was significant in the history of population issues in the discipline of psychology (David, 1998). At that meeting, Henry P. David, who at the time was Council representative for Division 18 (Psychologists in Public Service), joined with the Association for Women Psychologists to introduce a resolution declaring that termination of an unwanted pregnancy was a mental health and child welfare issue, making it a legitimate APA concern. The resolution also declared that termination of a pregnancy should be viewed as "a civil right of the pregnant woman" to be handled as any other medical or surgical procedure in consultation with the woman's physician. Division

18 (i.e., Dr. David) then moved a second resolution that the APA establish a Task Force on Psychology, Family Planning, and Population Policy. The resolution mandated the task force to prepare a review of the current state of psychological research related to "family planning and population policy" and to make recommendations for "encouraging greater research and professional service participation by psychologists in this emerging area of social concern" (McKeachie, 1970, p. 34).

Both resolutions passed by a substantial margin after what David (1998) characterized as "only brief discussion," thus placing the APA firmly in support of women's freedom of choice in reproduction well before the Supreme Court's 1973 abortion decision in *Roe v. Wade*. Both resolutions were controversial, and the case with which they were passed may need some explication. David (1998) suggested that this ease of passage can be understood in the context of Council deliberations on that day. Most of the morning had been devoted to various resolutions and suggestions for actions pertaining to the APA's public position on the Vietnam War. The debate had been "bitter," and each of the proposed resolutions and suggestions had been defeated. David (1998, xii) stated it became apparent that "Council members were wary of debate and wanted to show the association's awareness that professional expertise should be applied to topics of current social significance."

David was named chair of the Task Force on Psychology, Family Planning, and Population Policy. Members included James T. Fawcett, Deborah L. Matory, Sidney H. Newman, Edward M. Pohlman, Nancy F. Russo, and Vaida D. Thompson. Consultants named in the final report of the task force included Catherine Chilman, Harrison Gough, Mimi Keiffer, Janette Rainwater, M. Brewster Smith, and Helen Wolfers. The members and consultants came from diverse backgrounds but were a good cross-section of psychologists who were interested in population issues. Miriam Kelty coordinated the APA staff activities with the task force, with the assistance of Marsha Paller and Willo P. White. Leslie Hicks also served briefly in this capacity.

During its existence the Task Force on Psychology, Family Planning, and Population Policy and its members conducted numerous activities relevant to its mandate from the APA Council of Representatives. These activities were facilitated when the efforts of James Fawcett enabled the APA to obtain a small grant from the Population Council (a large multinational organization based in New York). The first major activity involved organizing workshops and conferences. The first workshop was convened in Washington in March of 1970 to review and discuss population-related activities by psychologists and to recommend future roles for psychologists. At that time fewer than a dozen American psychologists were working primarily in population-related endeavors, and this workshop seems primarily to have functioned to let them get acquainted with each other and each other's work (David, 1972). No major archival record was found for this workshop.

In 1971 the Conference on Psychological Measurement in the Study of Population Problems was convened in Berkeley, California, under the joint auspices of the task force and the Institute of Personality Assessment and Research (IPAR), University of California. Richard Crutchfield and Harrison G. Gough of the IPAR faculty played leading roles in this conference. The conference was designed to be interdisciplinary, and in addition to psychologists attracted representatives from anthropology, demography, sociology, obstetrics–gynecology, psychiatry, and public health (David, 1998). The *Conference Proceedings* were published by the IPAR (Gough, 1972), and subsequently a paper by Gough (1976) on the role of psychological methods in forecasting family-planning behavior was published in the compendium *Population Psychology: Research and Educational Issues* (Newman & Thompson, 1976).

A third workshop was held at the University of North Carolina Population Center under the combined auspices of the Task Force on Psychology, Family Planning, and Population Policy and the Center for Population Research, National Institute of Child Health and Human Development (NICHD). This workshop was intended to review the current status of educating psychologists in the population field and to make recommendations for the future. This review found that almost none of the psychologists working in the field entered it directly after completing their doctorates, and no psychology department in a U.S. institution had an undergraduate, graduate, or postgraduate program explicitly dealing with population issues (Thompson & Newman, 1974). These situations have not changed.

The workshop developed a number of recommendations for education in population psychology at all levels. These recommendations emphasized first educating students in a traditional field of psychology and adding rigorous training in population problems and procedures to this education. Vaida Thompson and Sidney Newman prepared a summary of these recommendations that was distributed to psychology department chairs and subsequently was published in *Population Psychology: Research and Educational Issues* (Thompson & Newman, 1976A). Implementation of these recommendations has been virtually nonexistent. There may be institutions that offer courses in population psychology, but recent editions of the compendium *Graduate Study in Psychology* (e.g., American Psychological Association, 1996) list no formal programs of study in the field. The reasons for the lack of implementation perhaps are that interest in population psychology is not extensive enough to sustain it as an independent field and that population issues do not fall very clearly under the rubric of any traditional field in psychology (Thompson, 1986). Also, federal support for academic programs in population psychology has been lacking. Vaida Thompson at the

University of North Carolina, Chapel Hill, has incorporated many of these ideas into her own teaching endeavors in the Department of Psychology, which as a consequence have produced many of the younger population psychologists. Some of her students, such as Lawrence Severy, Joseph Rodgers, and Christopher Agnew, have begun to train third-generation population psychologists.

During this period, the Task Force on Psychology, Family Planning, and Population established a close working relationship with the NICHD's Center for Population Research. This collaboration examined sources of external funding for psychological research on population issues. Although a variety of potential sources were identified, the Center for Population Research has been the dominant source. Three members of the Center staff, Sidney Newman, Gloria Kamenske, and Wendy Baldwin, strongly encouraged psychologists to submit proposals to the center, and a number of successful proposals were submitted. The center continues to be the most likely source of funding for research in population psychology.

Also during this period, task force members published two books (Fawcett, 1973; Newman & Thompson, 1976) designed to summarize the current state of the art in population psychology. These books identified a substantial number of researchers and research areas in the broad field of population research, but they do not appear to have been influential in attracting psychologists to population-related work. Vaida Thompson (1986) discussed possible reasons why this was the case. Her argument was rather complex but might be summarized as holding that population psychologists are neither fish nor fowl. They are not demographic scientists and also are not mainstream psychologists. Thus they have neither a clear audience for their work nor a clear disciplinary home base. It is difficult to recruit psychologists to sustained work—or for psychologists to do effective, sustained work in a field that has no disciplinary home.

As is the usual practice for task forces, considerable effort was devoted to developing sessions for the annual convention of the APA. Several symposia were organized for the 1970, 1971, and 1972 conventions, and each convention also included some form of open meeting for psychologists with an interest in population issues. Vaida Thompson and Sidney Newman (1976b) reviewed some of the more significant sessions. They direct attention especially to the 1972 symposium chaired by Dr. Thompson titled, "Issues for Psychologists Involved in Population Research." At this symposium James Palmore discussed the relevance of psychological research designs for demographic evaluation systems, James Fawcett discussed the psychological consequences of population change, and Mark Flapan discussed psychological research on family formation and marital relationships. In addition, Kurt Back discussed three ways in which demography and psychology interact: the transformation of a basic biological need to propagate into social values and symbolic expression, the fitting of crucial life events into a comprehensive view of life-span development, and the integration of micro- and macrosystem methodologies. These presentations point to problems of continuing importance but also support the neither-fish-nor-fowl view of population psychology.

As the last item in its mandate the task force addressed the issue of population policy. Back and Fawcett (1974) examined the relationship between population policy and the individual person, especially whether or not that relationship inevitably involved conflict. Also, the task force worked with M. Brewster Smith (1972) on the psychological aspects of the complex ethical problems inherent in establishing population policy.

The final report of the Task Force on Psychology, Family Planning, and Population Policy was submitted to the APA Council of Representatives in 1972. This report recommended that an APA division of population psychology be established. The necessary requirements were met in 1973, and the Council then approved the new division. The Division of Population Psychology became an official part of the APA's structure on January 1, 1974, with Thompson as its first president. The next four presidents (Fawcett, Russo, David, and Kelty) also had been members of the task force.

One of the early actions of the new division was to establish an official division journal, the *Journal of Population, Behavioral, Social, and Environmental Issues;* to negotiate a contract with Human Sciences Press for publication of the journal; and to appoint Thompson as its first editor. The initial volume of this journal appeared in 1978.

TASK FORCE ON ENVIRONMENT AND BEHAVIOR

Psychological research in the environmental area has a longer history prior to the establishment of Division 34 than does such research in the population area, and several comprehensive accounts of earlier environmental work have been published (Altman & Rogoff, 1987; Proshansky & Altman, 1979; Stokols, 1987). An ecological perspective also has a long history in psychological research, but this is treated more from a scientific point of view than from a social-problems point of view (Barker, 1965, 1968; Brunswick, 1955; Lewin, 1936). That is, populations and individuals inhabit environmental settings that are organized wholes, and a valid science of psychology must view behavior in the context of those settings. Such a psychology cannot view behavior solely in terms of intraorganism causes or of responses to discrete stimuli, and laboratory research must be ecologically valid in the sense that it is representative of the external world settings in which the behaviors under investigation are "embedded" (Stokols, 1987).

A formal field of environmental psychology began to emerge in the 1950s and 1960s (White, 1979). Because mental illness was (and continues to be) a substantial problem, and at that time was treated mainly in psychiatric hospitals, several germinal studies for environmental psychology focused on such hospitals and more particularly on psychiatric wards (Ittelson, Proshansky, & Rivlin, 1970; Osmond, 1957; Sommer & Becker, 1961). Another germinal event in the emergence of environmental psychology was the establishment of the architectural psychology program at the University of Utah by Calvin W. Taylor (Taylor, Bailey, & Branch, 1967). This program sponsored a series of national conferences, published an influential newsletter, developed a common curriculum for graduate students in architecture and psychology, and provided a prototype for other educational programs in environmental psychology.

From 1960 on research increasingly focused on questions that more obviously involved environmental psychology (e.g., Barker, 1965, 1968), and explicit use of the title "environmental psychology" emerged (Wohlwill, 1970). The field was facilitated when the journal *Environment and Behavior* was established with Gary Winkel as first editor. The first volume was published in 1969. The existence of this journal ensured a major outlet for the work of environmental psychologists was already available when the Task Force on Environment and Behavior was established.

When Kenneth Craik published a chapter with the title "Environmental Psychology" in the *Annual Review of Psychology* (Craik, 1973), environmental psychology received "institutional recognition as a legitimate field of research" (White, 1979). A second *Annual Review* article (Stokols, 1978) provided further support for the legitimacy of the field. Similar *Annual Review* chapters have appeared in later years (Holahan, 1986; Russell & Ward, 1982; Saegert & Winkel, 1990).

During this period the APA's Board of Scientific Affairs had appointed the Ad Hoc Committee on Newly Emerging Areas in Psychology. The purpose of this committee was to serve as a mechanism for supporting emerging areas of psychology that already had committed researchers (White, 1979). Environmental psychology met this criterion, and the Task Force on Environment and Behavior was established through this ad hoc committee. In April of 1973 an environmental psychology steering committee consisting of Irwin Altman, Joachim Wohlwill, Edwin Willems, and Robert Helmreich met to consider the desirability of an initiative under the newly emerging areas program. The steering committee met again in August 1973 to develop and submit a formal proposal to the ad hoc committee. This proposal was approved, and the Task Force on Environment and Behavior was established in January 1974. Altman was named chair. Members included Helmreich, Henry M. Parsons, Willems, and Wohlwill. The APA staff coordination was provided by Willo P. White.

The mandate of the task force was (a) to bring the research and scholarly potential of the area of environment and behavior to the attention of APA members, (b) to provide information about alternative models and courses of instruction in environment and behavior, (c) to develop interdisciplinary contacts in the area of environment and behavior, and (d) to promote practical applications and policy-oriented research on environment and behavior issues.

The first item in the mandate, bringing environment and behavior to the attention of APA members, was addressed through the traditional techniques of developing conferences and workshops and of sponsoring convention programs. Many of these activities centered on the 1975 and 1976 annual conventions of the APA (White, 1979). The task force organized and sponsored sessions at both of these conventions. In both of these years the task force also developed a preconvention workshop. The 1975 workshop was chaired by Edward Ostrander and titled "Social and Behavioral Data for Environmental Design Applications." The goal of this workshop was to improve communication between researchers and designers to promote translation of research findings into products of use to designers. The 1976 workshop was chaired by Andrew Baum and Daniel Stokols and was titled "Emerging Trends in Crowding Research and the Study of Environmental Stress." An important emphasis of this workshop was the distinction between *density* and *crowding*. A large number of environmental psychologists participated in these workshops, and White (1979) provided a complete list of participants.

In 1976 the Task Force on Environment and Behavior also cosponsored sessions at the conventions of regional psychological associations (White, 1979). This effort was coordinated by Stokols. The large number of psychologists who served as regional coordinators also are listed by White (1979). In 1975 two sessions were developed: a symposium on current research topics in environmental psychology and an open forum to discuss the activities of the task force. In 1976 the regional coordinators developed a symposium at each regional convention titled "The Utility of Theoretical Constructs in Environment Behavior Research."

As another way of bringing environmental issues to the attention of APA members, the task force also issued a newsletter under the editorship of White. A total of 11 issues were published. The primary purpose of the newsletter was to report task force activities, but it also provided information on conferences, legislation, research briefs, new publications, and job openings (White, 1979). Each edition also included a listing of 100-word statements by people working in the environment and behavior that described their backgrounds and interests. These listings were intended to be a resource for identifying colleagues and potential symposia participants, professors, and consultants. Statements were obtained from a substantial number of environmental psychologists, and more than 350 of these statements were reprinted in the book *Resources in Environment and Behavior* (White, 1979).

The next item in the mandate for the Task Force on Environment and Behavior was to provide information about alternative models and courses of instruction in environment and behavior. The task force appointed a committee with Gary Evans as chair to conduct a survey of graduate training in the field (White, 1979). Questionnaires were sent to 450 persons who were assumed be knowledgeable about graduate education in environment and behavior. A large number of programs with some relevance were identified, and these programs were listed in *Resources in Environment and Behavior* (White, 1979). Most of these programs had only a tenuous relationship to psychology, however, and fewer than 10 programs were identified specifically with environmental psychology. This situation has not changed; a 1986 survey by the Division 34 executive committee also identified fewer than 10 graduate programs in environmental psychology. The extent to which there is a market for such training obviously is a consideration. Nevertheless, opportunities for graduate study in either population or environmental psychology are limited, and this lack of opportunity may have been a factor in the failure of Division 34 to grow. Currently Division 34 has a "below-replacement fertility rate"—that is, the number of new members (and new PhDs in population and environmental psychology) is smaller than the number of members retiring or attaining dues-exempt status in the APA.

The task force also conducted other activities to provide information about environment and behavior as an academic discipline. It assisted the Environmental Design Research Association (EDRA) in developing a curriculum network to exchange instructional material, course outlines, teaching methods, and so forth (White, 1979). This network reached a size of 125 in 1975 but has remained primarily an EDRA enterprise with little direct impact on Division 34. The task force also developed lists of scientific and professional journals, federal and private funding sources, and scientific and professional organizations related to environment and behavior (White, 1979). Finally, the task force developed and published (White, 1979) an annotated bibliography of more than 60 scholarly books on issues related to environment and behavior.

The third element in the task force mandate was to develop interdisciplinary contacts. Donald Conway and White led the formation of the Interprofessional Consortium on Environment and Behavior that met for the first time in November 1974. The organizations that joined the consortium are listed by White (1979). However, the continued relevance or even existence of the consortium is doubtful. The division does not currently have an officially designated representative to the consortium, and no business items pertaining to the consortium have been on the agenda of the Division 34 executive committee meeting in many years.

The last item in the task force mandate was to promote application and policy-oriented research. John Archea led a project to identify mechanisms by which research on environment and behavior can influence policy and design decisions. The impact of a research finding from the "Michigan Research Project" was described in some detail (White, 1979). This project involved procedures for acclimating elderly individuals to a new nursing home by familiarizing them with the new environment and by such techniques as placing some of their treasured objects in the new home before they moved in.

In the last stages of its existence the Task Force on Environment and Behavior sought an organizational home for environmental psychology. In 1976 the task force surveyed persons in the environment and behavior area about their interest in affiliating with various APA divisions. On the basis of the survey results the task force negotiated primarily with Division 21 (Applied Experimental and Engineering Psychology) and Division 34 (then known as Population Psychology). The negotiations with Division 34 were successful, and in 1977 Division 34 officially became the Division of Population and Environmental Psychology. Most population psychologists were pleased with this change because the addition of environmental issues was consistent with their ecological perspective. Some environmental psychologists were unhappy with this arrangement, believing that a separate Division of Environmental Psychology was preferable. This tension has continued throughout the history of Division 34.

The journal was renamed *Population and Environment, Behavioral and Social Issues,* and Ralph Taylor was named coeditor for environment issues. In 1984 Burton Mindick replaced Thompson as coeditor for population issues. Some environmental psychologists became dissatisfied with the journal, partly because of unhappiness with the publisher Human Sciences Press, and partly because other journals, such as *Environment and Behavior,* seemed to be more appropriate outlets for their research. This dissatisfaction led Taylor to propose that *Population and Environment* be dropped as the official division journal. In 1986 the executive committee approved this proposal, leaving Division 34 with no official journal. (Human Sciences Press continued to publish the journal under the same title.) Many population psychologists, including the original editor Thompson, were opposed to this decision because they were left with no outlet specifically committed to population psychology research.

CHRONOLOGY OF EVENTS IN THE EARLY HISTORY

The events in the history of the two task forces are complex, and their timing may be hard to follow. Table 7 attempts to clarify this complexity

TABLE 7

Chronology of Events in the Early History of Division 34

1969	APA Council of Representatives passes resolution stating that termination of an unwanted pregnancy should be "a Civil Right of the pregnant woman."
1969	Task Force on Psychology, Family Planning, and Population Policy established by the APA.
1969	First volume of journal *Environment and Behavior* published, Gary Winkel editor.
1969	Book *The Psychology of Birth Planning,* Edward Pohlman, editor, published.
1970	With support from The Population Council, the Task Force on Psychology, Family Planning, and Population Policy convened a workshop to review and discuss current population-related activities by psychologists and to recommend future roles for psychologists.
1970	Book *Psychology and Population: Behavioral Research Issues in Fertility and Family Planning,* by James T. Fawcett, published.
1970	Task Force on Psychology, Family Planning, and Population Policy sponsored the APA convention sessions on population psychology for the first time.
1970	Paper by Joachim Wohlwill, "The Emerging Discipline of Environmental Psychology," published in the *American Psychologist.*
1970	Task Force on Psychology, Family Planning, and Population Policy began a newsletter.
1971	Conference on Psychological Measurement in the Study of Population Problems jointly sponsored by the Task Force on Psychology, Family Planning, and Population Policy and the Institute of Personality Assessment and Research, University of California, Berkeley.
1971	Workshop on Developing and Educating Psychologists for Work in the Population Area, cosponsored by Task Force on Psychology, Family Planning, and Population Policy and the Carolina Population Center, University of North Carolina, Chapel Hill.
1972	Final Report of Task Force on Psychology, Family Planning, and Population Policy published in *American Psychologist.*
1972	Task Force on Psychology, Family Planning, and Population recommends creation of a Division of Population Psychology.
1973	APA Council of Representatives admits Division of Population Psychology.
1973	Chapter on environmental psychology by Kenneth Craik published in *Annual Review of Psychology.*
1973	Environmental Psychology Steering Committee met twice to develop a proposal for an environmental task force and to submit it to the Ad Hoc Committee on Newly Emerging Areas in Psychology, APA Board of Scientific Affairs.
1974	Division of Population Psychology officially joins list of APA divisions. Task force newsletter becomes the *Population Psychology Newsletter.*
1974	Task Force on Environment and Behavior established by the APA under the aegis of the Ad Hoc Committee on Newly Emerging Areas in Psychology.
1974	Task Force on Environment and Behavior led in the formation of the Interprofessional Consortium on Environment and Behavior.
1975	Task Force on Environment and Behavior presented a pre-APA convention workshop titled, "Social and Behavioral Data for Environmental Design Applications."

(continued)

TABLE 7
(continued)

1975	Task Force on Environment and Behavior sponsored APA convention sessions on environmental psychology for the first time.
1975	Task Force on Environment and Behavior cosponsored sessions at meetings of the regional psychological associations, Daniel Stokols, coordinator.
1975	Task Force on Environment and Behavior initiated a newsletter.
1975	Subcommittee of the Task Force on Environment and Behavior, Gary Evans, chair, conducted a survey of graduate training programs in environmental psychology.
1976	Book *Population Psychology: Research and Educational Issues,* Sidney H. Newman and Vaida D. Thompson, editors, published by the APA.
1976	Task Force on Environment and Behavior presented a pre-APA convention workshop titled "Emerging Trends in Crowding Research and the Study of Environmental Stress."
1976	Task Force on Environment and Psychology sponsored sessions at the APA convention on environmental psychology.
1976	Task Force on Environment and Behavior surveyed environment and behavior researchers concerning the most appropriate APA division affiliation for environmental psychology. Division 34 viewed as the best available choice.
1976	APA Council of Representatives approved renaming Division 34 the Division of Population and Environmental Psychology.
1977	Division 34 officially becomes the Division of Population and Environmental Psychology. Newsletter renamed *The Population and Environmental Psychology Newsletter.*
1978	First volume of *Journal of Population, Behavioral, Social, and Environmental Issues* published, Vaida D. Thompson, editor.
1978	Chapter on environmental psychology by Daniel Stokols published in *Annual Review of Psychology.*
1979	Book *Resources in Environment and Behavior,* Willo P. White, editor, published by the APA. This book served as the final report of the Task Force on Environment and Behavior.
1980	Journal renamed *Population and Environment, Behavioral and Social Issues.* Ralph Taylor named coeditor for environment.

by presenting an overall chronology of events and dates in the early history of Division 34. There was only minor overlap between population-related events and environmental-related events, and most of the overlap involved events that were not part of the formal functioning of the task forces.

Handbook of Environmental Psychology

Publication of the *Handbook of Environmental Psychology* (Stokols & Altman, 1987) was an important milestone in the history of environmental psychology. The primary function of handbooks is to provide a comprehensive overview of current knowledge and state-of-the-art research methods in a given field, but handbooks also function to validate the maturity of the field in question. The *Handbook of Environmental Psychology* did an excellent job of performing both functions. The content was diverse, including 43 chapters by 68 authors. These chapters were organized in terms of six broad categories. The categories covered in Volume 1 were (a) Origins and Scope of Environmental Psychology, (b) Processes of Person–Environment Transaction, and (c) Levels of Environmental Analysis: Situations, Settings, and Places. The categories covered in Volume 2 were (d) Application of Environmental Psychology to Community Psychology, (e) International Perspectives on Environmental Psychology, and (f) Environmental Psychology: Prospects for the Future.

Other Major Publications

Several serial publications have been established in both population and environmental psychology. Altman, in collaboration with Wohlwill and various other environmental psychologists, has edited a series of volumes under the title *Human Behavior and Environment: Advances in Theory and Research*. Thirteen volumes have been published over a 20-year period. Thematic issues have included such topics as children and the environment, natural environments, the elderly population and the environment, place attachment, women and the environment, and home environments.

Lawrence Severy has edited a series of volumes under the title *Advances in Population: Psychosocial Issues*. In addition to current research, the series attempts to focus on theory, methodological problems and approaches, and policy issues. Specific topics have included adolescents, couple decision making, HIV–AIDS, contraceptive choice and use, fertility theory, prostitution, and other similar psychosocial issues.

In 1980 the *Journal of Environmental Psychology* was established with David V. Canter as first managing editor. Although this journal is edited and published in the United Kingdom, it provides a second major outlet for the environmental work of Division 34 members.

MEMBERSHIP

Membership began with a relatively modest number of 302, and the number of members has remained small and relatively constant. Time trends for membership are summarized in Table 8. There was an increase in the number of members following the addition of environmental psychologists, with membership reaching a peak of 501 in 1981. Since that time membership has fluctuated somewhat, but overall has declined until the present number of members is close to the number in the division's first year. All of this has taken place in a period in which the total membership of the

TABLE 8
Historical Trends in Division 34 Membership

Year	Number of members	Year	Number of members
1974	302	1987	456
1975	301	1988	426
1976	297	1989	382
1977	342	1990	393
1978	411	1991	491
1979	468	1992	435
1980	484	1993	418
1981	501	1994	376
1982	494	1995	355
1983	483	1996	355
1984	452	1997	351
1985	466	1998	315
1986	462		

APA more than doubled from 39,411 in 1975 to 82,938 in 1998. As a consequence, Division 34 membership as a percentage of total APA membership has declined from 0.8% to 0.4% over the same period. In other words, an interest in population and environmental issues is, and always has been, characteristic of a small minority of psychologists. Throughout its history the division bylaws have made it possible for population and environmental scientists and activists who are not members of the APA to join the division as affiliate members. No archival record of the number of affiliates over time was found, but financial information indicates the number has been a relatively constant 100 to 150. Thus affiliates represent a quarter to a third of past and present membership. In 1998 the division bylaws were changed to grant affiliates equal status with APA members who are members of the division, making affiliates eligible to vote in all division elections and to be elected to all division offices.

RELATIONSHIP TO APA'S DIVISIONAL STRUCTURE

The relationship of Division 34 to other divisions was examined in terms of the structure found in factor analytic research (Adkins, 1954, 1973; Rodgers, 1988). The specific factors that were included and the divisions with substantial loadings on each were clinical (12, 13, 27, 29, 31), social–developmental (7, 8, 9, 20), experimental (3, 6, 25, 28), general (1, 2, 10, 24, 26), military–engineering (19, 21), industrial (14, 23), and measurement (5, 15, 16, 17). The source of data was the APA *Directories* that have been issued since Division 34 was established. The percentage of Division 34 members who also were members of each of these divisions was compared with the percentage of APA members who were members of at least one division (only about 50% of all APA members) who were members of each of these divisions. The pattern of divisional memberships was highly consistent over time, and indicated Division 34 members differed from APA members in general only in being more likely to be members of divisions on the social-developmental factor, especially Division 8 (Society for Personality and Social Psychology) and Division 9 (Society for the Psychological Study of Social Issues). The most surprising element in this pattern is how similar Division 34 members have been to other psychologists.

OFFICERS

The psychologists who have served as president of Division 34 are listed in Table 9. This list includes a number of psychologists who have distinguished records, both in the population and environment area and in psychology in general. As might be expected, the first six presidents came primarily from the population area. Six of the next seven presidents, however, came from the environmental area, presumably a reflection of the number of members who were interested in environmental psychology versus population psychology. This disparity was viewed by some members as problematic for the overall welfare of division, and Joseph L. Rodgers proposed the bylaws be changed to provide that whenever two successive presidents came from the same wing of the divisions all candidates for president in the next election must come from the other wing. This bylaw change was approved at the 1988 business meeting of the division and has worked well since. A pattern has emerged in which two presidents from environmental psychology are followed by one president from population psychology.

From 1974 to 1983 the division had two other major officers: the secretary–treasurer and the *Newsletter* editor. In 1983 the membership voted to separate two functions and to elect both a secretary and a treasurer. The intent was for each of these two officers to serve a three-year term, but because of various contingencies this pattern has not always been followed. The division members who have filled these offices in various years are also listed in Table 9.

ROLE OF THE DIVISION FOR MEMBERS

In the summer of 1986, the division conducted a mail survey of all of its members (Richards, 1986), which was intended to explore the role the

TABLE 9
Officers of Division 34

Year	President	Year	President
1974	Vaida D. Thompson (pro tem)	1988	Robert Bechtel
1975	Vaida D. Thompson	1989	Ralph Taylor
1976	James T. Fawcett	1990	Carol Werner
1977	Nancy F. Russo	1991	Linda Beckman
1978	Henry P. David	1992	Seymour Wapner
1979	Miriam Kelty	1993	Richard Wener
1980	Nancy Adler	1994	Paul Bell
1981	Stuart Oskamp	1995	Joseph L. Rodgers
1982	Irwin Altman	1996	Patricia A. Parmelee
1983	Daniel Stokols	1997	George Cvetkovich
1984	Kenneth Craik	1998	James M. Richards, Jr.
1985	Toni L. Falbo	1999	Robert D. Gifford
1986	Allan W. Wicker	2000	Robert Sommer
1987	Susan C. Saegert	2001	S. Marie Harvey

Year	Secretary-Treasurer	Newsletter Editor
1974	Sidney H. Newman (pro tem)	Nancy F. Russo
1975	Nancy F. Russo	Nancy F. Russo
1976	Nancy Adler	Toni Falbo
1977	Nancy Adler	Toni Falbo
1978	Nancy Adler	Toni Falbo
1979	Linda J. Beckman	Toni Falbo
1980	Linda J. Beckman	James M. Richards, Jr.
1981	Linda J. Beckman	James M. Richards, Jr.
1982	Toni Falbo	James M. Richards, Jr.
1983	Toni Falbo	James M. Richards, Jr.

Year	Secretary	Treasurer	Newsletter Editor
1984	Lawrence J. Severy	Charles J. Holahan	James M. Richards, Jr.
1985	J. J. Card	Charles J. Holahan	James M. Richards, Jr.
1986	Joseph L. Rodgers	Barbara Brown	David E. Campbell
1987	Carol Werner	Barbara Brown	David E. Campbell
1988	Carol Werner	Barbara Brown	Patricia A. Parmelee
1989	Carol Werner	Barbara Brown	Patricia A. Parmalee
1990	Richard E. Wener	Paul A. Bell	Patricia A. Parmelee
1991	Richard E. Wener	Paul A. Bell	Dorothy Kagehiro
1992	Patricia A. Parmelee	Paul A. Bell	Dorothy Kagehiro
1993	Patricia A. Parmalee	S. Marie Harvey	Dorothy Kagehiro
1994	Patricia A. Parmelee	S. Marie Harvey	Jill Greenwald
1995	Gregory H. Wilmoth	S. Marie Harvey	Jill Greenwald
1996	Gregory H. Wilmoth	Jennifer A. Veitch	Jill Greenwald
1997	Gregory H. Wilmoth	Jennifer A. Veitch	George Cvetkovich
1998	Gregory H. Wilmoth	Jennifer A. Veitch	Division Officers
1999	Gregory H. Wilmoth	Peter Walker	Jennifer A. Veitch

division played in their professional lives. Completed questionnaires were returned by 290 members for an overall response rate of about 42%. Results suggested that population and environmental issues were, at best, secondary concerns for many members at the time of the survey. Division 34 was the most common primary affiliation within the APA but was chosen by only 28% of respondents. Out of every 10 members, 2 indicated that environmental issues currently were their most important personal and professional interest and 1 in every 10 indicated population issues were their most current important interest. About half of the respondents devoted 10% or more of their "normal working time" to population or environmental issues, but 60% of respondents devoted no working time to population issues and 34% devoted no working time to environmental issues. The APA convention programs suggest this pattern has changed very little in subsequent years.

ACTIVITIES OF MEMBERS RELATED TO POPULATION AND ENVIRONMENT

The 1986 survey of members also addressed the issue of what Division 34 members actually do that is related to population and environment (Richards, 1987). Members reported their activities on a 29-item checklist. This checklist was designed to conform to standards of good practice derived from earlier checklist research (Holland & Richards, 1965; Richards & Gottfredson, 1984). It consisted of socially relevant activities that require competence, persistence, and originality; that frequently involve public recognition; and that, at least in principle, are verifiable. The percentage of members performing each activity is shown in Table 10. The percentage ranged from 66% to 12%, with a median of 28%. Thus members have been quite active in population and environment issues (especially the 50% of members who devote working time to these issues). Members were most likely to have performed activities related to the scientific aspects of population and environmental issues and least likely to have performed activities directly related to Division 34. This pattern probably also has not changed in subsequent years.

CONCLUSION

The process of writing this history identified several themes that are likely to be important in psychological work on population and environmental issues. The future work of environmental psychologists may address such themes as natural environments (especially forests), perception of environmental risks, indoor environments, workplace design, women and

TABLE 10
Activities of Division 34 Members Related to Population and Environment (in percentages)

Activity	Percentage
Was author or coauthor of one or more articles dealing with population or environmental issues published in a scientific journal.	66
Presented a paper, symposium, etc., dealing with population or environmental issues at a regional or national convention of a scientific society other than the APA.	56
Reviewed one or more manuscripts that were being considered for a publication concerned with population or environmental issues.	54
Taught a course or seminar in population or environmental psychology.	53
Received tenure or its equivalent.	51
Gave a talk about population or environmental issues to a community group or organization.	49
Was member of a public or community organization concerned with population or environmental issues.	44
Served as a principal investigator for a scientific project in the population or environmental area that had a budget of $15,000 or more.	40
Served as a consultant (paid or unpaid) to a scientific project in the population or environmental area.	39
Appeared on radio or television as an expert on population or environmental issues.	35
Presented a paper, symposium, etc., at a Division 34 session at an APA convention.	34
Supervised a staff of three or more persons working on a project or program in the population or environmental area.	34
Served as a consultant (paid or unpaid) to a community organization or project in the population or environmental area.	32
Served as a review panel member, consultant, etc., for a governmental agency concerned with population or environmental issues.	29
Chaired a doctoral committee in the population or environmental area.	28
Was author or editor (or coauthor or coeditor) of a book that was published in the population or environmental area.	28
Was editor or member of the editorial board of a publication concerned with population or environmental issues.	26
Served on the staff of a community-based effort whose goal was to help solve population or environmental problems.	23
Author or coauthor of one or more published reviews of books dealing with population or environmental issues.	23
Worked for two or more years in a nonacademic setting concerned with population or environmental issues.	23
Served as an officer, committee member, etc., of an organization other than Division 34 concerned with population or environmental issues.	22
Participated in a formal effort by a scientific or community organization to affect public policy in the population or environmental area.	20

(continued)

TABLE 10
(continued)

Author or coauthor of one or more articles dealing with population or environmental issues published in a popular newspaper or magazine.	20
Was elected a fellow of Division 34.	19
Testified before a legislative committee, in a public hearing, etc., about population or environmental issues.	16
Chaired a Division 34 session at an APA convention.	15
Received a prize or award for research, teaching, or service contributions in the population or environmental area.	15
Was author or coauthor of one or more articles published in *Population and Environment*.	13
Served as an officer, committee member, etc., of Division 34.	12

the environment, and aging and the environment. A "greening" perspective seems to be increasing. This perspective stresses the need and procedures for reducing negative impacts of humans on our environment. This trend has been greeted with ambivalence by scientifically oriented environmental psychologists. Similarly, the future work of population psychologists may address such issues as emergency contraception, methods for improving the reliability of "natural" family planning, developmental aspects of adolescent sexuality, the reasons for contraceptive failure, abortion in all of its ramifications, and reproductive behavior in international context. Several attempts to develop specific psychological theories of reproductive behavior are in progress.

Division 34 members have active research programs in each of these important and interesting areas, and these programs present a more optimistic picture of the future of population and environmental psychology than was seen in some previous sections of this history.

REFERENCES

Adkins, D. (1954). The simple structure of the American Psychological Association. *American Psychologist, 9,* 175–180.

Adkins, D. (1973). A simpler structure of the American Psychological Association. *American Psychologist, 28,* 47–54.

Altman, I., & Rogoff, B. (1987). World views in psychology: Trait, interactional, organismic, and transactional perspectives. In D. Stokols & I. Altman (Eds.), *Handbook of environmental psychology.* New York: John Wiley.

American Psychological Association. (1996). *Graduate study in psychology.* Washington, DC: Author.

APA Task Force. (1972). Report of the task force on psychology, family planning, and population policy. *American Psychologist, 27*, 1100–1105.

Back, K. W., & Fawcett, J. W. (Eds.). (1974). Population policy and the person: Congruence or conflict. *Journal of Social Issues, 30* (40) [Special edition], 1–295.

Barker, R. G. (1965). Explorations in ecological psychology. *American Psychologist, 20*, 1–14.

Barker, R. G. (1968). *Ecological psychology.* Stanford, CA: Stanford University Press.

Beckman, L. J., & Harvey, S. M. (Eds.). (1998). *The new civil war: The psychology, culture, and politics of abortion.* Washington, DC: American Psychological Association.

Brunswick, E. (1955). Representative design and proabilistic theory in a functional psychology. *Psychological Review, 3*, 193–217.

Craik, K. H. (1973). Environmental psychology. *Annual Review of Psychology, 24*, 403–422.

David, H. P. (1972). Remarks. In H. G. Gough (Ed.), *Conference proceedings: Psychological measurement in the study of population problems.* Berkeley: Institute of Personality Assessment and Research, University of California.

David, H. P. (1986). Reflections on the psychosocial workshop. *P.A.A. Affairs (Fall),* 2–3.

David, H. P. (1992). Born unwanted: Long-term developmental effects of denied abortion. *Journal of Social Issues, 3*(3), 163–181.

David, H. P. (1998). Foreword. In L. J. Beckman & S. M. Harvey (Eds.), *The new civil war: The psychology, culture, and politics of abortion.* Washington, DC: American Psychological Association.

Ehrlich, Paul R. (1968). *The population bomb.* New York: Ballantine Books.

Fawcett, J. T. (1970). *Psychology and population: Behavioral research issues in fertility and family planning.* New York: Population Council.

Fawcett, J. T. (Ed.). (1973). *Psychological perspectives on population.* New York: Basic Books.

Gough, H. G. (Ed.). (1972). *Conference proceedings: Psychological measurement in the study of population problems.* Berkeley: Institute of Personality Assessment and Research, University of California.

Gough, H. G. (1976). Some methodological explorations in forecasting family-planning behavior. In S. H. Newman and V. D. Thompson (Eds.), *Population psychology: Research and educational issues.* (DHEW Publication No. (NIH) 76-574) Washington, DC: National Institute of Child Health and Human Development, Center for Population Research.

Hardin, G. (1993). *Living with limits: Ecology, economics, and population taboos.* New York: Oxford University Press.

Holahan, C. J. (1986). Environmental psychology. *Annual Review of Psychology, 37*, 381–407.

Holland, J. L., & Richards, J. M., Jr. (1965). Academic and nonacademic accomplishment: Correlated or uncorrelated? *Journal of Educational Psychology, 56,* 165–174.

Howard, G. S. (1997). *Ecological psychology: Creating a more earth-friendly human nature.* Notre Dame, IN: University of Notre Dame Press.

Ittelson, W. H., Proshansky, H. M., & Rivlin, L. G. (1970). A study of bedroom use on two psychiatric wards. *Hospital and Community Psychiatry, 21,* 177–180.

Lewin, K. (1936). *Principles of topological psychology.* New York: McGraw-Hill.

Malthus, R. T. (1798). *An essay on the principle of population.* Reprinted in G. Hardin (Ed.) (1969), *Population, evolution, and birth control.* San Francisco: Freeman.

McKeachie, W. J. (1970). Proceedings of the American Psychological Association of the year 1969: Minutes of the annual meeting of the Council of Representatives. *American Psychologist, 25,* 13–37.

Newman, S. H., & Thompson, V. D. (Eds.). (1976). *Population psychology: Research and educational issues.* (DHEW Publication No. (NIH) 76-574). Washington, DC: National Institute of Child Health and Human Development, Center for Population Research.

Osmond, H. (1957). Function as the basis of psychiatric ward design. *Mental Hospitals, 8,* 23–30.

Pohlmar, E. (Ed.). (1969). *The psychology of birth planning.* Cambridge, MA: Schenkman.

Proshansky, H., & Altman, I. (1979). Overview of the field. In W. P. White (Ed.), *Resources in environment and behavior.* Washington, DC: American Psychological Association.

Richards, J. M., Jr. (1986). Results of the Division 34 membership survey: I. Response rates, primary interests, and division services. *Population & Environmental Psychology Newsletter, 13*(3), 13–16.

Richards, J. M., Jr. (1987). Results of the Division 34 membership survey. II. Activities and accomplishments. *Population & Environmental Psychology Newsletter, 14*(1), 13–16.

Richards, J. M., Jr., & Gottfredson, G. D. (1984). Patterns of accomplishment among psychologists. *American Psychologist, 39,* 1352–1356.

Rodgers, J. L. (1988). Structural models of the American Psychological Association in 1986. *American Psychologist, 43,* 372–382.

Russell, J. A., & Ward, L. M. (1982). Environmental psychology. *Annual Review of Psychology, 33,* 651–688.

Saegert, S., & Winkel, G. (1990). Environmental psychology. *Annual Review of Psychology, 41,* 441–477.

Severy, L. J. (1975). Ecosystems: Populations in environments. *Population Psychology Newsletter, 2,* 15–18.

Smith, M. B. (1972). Ethical implications of population policies: A psychologist's view. *American Psychologist, 27,* 11–15.

Sommer, R., & Becker, H. (1961). Symptoms of institutional care. *Social Problems, 8*, 254.

Stokols, D. (1978). Environmental psychology. *Annual Review of Psychology, 29*, 253–295.

Stokols, D. (1987). Conceptual strategies of environmental psychology. In D. Stokols & I. Altman (Eds.), *Handbook of environmental psychology*. New York: John Wiley.

Stokols, D., & Altman, I. (Eds.). (1987). *Handbook of environmental psychology*. New York: John Wiley.

Taylor, C. W., Bailey, R., & Branch, C. H. H. (Eds.). (1967). *National conference on architectural psychology*. Salt Lake City: University of Utah.

Thompson, V. D. (1986). Where is population psychology? *Population and Environment Newsletter, 13*(2), 12–15.

Thompson, V. D., & Newman, S. H. (Eds.). (1974). Educating psychologists to work in the population field. *Professional Psychology, 5*, 320–324.

Thompson, V. D., & Newman, S. H. (1976a). Developing psychologists for work in the population field: Workshop report. In S. H. Newman & V. D. Thompson (Eds.), *Population psychology: Research and educational issues*. (DHEW Publication No. (NIH) 76-574) Washington, DC: National Institute of Child Health and Human Development, Center for Population Research.

Thompson, V. D., & Newman, S. H. (1976b). Population psychology in the process of development: An overview. In S. H. Newman & V. D. Thompson (Eds.), *Population psychology: Research and educational issues* (DHEW Publication No. (NIH) 76-574) Washington, DC: National Institute of Child Health and Human Development, Center for Population Research.

Westoff, C. F., Potter, R. G., Jr., Sagi, P. C., & Mishler, E. G. (1961). *Family growth in metropolitan America*. Princeton, NJ: Princeton University Press.

White, W. P. (Ed.). (1979). *Resources in environment and behavior*. Washington, DC: American Psychological Association.

Winter, D. D. (1996). *Ecological psychology, healing the split between planet and self*. New York: Harper Collins.

Wohlwill, J. F. (1970). The emerging discipline of environmental psychology. *American Psychologist, 25*, 303–312.

6

A HISTORY OF DIVISION 40 (CLINICAL NEUROPSYCHOLOGY)

ANTONIO E. PUENTE and ANN C. MARCOTTE

Neuropsychology can be broadly defined as the study and practice of brain–behavior relationships. The roots of neuropsychology can be traced to clinical and physiological psychology, as well as to the study of individual differences. In addition, the discipline has strong ties with medicine, especially neurology and neuroscience. Whereas several accounts are available regarding the history of neuropsychology, almost all the published material focuses on older and more experimentally oriented information—and often from a personal perspective (e.g., Finger, 1992). For example, efforts by pioneers such as Benton (1992), Costa (1976, 1998), Goldstein (1985), and Meier (1992) have provided personal reflections on recent developments of neuropsychology as a professional discipline. The early organizational development, especially of the International Neuropsychological Society, is also well-described by Meier (1992). Puente (1992) provided some of the background regarding the development of neuropsychology as a professional discipline, also. However, relatively little has been documented regarding the establishment of either of the two organizations involved with clinical (versus experimental) neuropsychology—namely the National Academy of Neuropsychology (NAN) and the Division of Clinical Neuropsychology (Division 40) of the American Psychological Association (APA). This chapter reports on the history of one of the most recent additions to the division structure of the APA, as well as one of the largest and most active.

A chapter of this type is difficult to write for several reasons. First, large amounts of data should be included for archival purposes. Second, critical information pertaining to the division was not stored and often not documented. Division 40, however, established an archival depository for its records in August 1998. Archives will now be housed at the Louisiana and Lower Mississippi Valley Archival Collection, Louisiana State University Libraries, Baton Rouge, Louisiana. With a recent grant from the executive committee of the division, existing archival records have now been digitized and are retrievable through the Internet at http://diglib.lsu/edu/digitallibrary. Though not historical in content, the general Web site for the division is http://www.Div40.org. Finally, history is not written without a contextual background, potentially with particular biases. Although we trust that such biases have been held constant, we similarly realize the vagaries of writing a history, especially of a specialty in rapid evolution. Thus we trust that this chapter serves as a first approximation to what is considered to be important while expecting that future colleagues and students will help to reevaluate what has already transpired and what exciting developments will come to fruition.

ESTABLISHING THE DIVISION

In an invited address delivered at the 1997 APA annual convention, in honor of the Golden Anniversary of divisions within the APA, Louis Costa provided a retrospective review of the early years in the professionalization of neuropsychology (Costa, 1998). He noted that Division 40 was a direct outgrowth of the first formal organization in neuropsychology, The International Neuropsychological Society (INS). In fact, the histories of the INS and Division 40 are intricately interwoven. The earliest informal meeting of what would become the INS was held as part of the annual APA convention in 1965. This meeting occurred in part, according to Meier (1998), because a small group had been convened at the University of Minnesota. Starke Hathaway (known for his work on the MMPI) was then director of clinical psychology at the University of Minnesota. He obtained funds to convene a meeting in Minneapolis in 1965 of Costa, Hallgrim Klove, Charles Matthews, Manfred Meier, Ralph Reitan, and Paul Satz. Approximately 48 neuropsychologists attended a meeting at the APA convention to explore the formation of a formal association. A steering committee under the direction of Raymond Dennerll was developed (partially at the urging of Aaron Smith). In October 1976, the first edition of *Neuropsychology Bulletin* was published and the INS was formally organized.

The purpose of the organization was to promote research, service, and education in a multidisciplinary context. The group continued to meet as part of the APA convention between 1967 and 1972, with the first independent meeting occurring in 1973 (New Orleans).

As the field of clinical neuropsychology continued to evolve during the 1960s, professional issues emerged, particularly those germane to the training and education of clinical neuropsychologists. Costa made this the central issue of his 1976 INS presidential address (Costa, 1976). His position was that clinical neuropsychology was a specialty and not a proficiency of clinical psychology. He commented on the need for training guidelines and standards for the field and argued for the need for an organization independent of the INS to "optimize the realization of the professional and societal goals" of clinical neuropsychology (Costa, 1976, p. 6). Although recognizing that Division 12 (Society of Clinical Psychology) had been supportive of clinical neuropsychology's efforts, Costa raised concerns that the field not be entrenched within clinical psychology, noting, "Perhaps we would best be independent guardians of our professional interests" (Costa, 1976, p. 7). He then went on to propose the formation of a division of clinical neuropsychology within the APA.

In his reflections of the early years of the field, Costa (1998) reported that the reception of this idea was enthusiastic, although the INS executive board's support for the creation of a new division within the APA to address professional and training issues was less well-received. Nevertheless, by 1978 the INS created the Task Force on Education, Accreditation, and Credentialing of Clinical Neuropsychologists. In 1979 the INS board finally endorsed Costa's 1976 proposal to create a new division within the APA devoted to clinical neuropsychology. Costa (1998) noted that there was some discussion by the INS executive board about the use of the term "clinical" in naming the division, but that point was eventually quickly resolved. An application was subsequently filed with the APA petitioning for a new division. The 1979 *Proceedings of the APA* (Conger, 1980, p. 159) document that at its September 1979 meeting the APA Council of Representatives approved the creation of Division 40 (Clinical Neuropsychology) effective January 1, 1980. There apparently was little dissent to the formation of the new division. However, the *Proceedings* document that "a representative of Division 6 (then Physiological and Comparative Psychology) noted that Division 6 did not oppose the establishment of Division 40 but suggested that the proliferation of divisions is of itself inimical to all Divisions, and signals a need for reorganization of APA" (Conger, 1980, p. 159). The INS task force quickly became the joint INS–Division 40 Task Force on Education, Accreditation, and Credentialing. The first report was published in 1981, marking the first published guidelines for training in clinical neuropsychology. The culmination of these efforts occurred in 1996 when the APA Council of Representatives approved the application of clinical neuropsychology as the first specialty within psychology.

ORGANIZATIONAL STRUCTURE AND OFFICERS

The organization of the division has changed relatively little during the first 20 years of existence. In fact, the number of individuals involved with governance has been relatively small. However, some growth within its structure has occurred as a result of the increase in Council representatives.

Executive Committee

The organizational structure and the officers of the division and their delineated duties are described in the division bylaws. Originally written in 1980 after the founding of the division, the bylaws were updated and approved by the membership for the first time in 1997. However, the structure and function of the division has remained relatively intact. The bylaw changes reflect more of an adjustment to minor changes over time (e.g., the phasing out of a committee) than a major paradigm shift. The governing body of Division 40 is the executive committee, which meets twice a year in a mid-winter meeting (traditionally held prior to the INS annual meeting) and a meeting held in conjunction with the annual convention of the APA. The executive committee is mandated by divisional bylaws to supervise the affairs of the division. The committee is composed of the division officers, the division's representative(s) to the APA Council, and three members at large. According to the bylaws of the division, the officers of Division 40 shall be a president, president-elect, past president, secretary, and treasurer. All executive committee members are elected by the membership of the division in elections conducted and regulated by the APA. All division officers and members at large assume their positions at the close of the annual business meeting held at the APA annual convention and maintain the position until their successors are seated. The number of Division 40 representatives (four in 1999) to the APA Council is determined each year by the number of votes designated for Division 40 representation by APA members in the annual apportionment vote. Committee chairs, appointed by the president, also are invited to attend the executive committee meetings and make reports of committee activities, but they are not allowed to vote.

Although the membership of the division is more than 4300, slightly more than 30 individuals have held elected offices during its close to 20-year history. There have been 18 presidents, 4 secretaries, 6 treasurers, 20 members at large, and 11 Council representatives. Of the 11 Council representatives, 3 have not been president of the division. Even though only one member has been reelected or held an office longer than the stated term in the president's office, all other offices have had individuals with multiple terms. It is worth noting that of the 35 individuals who have served as elected officers, 3 have been women and 2 have been ethnic minorities. The lack of women and ethnic minorities within the executive committee is a reflection of the demographics of clinical neuropsychology. A summary of the elected officials of Division 40 from 1979 to 1999 is presented in Table 11.

The president serves as the chair of the executive committee and begins his or her respective term after completing one year as the president-elect. No person is allowed to serve in this position for more than one term. The exception to this rule, however, was the division's first president, Harold Goodglass, who served from the founding of the division in September 1979 to August 1980, and then again for a full term that ended in August 1981. The president is empowered to make committee appointments and to name chairs of committees in consultation with the executive committee. The president also can create task forces with the approval of the executive committee to address specific topics of interest to the division. In the division's 20-year history, only two women, Edith Kaplan (1986–1987) and Eileen Fennell (1996–1997) have served as president; no ethnic minorities have served. All but two former Division 40 presidents are alive at the time of this chapter's publication, and all remain active in the field of clinical neuropsychology. Nelson Butters died in November 1995 and Matthews died in May 1998. A book honoring the life and work of Butters was published (Cermark, 1996) and a series of short articles commemorating Matthews was printed in the Division 40 newsletter in the last issue of 1998.

The president-elect performs duties traditionally assigned to a vice-president. The past-president is the most recently retired division president. In addition to being a voting member of the executive committee, the past-president also serves as chair of the elections committee, overseeing the development of the election slate and reporting on election results.

The secretary and treasurer of the division are elected to three-year terms but can hold these positions for no more than two consecutive terms. When the division was founded in September 1979, these two positions were combined into one joint position, which was filled by Gerald Goldstein. In August 1980 the decision was made to separate the two positions. The treasurer oversees the daily financial running of the division and aids the president and president-elect in developing the annual budget. Six different Division 40 members have served as treasurer: Goldstein, Butters, Larry Squire, Raymond Dean, Roberta White, and Wilfred Van Gorp. The secretary of the division is responsible for keeping the membership informed of

TABLE 11
Elected Officials of the Division 40: 1979–1999

Years[a]	Presidents	Secretaries	Treasurers	Members at Large	Council Representatives
1979	Harold Goodglass	Gerald Goldstein	Gerald Goldstein	Edith Kaplan Oscar Parsons Byron Rourke	Manfred Meier
1980	Harold Goodglass	Gerald Goldstein	Nelson Butters	Edith Kaplan Oscar Parsons Byron Rourke	Manfred Meier
1981	Louis Costa	Gerald Goldstein	Nelson Butters	Edith Kaplan Charles Matthews Kenneth Adams	Manfred Meier
1982	Nelson Butters	Gerald Goldstein	Larry Squire[b]	Charles Matthews Kenneth Adams Byron Rourke	Thomas Boll
1983	Thomas Boll	Gerald Goldstein	Raymond Dean	Kenneth Adams Byron Rourke Linas Bieliauskas	Thomas Boll
1984	Lawrence Hartlage	Gerald Goldstein	Raymond Dean	Byron Rourke Linas Bieliauskas Cecil Reynolds	Thomas Boll
1985	Manfred Meier	Kenneth Adams	Raymond Dean	Cecil Reynolds Roberta White[c] Jeffrey Barth	Linas Bieliauskas Manfred Meier
1986	Edith Kaplan	Kenneth Adams	Raymond Dean	Cecil Reynolds Jeffrey Barth Jack Fletcher	Linas Bieliauskas Manfred Meier
1987	Byron Rourke	Kenneth Adams	Raymond Dean	Jeffrey Barth Jack Fletcher Antonio Puente	Linas Bieliauskas Manfred Meier
1988	Gerald Goldstein	Kenneth Adams	Raymond Dean	Jack Fletcher Antonio Puente Gordon Chelune	Nelson Butters Robert Heaton
1989	Charles Matthews	Kenneth Adams	Roberta White		

Year					
1990	Raymond Dean	Kenneth Adams	Roberta White	Antonio Puente Gordon Chelune Jeffrey Barth	Nelson Butters Robert Heaton
1991	Steven Mattis	Robert Bornstein	Roberta White	Gordon Chelune Jeffrey Barth Jim Hom	Robert Heaton Kenneth Adams
1992	Oscar Parsons	Robert Bornstein	Roberta White	Jeffrey Barth Jim Hom George Prigitano	Kenneth Adams Gerald Goldstein
1993	Robert Heaton	Robert Bornstein Ann Marcotte[d]	Roberta White	Jim Hom George Prigitano Thomas Hammeke	Kenneth Adams Gerald Goldstein
1994	Carl Dodrill	Ann Marcotte	Wilfred Van Gorp	George Prigitano Thomas Hammeke Jill Fischer	Gerald Goldstein Antonio Puente
1995	Kenneth Adams	Ann Marcotte	Wilfred Van Gorp	Thomas Hammeke Jill Fischer Kerry Hamsher	Gerald Goldstein Antonio Puente Thomas Boll
1996	Eileen Fennell	Ann Marcotte	Wilfred Van Gorp	Jill Fischer Kerry Hamsher Richard Berg	Gerald Goldstein Antonio Puente Thomas Boll
1997	Linas Bieliauskus	Ann Marcotte	Wilfred Van Gorp	Kerry Hamsher Richard Berg Munro Cullum	Gerald Goldstein Thomas Boll Antonio Puente
1998	Cecil Reynolds	Ann Marcotte	Wilfred Van Gorp	Richard Berg Munro Cullum Lloyd Cripe	Thomas Boll Theodore Blau Kerry Hamsher Antonio Puente
1999	Gordon Chelune	Ann Marcotte	Wilfred Van Gorp	Munro Cullum Lloyd Cripe Keith Yeates	Thomas Boll Theodore Blau Kerry Hamsher Antonio Puente

Notes. The first full election for Division 40 officials was held in 1980, following the founding of the division in September 1979. The positions of secretary and treasurer were separated in August 1980.
[a] A year of term begins in August of the year indicated, immediately following the annual business meeting held at the APA convention, and ends at the conclusion of the annual business meeting of the following calendar year.
[b] Squire was elected to complete the third year of Butters's term as treasurer, because Butters had to resign from the position to become division president.
[c] White was elected to complete the third year of Bieliauskas's term as member at large, because he had to resign from the position to become division's Council representative.
[d] Bornstein resigned as secretary in January 1994; Marcotte was elected to complete the remaining 8 months of his term.

the actions of the executive committee. The secretary takes the minutes for each executive committee meeting and the annual business meeting, which are published in the *Division 40 Newsletter*. The secretary of the division also serves as a vital link for the division to the APA Central Office and is the person individuals seeking information about clinical neuropsychology from the APA are placed in contact with to receive pertinent information or to have questions answered. In the division's approximately 20-year history, only four individuals have served as secretary: Goldstein, Kenneth Adams, Robert Bornstein, and Ann Marcotte. Originally, the secretary also served as the division's newsletter editor. In 1984, however, the decision was made to create a new position of editor independent of the secretary. White served as the division's newsletter editor from 1984 to 1995. John DeLuca succeeded White as editor.

The number of Division 40 representatives to the APA Council has changed over the years, with increases in division membership frequently reflecting increases in the number of representatives elected. From 1980 to 1986, the division had one Council representative; since 1986, the division has consistently received enough votes on the apportionment ballot to elect two representatives to Council. After a concerted effort on the part of the division to increase representation, the division representation to the APA Council of Representatives was increased to three in 1995; unfortunately, the third position was not maintained in the next apportionment ballot, and the divisional representation dropped back to two representatives in 1996. Through a concerted effort to recruit additional Council representation, the lost seat was regained in 1997, and in 1998 one other was added for a total of four representatives. Each representative is elected to complete a three-year term of office. In 1989, however, the executive committee of the division discussed the need for staggered terms for Council representatives to ensure smoother representation. It was decide that Butters, who was elected along with Robert Heaton to this position, would only serve two of his three years of appointment, with a new representative to be elected at the end of his second year. Since that time, a staggered term for representatives has been maintained.

There are three members at large to the executive committee, who are allowed to serve up to two consecutive terms of three years each. In the earliest years of the division, Kaplan, Oscar Parsons, and Byron Rourke filled these positions. In 1982 two of these original members at large rotated off the executive committee after only two years of service to begin to attain a staggered term among the three positions. To help fully actualize this plan, in 1984 Matthews was rotated off as member at large after serving two of his three years of office. Thus by the time of the 1984 elections, the staggered plan of election of a new member at large each year was attained.

In all, 21 different Division 40 members have been elected to serve as a member at large to the executive committee.

Standing Committees

In addition to the executive committee, the Division 40 bylaws called for the formation of four standing committees to address specific activities central to the operations of the division. These four committees are elections, membership, fellowship, and program.

The elections committee is chaired by the past-president of the division and has at least two other past-presidents appointed by the chair of the committee. The committee is charged with securing the nominations for elected divisional appointments by a mail ballot from all voting Division 40 members and to ensure that all nominees meet requirements to hold office and indeed wish to run for the position. Any person who receives nominations totaling at least 1% of the current voting membership is included on the ballot, if so qualified to hold office. The elections committee is also empowered by the division bylaws to place the name of one more person on the ballot for each office for which election is being held.

The membership committee is responsible for securing and reviewing evidence concerning the qualifications of all candidates for membership or change in membership status in the division. The minimum qualifications for election to membership are the attainment of member or fellow status within the APA and demonstrated interest in the field of neuropsychology and its development. After reviewing the credentials of candidates, the membership committee submits the names of all candidates to the general Division 40 membership at the annual business meeting for approval.

The fellowship committee was developed to receive all applications for fellow status in the division, to collect and consider such supporting materials as are necessary, and to make nominations for fellow status in the division. The definition of fellows involves the identification of neuropsychologists who have made "outstanding activities, contribution, performance that have had a sustained, discernible, and salutary effect on the development of neuropsychology as a science and/or a profession." The executive committee votes to ratify each of the fellow's nominations, which is then passed on to the APA for final consideration. Potential fellows must be recommended by three current Division 40 fellows and be able to demonstrate that they have made a substantial contribution to the science or the profession of neuropsychology. As of 1999, there were 109 fellows in Division 40.

The program committee is charged with the planning and coordination of the division's programming of activities held in conjunction with the annual APA convention. This committee was developed to meet two of the four original purposes of the division: (a) to advance the contribution of psychology in understanding the neurological bases of normal and dysfunctional behavior by encouraging basic and clinical research, and (b) to inform psychologists, members of related fields, and the general public of the results of current research and service activities relating to clinical neuropsychology. Each year since 1980 a program of events to meet these two objectives has been sponsored by Division 40. Seven Division 40 members have served as chair of the program committee: Parsons (1980–1982), Linas Bieliauskas (1983–1986), Polly Pechstedt (1987–1989), Carl Dodrill (1990–1992), Ann Marcotte (1992–1994), Max Trenerry (1994–1996), Keith Yeates (1996–1997), Mark Bondi (1997–1998), Glenn Smith (1998–1999), and Paula Shear (2000–2001). Formal terms of appointment for the chair of this committee were delineated in 1991 during the tenure of Dodrill as chair. Beginning with Dodrill, the chair was appointed to serve a three-year term of duty, with the first year spent as cochair with the outgoing program chair and the third year spent as chair acting as a mentor to the incoming cochair. This three-year plan, however, was discontinued in 1996, and replaced with two-year appointments. Under the new system, the first year of appointment is spent as cochair and the second as chair. The chair of the program committee recruits Division 40 members to serve as committee members, whose task is to review all anonymous submissions to the division program. As the membership of Division 40 grew significantly during the mid- to late 1980s, so too did the number of paper, poster, and symposia submissions to the division program committee. To meet the increasing demands, the size of the program committee membership has also greatly increased in number, such that in 1999 there were 16 members serving on this committee.

To better understand the role and functions of committees, a review of the minutes was completed. This review suggested that the executive board and its committees has primarily been focused on specific issues at their regular meetings, including increasing participation from the membership and developing strategic planning for the future of the division as well as for clinical neuropsychology. Over the years the following topics have been the focus of executive board meetings: *Psychology Today*, APA reorganization, relationship with the APA, publications (including the development of *Neuropsychology*), and regular contact and interaction with APA representatives from the practice as well as the science Directorates. The development of the journal *Neuropsychology* was initiated by the APA's publication office and not the division. A small committee headed by Butters (and including the senior author) was formed to address APA's interest. An existing journal was purchased (for the sake of the title of the journal, *Neuropsychology*) and Butters was given the charge as the first editor to incorporate both experimental and clinical neuropsychology. After Butters's death, his colleague Laird Cermak took over as editor. It should be noted that the journal is not the official journal of the division and that most of the position papers as well as convention abstracts are published in *The Clinical Neuropsychologist*. In addition, practice issues have become increasingly important to the division's executive committee. Topics that have been discussed include the use of nondoctoral technicians, credentialing of neuropsychologists and of educational and training programs, definition of a *neuropsychologist*, managed care and reimbursement, and forensics.

Finally, at their regular board meetings the executive committee works diligently at conducting its business. This work is categorized in one of three ways: information (to and from the APA and its members), ongoing business, and development of new agendas. During the 1980s, the meetings took almost three days, whereas now the meetings have been held over a three- to four-hour period. This is, in part, because the meetings have focused on decision making, with information items being distributed in the form of written reports, often before the meetings.

Ad Hoc Committees and Task Forces

As part of neuropsychology's ongoing development as a specialty area in psychology, Division 40 has helped to define the field. The division set standards for practice, education, training, research, and the advancement of neuropsychology in the public interest through the work of several important task forces and ad hoc committees. These task forces and committees have been created by the president and the executive committee of Division 40, each mandated with specific goals and objectives. Task force and committee reports have been published in *The Clinical Neuropsychologist* or the *Division 40 Newsletter*. *The Clinical Neuropsychologist* is an independently published, peer-reviewed journal devoted to the science and profession of neuropsychology. In contrast, the Division 40 Newsletter is the quarterly and official publication of the division. The following is a review of some of the accomplishments of these groups that have served to help advance clinical neuropsychology.

One of the most important tasks in a new profession is to establish standards for education and training. In part, the founding of Division 40 as an entity was based on a need for such professional training and practice guidelines for clinical neuropsychologists in the late 1970s. The INS, the primary organization joined by neuropsychologists at that time, viewed these growing needs to be outside the scope of their multidisciplinary and more experimentally oriented organization. Division 40 was, in part, established to meet these new professional needs of clinical neuropsychologists. One of the earliest task forces established after the founding of the division was the INS/Division 40 Task Force on Education, Accreditation and

Credentialing (see Costa, 1998, and Meier, 1992, 1998). At various times task forces worked toward defining the standards for training for clinical neuropsychologists at the doctoral, internship, and postdoctoral fellowship level. Reports of these subcommittees were reviewed and approved and published in the *Division 40 Newsletter* (Division 40/INS Task Force on Education, Accreditation and Credentialing, 1984; INS-Division 40 Task Force on Education, Accreditation and Credentialing, 1986). A final report of the joint INS/Division 40 Task Force summarizing guidelines for training at each of these levels was published in 1987 (Reports of the INS/Division 40 Task Force on Education, Accreditation and Credentialing, 1987). This report has come to serve as the standard for programs offering training in clinical neuropsychology.

With the final report of this task force filed and published in 1987, the board of directors of the INS announced its intent to withdraw from any future activities of this task force. The executive committee of Division 40 therefore created an independent Task Force on Education, Accreditation and Credentialing, which continued to address issues in these three broad areas. Robert Bornstein chaired the task force until 1992, at which time it was temporarily disbanded. Issues addressed included the development of guidelines for continuing education in clinical neuropsychology (Bornstein, 1988), the use of nondoctoral personnel in clinical neuropsychological assessment (Report of the Division 40 Task Force on Education, Accreditation and Credentialing, 1989), and recommendations for the training of such nondoctoral personnel (Report of the Division 40 Task Force on Education, Accreditation and Credentialing, 1991).

Emerging from these early efforts came the increasing awareness of the need for a definition of a *clinical neuropsychologist*. In 1988, this task was put to the newly developed Professional Affairs Committee, chaired by Bieliauskas. A definition was drafted by the committee and discussed by the Division 40 executive committee, which adopted the definition on August 12, 1988. It was published in *The Clinical Neuropsychologist* (Definition of a Clinical Neuropsychologist, 1989). However, this definition was considered by some to be controversial and, as a consequence, is under review at present. In the early 1990s, the Professional Affairs Committee surveyed Division 40 members' attitudes about prescription privileges for psychologists, and results were published in the *Division 40 Newsletter* in 1991. Over the course of the past few years, under the leadership of Joseph D. Eubanks, this committee has focused efforts on developing a recently published informational pamphlet for the general public, insurance companies, businesses, and health care providers that outlines the practice of clinical neuropsychology.

Another task force developed early in the history of Division 40 was the Task Force on the Use of Computer Technology in Evaluation and

Rehabilitation in Neuropsychology. This task force was established in 1984 and was chaired by Matthews throughout its existence. Given the broad scope and complexity of the mission put to this task force, the group completed its work in two phases, filing reports at the conclusion of each phase. The first report (Division 40: Task Force Report on Computer-Assisted Neuropsychological Evaluation, 1987) expanded on the Guidelines for Computer-Based Tests and Interpretations (INS-Division 40, 1986) published jointly by the APA Committee on Professional Standards and the Committee on Psychological Tests and Assessment. Division 40 provided minor additions designed to focus the reader's attention to specific applicability of the guidelines to the practice of clinical neuropsychology. In its second phase of work, the task force prepared guidelines for the use of computer-assisted retraining–remediation procedures in neuropsychology. In this portion of the task force's assignment, J. Preston Harley joined Matthews as cochair. An official report was published in 1991 (Matthews, Harley, & Malec, 1991).

Another priority for the emerging field of clinical neuropsychology was maintaining and disseminating information pertaining to programs offering training in clinical neuropsychology. In the early 1980s Goldstein, then acting secretary of the division, kept an informal list of such information. In 1986, however, Lloyd Cripe proposed developing and maintaining a database of such doctoral, internship, and postdoctoral training programs with the goal of publishing the listing on a periodic basis. The executive committee accepted Cripe's proposal and appointed him chair of the ad hoc Training Database Committee. The listing of training programs has been published every two years (Cripe, 1989, 1991, 1993, 1995, 1997), with each new listing offering expanded information about the programs. In 1995 this information was also put on the World Wide Web (http://www.Div40 .org) allowing interested students easy access to the listing through computer technology. The 1995 listing summarized the offerings of 30 doctoral training programs, 43 clinical internships, and 66 postdoctoral fellowship programs in clinical neuropsychology. This list is being regularly updated, and the latest version can be found in The Clinical Neuropsychologist as well as on the division's Web page.

Other early ad hoc committees formed by Division 40 often grew out of appointments of individual members to serve as a Division 40 liaison to APA committees. Other early ad hoc Division 40 Committees included the Legislative Committee (which in 1987 evolved into the Professional Affairs Committee), the Committee on Women in Psychology (disbanded in 1986 but resurrected in 1997), and the Committee on Gay and Lesbian Concerns. Another committee established shortly after the founding of the division was the Committee on Ethnic Minority Affairs. Originally chaired by Alonzo Campbell (1983–1986), it was subsequently chaired by Antonio Puente

(1987–1993), Tony Strickland (1993–1996), and Duane Dede (1997–present). The missions of this ad hoc committee are to identify minority members, consider ways to increase minority involvement in neuropsychology, and to promote awareness of minority and ethnic issues important to the practice of clinical neuropsychology. Over the years, this committee has developed events presented at the APA convention to increase Division 40 members' awareness of these issues. Finally, an ad hoc ethics Committee was established in 1986 to review ethical problems facing the practice of neuropsychology and to assist in the interpretation of the APA *Ethical Principles* (APA, 1990) to neuropsychology. This committee has been chaired by Kenneth Adams (1986–1993), John McSweeny (1993–1995), and Bruce Becker (1995–present). This committee has also sponsored events as part of the Division 40 Program at the APA convention. In 1995 McSweeny also introduced a column published in *The Clinical Neuropsychologist* in which debates concerning ethical practice issues are considered.

In response to the changing needs of the division several new ad hoc committees and task forces were created. In 1993, then President Parsons reactivated the Task Force on Education, Accreditation and Credentialing, naming Bruce Crosson as chair. The task force was charged with the mission of reviewing and clarifying aspects of the definition of a clinical neuropsychologist, and, if necessary, of offering a revised definition for consideration. The task force presented its report to the executive committee in August 1995; this report was used as a working document while additional issues become resolved. A formal report was approved in August1997 but never published.

Partially in conjunction with the Practice Directorate of the APA as well as the National Academy of Neuropsychology (an independent organization founded in 1980 to further the science and practice of clinical neuropsychology), efforts have been made to further the development of professional neuropsychology. Primary concerns have focused on work with the American Medical Association (AMA) and the Health Care Financing Administration (HCFA), the federal government's policy-setting agency for health insurance and related matters. Puente has headed the Current Procedural Terminology (CPT) Committee and has acted as liaison for with both the AMA and the Health Care Financing Administration (HCFA) to establish billing codes and reimbursement guidelines for neuropsychological services. In addition, model reimbursement strategies have also been proposed. Recently one aspect of the reimbursement issue, "incident to," became problematic in that the HCFA indicated that technical time was not reimbursable in inpatient settings. To address this issue, Bieliauskas asked Puente to develop a task force on "incident to"; this task force was recently expanded and is now chaired by Bieliauskas. "Incident to" is defined as any professional service provided by a nonprofessional (e.g., technician) in response to a direct request and under the direct supervision of the provider.

The 1990s also saw growing interest within the APA in international psychology. The APA established the Committee on International Relations in Psychology, and Robert Heilbronner was appointed to serve as liaison. An ad hoc committee on international relations in psychology was established in Division 40 in 1993. This committee has actively assessed division members' interest in international psychology, and has been completing work on establishing a listing of neuropsychologists proficient in languages other than English who are able to receive non–English-speaking referrals.

Awards and Honors

In 1989 Division 40 established the Student Award, given to the best student submission to the annual Division 40 program. In 1993, the American Psychological Foundation (APF) announced the formation of the Henri Hecaen Scholarship, the recipient of which would be a graduate student pursuing studies in neuropsychology who has distinguished him- or herself in scholarly neuropsychological work. Kerry Hamsher was appointed to chair the division's Hecaen Award Committee, and the first award was granted in 1994. In 1994, Division 40 formed an Awards Committee, chaired by Ida Sue Baron, in response to the development of two new awards to honor neuropsychologists to be administered through Division 40. The Robert A. and Phyllis Levitt Early Career Award was developed to honor the Levitts's generosity to the division. The executive committee decided that this award would honor a clinical neuropsychologist who has achieved the doctoral degree not more than 10 years previously and who has made a distinguished contribution to neuropsychology in research, scholarship, or clinical work. To date the awards have been given to Max Trenerry (1995), John Gabrielli (1996), John DeLuca (1997), Marlene Behrmann (1998), and Mark Bondi (1999). In addition to receiving an honorarium, the Levitt Award recipient is invited to make a presentation at the APA annual convention. Also in 1994, the APF announced the first Arthur L. Benton Lectureship. The recipient of this award is selected by the Division 40 Awards Committee and approved by the APF. The award is bestowed annually to a senior neuropsychologist who receives an honorarium and delivers a lecture at the APA convention. The recipients have been Costa (1995), Matthews (1996), Parsons (1997), Harold Goodglass (1998), and Ottfried Spreen (1999). In 1997, a new award was administered through the APF with the assistance of Division 40. The Manfred A. Meier Award was created to honor the contributions of Meier to clinical neuropsychology. The award is given annually to graduate students pursuing studies in a neuropsychology field. In 1999 the recipient was Sheryl Reminger.

MEMBERSHIP

Division 40 was established in 1980 with 433 charter members. By 1999 membership had increased ten-fold to 4312. Although associates have always been a small segment of the membership, student membership has increased substantially in recent years. Another segment of the membership that has increased substantially (but remains at a low level) are fellows. Six fellows were voted in 1981 and 109 were included by 1999. Although this represents a large increase, the total number of fellows to members remains at a very low 2%. In addition, women (17%) and ethnic minorities (less than 1%) represent a small segment of this pool of recognized individuals: There are 1315 women and only 215 ethnic-minorities. This represents 30% and .01%, respectively, of the membership.

The APA Research Office gathers and disseminates information about the demographic characteristics of division members as indicated in their responses to questions for the APA *Membership Register* (APA, 1996). The following information about Division 40 members was based on the 1993 update of the *Register*, with new member updates for 1994 and 1995. This information is based on the reporting of some 3880 division 40 members.

Geographically, the largest concentrations of Division 40 members reside on the Pacific coast (16.9%), Middle Atlantic (16.9%), and South Atlantic (16.3%) regions. The gender representation in Division 40 differs significantly from the 54.1% male to 45.9% female ratio within the APA as a whole; 66.6% of Division 40 members are male, and 33.3% are female. The vast majority of Division 40 members indicate their ethnic group as White (81%), followed by not specified (13.6%), Hispanic (2.4%), Asian (0.3%), Black (0.9%), American Indian (0.7%), and other (0.2%). The mean age of a Division 40 member is 48.0 years (SD = 9.49 years), and the average member has been postdegree 16.3 years (SD = 12.6 years).

The vast majority of Division 40 members hold a PhD (80.8%), with 6.0% of the division having earned PsyD degrees and 3.2% EdD degrees. Eighty-one percent of Division 40 members report being licensed to practice psychology, and 67% belong to their state's psychological association. By far, most Division 40 members are also members in other APA divisions; 28% of members, however, belong solely to Division 40. The most popular divisions for Division 40 members to hold membership in are Division 12 (Society of Clinical Psychology; 21.3%), Division 42 (Psychologists in Independent Practice; 21.3%), Division 22 (Rehabilitation Psychology;

15.5%), Division 38 (Health Psychology; 10%), and Division 29 (Psychotherapy; 9.7%).

In terms of employment, results suggest that the majority of Division 40 members view themselves as clinical service providers. Broken down by site, 35% of the division membership are independent practitioners, whereas 24.3% are employed in hospital-based settings and 8.1% are employed in other human service settings. Approximately 19% of the members indicated an academic setting as their primary employment setting, with 10.8% in medical schools and 8.6% in either a four-year college or university setting. Despite the majority of members engaging in clinical activities, 42% also indicated that they conduct research in their work settings and 45% provide educational instruction.

In a 1995 survey commissioned by the Committee for the Advancement of Professional Practice of the Practice Directorate of the APA, 809 members of the division were surveyed (Phelps, 1998). Of these, 522 endorsed the division as being their primary affiliation. Approximately 41% of the respondents indicated that their primary professional activity was assessment, with 19% in therapy or rehabilitation activities followed by supervision or teaching at 10%. Research accounted for 7% of their time. Medical settings was the predominant location of professional activities at 39%. Of the respondents surveyed, the most critical professional concerns were (a) managed care affecting professional activities, (b) difficulty with reimbursement, (c) excessive restrictions (e.g., precertification) for professional practice, (d) decreased income as a result of managed care, and (e) ethical dilemmas posed by managed care. (See Table 12 for further information on issues of importance.)

PLANNING COMMITTEE REPORT OF 1994

In 1994, during his tenure as president of Division 40, Robert Heaton called for the formation of a planning committee. The missions of this committee were to develop a long-range plan for the division, to articulate its mission, and to define an agenda with goals for neuropsychologists within the APA. Chaired by former Division 40 representative to Council and past-president Meier, the planning committee was composed of 14 division leaders. The committee met over two days in April 1994 in Chicago, and engaged in much discussion about the division's past history, the division's relationship to the APA and other organizations, and the future of clinical neuropsychology. The image of Division 40 within the APA and outside organizations was examined, problems identified, and plans were developed to improve relationships with these groups. Given the zeitgeist of increasing

TABLE 12
Division 40 Membership Growth (1980–1999)

Years	Fellows	Members	Associates	Total
1980		433		433
1981	6	608	22	636
1982	23	723	40	786
1983	26	918	65	1009
1984	34	1332	103	1469
1985	43	1608	134	1785
1986	49	1829	153	2031
1987	53	2111	170	2334
1988	55	2251	157	2463
1989	57	2390	159	2606
1990	61	2574	144	2779
1991	60	2889	150	3099
1992	70	3158	158	3386
1993	75	3235	140	3450
1994	84	3388	133	3605
1995	86	3587	144	3817
1996	85	3601	133	3819
1997	89	3630	126	3845
1998	99	3849	108	4056
1999	109	4101	102	4312

consolidation of power by clinical divisions within the APA, the Planning Committee quickly articulated a crucial goal for the division and the field of clinical neuropsychology was the recognition by the APA of clinical neuropsychology as a distinct specialty area within psychology. After discussion, a new mission statement was created for the division. The committee next formulated goals organized around the APA Directorate structure, with goals and objectives developed for science, education, practice, and public interest. The final report of the planning committee was written by Ann Marcotte, Meier, and Robert Heaton and was presented to the division executive committee in August 1994. The report was published in 1995 (Report of the Division 40 Planning Committee, 1995).

With the approval of the planning committee's report, Division 40 has a new agenda driving its activities. The executive committee is undergoing reorganization, and some existing task forces and ad hoc committees have been incorporated into the four new advisory committees developed to implement each of the four sections of goals outlined in the planning committee report. The four advisory committees focus on science, education, practice, and public interest. Division 40 members responded to a broad appeal set out from the executive committee for members not previously active in divisional affairs to volunteer to serve on the four new advisory committees.

CONVENTION PROGRAMS

Arguably the centerpiece of Division 40 activities has been the convention program. Although the APA comprises more than 50 divisions, the size and scope of Division 40 has resulted in a surprisingly large convention program spread over almost a week of activities.

Paralleling the growth in membership of Division 40, the division has been allotted increasing hours for presentations at the annual APA convention. In recent years, Division 40 was assigned more than 40 hours for programming, ranking it among the largest of the APA divisions in visibility at the convention. The Division 40 program consists of paper and poster presentations, symposia, conversation hours, invited addresses delivered by prominent neuropsychologists and neuroscientists, awards addresses, a presidential address, and the annual business meeting. Division 40 has also in the past participated in APA's Science Weekend Program at the convention, both in donating hours to this programming as well as directly organizing events. Beginning with the 1987 Division 40 program, abstracts for all division-sponsored presentations have been published in *The Clinical Neuropsychologist*. A student award was initiated in 1989 to honor the top student submission to the Division 40 program. In 1999 the science committee created two research awards. As a result there has been an increase in the number of student research submissions and presentations in the program.

The convention programs of Division 40 of 1984–1996 were analyzed. The year 1984 was chosen as a starting point because that is when the division newsletter started publishing the convention program. Indeed, convention programs have always been found not only in the usual APA program book but within the pages of the *Division 40 Newsletter*. Program activities have slowly evolved to center around the weekend (because the convention starts on Friday morning and ends Tuesday afternoon). Activities have included primarily papers (often arranged into symposia) as well as posters. Other functions have included invited addresses, presidential addresses, and several conversation hours. Executive committee meetings as well as specific committee (e.g., program) meetings have typically been included as part of the program.

Numerous neuropsychologists have accepted the division's invitations to speak. A sampling during the 1980s and 1990s includes Arthur Benton, Butters, Costa, Jeffrey Cummings, Alan Mirsky, Reitan, Rourke, and Satz. Conversation-hour topics have ranged from economic issues to forensics. As Table 13 indicates, a wide variety of topics are covered within the programs. As can be seen in the table the most active issues include, in order of appearance, syndromes, assessment, and developmental issues. History is the least represented of all the topics. It is important to note that a qualitative

TABLE 13
Convention Activities: 1984–1996

Topic	Frequency of total number of presentations
Syndromes (e.g., head injury, dementia, AIDS)	41
Assessment (e.g., memory)	35
Developmental (e.g., child, elderly)	33
Anatomy (e.g., laterality, frontal lobe)	19
Treatment/recovery	19
Professional issues (e.g., education/training, practice)	18
Psychopathology (e.g., schizophrenia, depression)	14
Forensics	7
History	3
Miscellaneous	35

inspection of the programs suggests an evolution. For example, no presentations on economic issues were given prior to the 1990s, whereas such issues were prominent in recent meetings.

NEWSLETTER

The newsletter has been published regularly since 1983. It is published usually at the beginning of the year and immediately before the APA annual convention. Every newsletter reviewed contained minutes from the prior Executive Committee meeting and about two thirds contained a column from the president. In order of prominence, the following other topics were found printed in the newsletter: nominations and elections, convention programs, task force reports, general information or policy statements, and notice of awards and award recipients.

INTEGRATING THE PAST AND THE FUTURE

Division 40 has clearly been active, especially with convention activities and liaisons with other groups, namely segments within the APA. However, to determine the accomplishments, current issues, and future directions, all elected officials from 1980 to present were surveyed. Of the 32 elected officials, 2 were not able to complete the questionnaire because of illness or death and 24 did submit their responses. As Table 14 indicates, patterns were present at one point but have evolved. For example, credential-

TABLE 14

Survey of Past, Current, and Future Issues Facing Neuropsychology
(according to Division 40 elected officers, 1980–1996)

Issues	Past	Current	Future
Certification	8	6	0
Definition	6	4	0
Economic issues	1	12	12
International issues	5	2	2
Practice issues	1	1	9
Relationship to the APA	5	1	0
Relationship to others	4	3	2
Training and education	5	2	2

Note: N = 24 (out of a possible 32).

ing and certification have been and are critical issues but are not expected to continue being critical. In contrast, economic and practice issues have not previously been considered to be important. However, such pragmatic issues now rank far and away as the most important concerns of the division members.

Qualitative analysis suggests that *a* definition of a neuropsychologist had been important, and now executive committee members believe that formulating a *relevant* definition is critical. In terms of relationships to others, initially concern was raised about interactions with the ASHA, later the concerns were directed with the NAN, and people expect that the certification board issue will be the focus of future concerns. Finally, in terms of training and education, respondents reported that standards are now the focus for a number of neuropsychologists.

Over the past 20 years, clinical neuropsychology has expanded quickly. Unfortunately, the field has not been as cohesive as could have been anticipated. Initially, differences between factions were evident in the differences between the INS and the NAN, with Division 40 being the melting pot of ideas and personalities. Over time, the INS has clearly focused on multidisciplinary and experimental approaches to neuropsychology. In contrast, the NAN has become more interested in the clinical and professional aspects of the discipline. Two theoretical camps were represented. For example, initially if one was interested in performing evaluations with the Halstead-Reitan Neuropsychological Battery, he or she tended to be a member of the INS. If, in contrast, the person used the Luria-Nebraska Neuropsychological Battery, the neuropsychologist was more likely to be a member of the NAN. Again, the melting pot was Division 40, with personal and intellectual battles sometimes fought at the APA convention floor in the form of presentations or more subtlety in the division executive committee meeting.

During the first decade of the division's life, the executive committee tended to reflect the views of the INS. During the 1990s, however, the committee has elected members that reflect the INS and the NAN, as well as a number of individuals whose allegiance has been to the field at large rather than to an organization. Unfortunately many of these battles have continued, sometimes at personal levels and often disguised as intellectual differences. Two of the most significant involve the definition of a clinical neuropsychologist and the existence of two credentialing boards, with apparently similar objectives.

CONCLUSION

Division 40 has been one of the fastest growing and most active divisions within the APA. Further, its growth has paralleled exciting scientific and professional developments in the field. Although it is anticipated that the division growth will taper off somewhat, there are no signs of that occurring at present. However, significant problems continue to exist that may affect the current growth and development of the field and the division. Foremost is the issue of economic pressures facing practitioners of neuropsychology, as evidenced by survey results and programming activities. Personal and theoretical differences within the ranks of professional neuropsychology, especially with the issue of definition of a neuropsychologist and board certification, threaten to undermine the unusual and unparalleled growth of the field. Costa (1976) proposed that the field was headed toward an "exciting and exhilarating period." Indeed the nearly 25 years following his prediction have been "exciting and exhilarating." What will it take for the division and the field to continue such growth?

As Hebb (1949) has proposed, neuropsychology is a "loose assemblance" of separate ways of thinking that should not be pursued in isolation from mainstream psychology. The division experienced particularly gratifying support recently when the Commission for the Recognition of Specialties and Proficiencies in Psychology recommended and the APA Council of Representatives at its winter 1996 meeting approved clinical neuropsychology as a specialty. This is particularly important not only because it officially validates the discipline within the APA but it is the first specialty to have been recognized (see Meier, 1998, for additional information). Thus the future of the discipline and of Division 40 appears promising. Assuming that the representational, economic, definitional, and board issues can be resolved, both neuropsychology and Division 40 can expect a successful future and increased involvement within the APA and the field of psychology.

REFERENCES

American Psychological Association. (1996). *APA membership registry—1996*. Washington, DC: American Psychological Association.

Benton, A. L. (1964). Contributions to aphasia before Broca. *Archives of Neurology and Psychiatry, 54,* 212–216.

Benton, A. L. (1992). Clinical neuropsychology: 1960–1990. *Journal of Clinical and Experimental Neuropsychology, 14,* 407–417.

Bornstein, R. A. (1988). Reports of the Division 40 Task Force on Education, Accreditation and Credentialing: Guidelines for continuing education clinical neuropsychology. *The Clinical Neuropsychologist, 2,* 25–29.

Cermak, L. A. (1994). *Neuropsychological explorations of memory and cognition.* New York: Plenum Press.

Costa, L. (1976). Clinical neuropsychology: Respice, adspice, and prospice. *The INS Bulletin,* 1–9.

Costa, L. (1998). Professional of neuropsychology: The early years. *The Clinical Neuropsychologist, 12,* 1–7.

Cripe, L. I. (1989). Listing of training programs in clinical neuropsychology—1989. *The Clinical Neuropsychologist, 3,* 116–128.

Cripe, L. I. (1991). Listing of training programs in clinical neuropsychology—1991. *The Clinical Neuropsychologist, 5,* 226–237.

Cripe, L. I. (1993). Listing of training programs in clinical neuropsychology—1993. *The Clinical Neuropsychologist, 7,* 371–419.

Cripe, L. I. (1995). Listing of training programs in clinical neuropsychology—1995. *The Clinical Neuropsychologist, 9,* 327–398.

Cripe, L. I. (1997). Listing of training programs in clinical neuropsychology—1997. *The Clinical Neuropsychologist, 11,* 332–389.

Conger, J. J. (1980). Proceedings of the American Psychological Association, Incorporated, for the year 1979: Minutes of the Annual Meeting of the Council of Representatives. *American Psychologist, 35,* 501–536.

Definition of a Clinical Neuropsychologist. (1989). Definition of a clinical neuropsychologist. *The Clinical Neuropsychologist, 3,* 22.

Division 40/INS Task Force on Education, Accreditation and Credentialling. (1984). Report of the subcommittee on psychology internships.

Division 40 Newsletter, 2(1), 7.

Division 40: Task Force Report on Computer-Assisted neuropsychological evaluation. (1987). *The Clinical Neuropsychologist, 2,* 161–184.

Finger, S. (1994). History of neuropsychology. In D. Zaidel (Ed.), *Neuropsychology* (pp. 1–28). San Diego, CA: Academic Press.

Goldstein, G. (1985). The history of clinical neuropsychology: The role of some American pioneers. *International Journal of Neuroscience, 25,* 273–275.

Hebb, D. O. (1949). *The organization of behavior.* New York: Wiley.

Matthews, C. G., Harley, J. P., & Malec, J. F. (1991). Task Force Report Division 40—Clinical Neuropsychology of the American Psychological Association: Guidelines for computer-assisted neuropsychological rehabilitation and cognitive remediation. *The Clinical Neuropsychologist, 5,* 3–19.

INS-Division 40 Task Force on Education, Accreditation and Credentialling. (1986). Guidelines for doctoral and post-doctoral training programs in clinical neuropsychology. *Division 40 Newsletter, 4(2),* 4–5.

Meier, M. J. (1992). Modern clinical neuropsychology in historical perspective. *American Psychologist, 47,* 2, 550–558.

Meier, M. J. (1998) On the emergence of clinical neuropsychology as a specialty. *Division 40 Newsletter,* 4 (Spring), 7–8.

Phelps, R. (1997). Profiling Division 40 members: The CAPP practitioner survey. *Division of Clinical Neuropsychology Newsletter, 15,* 5–7.

Puente, A. E. (1992). Historical perspectives in the development of neuropsychology as a professional psychological specialty. In C. R. Reynolds & E. Fletcher-Janzen (Eds.), *Handbook of child clinical neuropsychology.* New York: Plenum Press.

Report of the Division 40 Planning Committee. (1995). *Division 40 Newsletter,* 10(1), 6–9.

Report of the Division 40 Task Force on Education, Accreditation and Credentialing. (1989). Guidelines for the use of non-doctoral personnel in clinical neuropsychological assessment. *The Clinical Neuropsychologist, 3,* 23–24.

Report of the Division 40 Task Force on Education, Accreditation and Credentialing. (1991). Recommendations for education and training of non-doctoral personnel in clinical neuropsychology. *The Clinical Neuropsychologist, 5,* 20–23.

Report of the INS-Division 40 Task Force on Education, Accreditation and Credentialling. (1987). Guidelines for doctoral training programs in clinical neuropsychology. *The Clinical Neuropsychologist, 1,* 29–34.

7

A HISTORY OF DIVISION 50 (ADDICTIONS)

RAYMOND F. HANBURY, JR., JALIE A. TUCKER,
and RUDY E. VUCHINICH

The approval of an APA Division on Addictions in 1993 was a reflection of numerous forces that had been developing for several decades within American society and within the scientific and practice communities of psychology. These forces became readily apparent as the relatively sedate and stable 1950s gave way to the tumultuous 1960s and 1970s. During this time, the availability and use of illicit drugs rose dramatically, and the enormity of the various costs associated with the excessive use of alcohol and cigarettes was becoming clear (Secretary of Health, Education, and Welfare, 1971; U.S. Department of Health, Education, and Welfare and U.S. Public Health Service, Center for Disease Control, 1964). Currently substance use disorders have the highest lifetime prevalence (26.6%) among the diagnosable mental health conditions; the next most prevalent conditions, anxiety and affective disorders, have a lifetime prevalence of 24.9% and 19.3%, respectively (Kessler et al., 1994). Each pack of cigarettes smoked and each alcoholic drink consumed is estimated to cost the U.S. economy $.15 and $.22, respectively, for a total cost in the hundreds of billions of dollars (Manning, Keeler, Newhouse, Sloss, & Wasserman, 1991). The epidemic of Acquired Immune Deficiency Syndrome (AIDS) beginning in the 1980s and continuing into the 21st century increased the gravity of addictive behaviors, because injection drug users now are a major pathway of Human Immunodeficiency Virus (HIV) infections into the general population.

Although the historical location of addictive behavior research and practice was well outside the mainstream of psychology and medicine, other forces during this same time period prompted the initiation of some integration, which remains incomplete. First, the creation of community mental health centers during the 1960s offered new job opportunities for clinical psychologists and other mental health professionals, and many of these centers had substance abuse treatment programs. Second, during the 1970s and 1980s inpatient substance abuse treatment services enjoyed a period of relatively favorable insurance reimbursement that led to a proliferation of "chemical dependency" treatment programs. Although the reductions in reimbursement that were later implemented by managed care organizations led to inpatient program closures or shifts to ambulatory care, the rapid, though transient, development of the addictions treatment industry was accompanied by growth in the numbers and kinds of health care professionals involved in addictions treatment and research. Third, and perhaps most important, the U.S. government formed the National Institute on Alcohol Abuse and Alcoholism (NIAAA) and the National Institute on Drug Abuse (NIDA) in the early 1970s and began channeling financial and scholarly resources toward addressing the problems of alcohol and drug abuse.

These were watershed developments for the psychology of addictive behaviors. Prior to these events, substance abuse clinical services were rare, little was known about useful assessment strategies or the efficacy of clinical treatments, and funding for substance abuse research paled in comparison to that for other health and mental health disorders. The NIAAA and the NIDA provided much needed funding for research, clinical services, prevention, and education to a broad range of scientific and professional disciplines that were concerned with addictive behaviors. Psychologists have capitalized on the opportunities created by the increased availability of substance abuse services and by NIAAA and NIDA funding. Given that addictive behaviors are first and foremost behavioral problems, psychologists have been at the forefront of both developing a scientific database regarding addictive behaviors and designing and delivering clinical services to address the problems posed by excessive consumption. A subset of these psychological scientists, scientist–practitioners, and practitioners are the individuals who formed APA's Division 50 on addictions.

DIVISION 50'S PRECURSOR:
THE SOCIETY OF PSYCHOLOGISTS
IN ADDICTIVE BEHAVIORS

In 1975, a small group of like-minded psychologists formed the Society of Psychologists in Substance Abuse, with an initial purpose "to promote human welfare through encouragement of scientific and professional activities and communication among psychologists and others working in any capacity in the areas of substance abuse or dependence, and/or other addictive behaviors." In the early 1980s, the name was changed to the Society of Psychologists in Addictive Behaviors (SPAB). The name change reflected the expanded conception of addictive behaviors as encompassing, but as not limited to, behaviors that involve psychoactive substance use, and it opened the organization to psychologists with interests in obesity, eating disorders, gambling, sexual addiction, and other behaviors of excess. The choice of the term "addictive behaviors" rather than "addiction" was deliberate and meaningful. The former term was strongly preferred by psychologists with scientific training and a behavioral background, broadly defined, who were active in developing the applied research base of psychological knowledge about these disorders beginning in the 1960s. The older term "addiction," although more commonplace, has a stronger association with medical, disease-oriented perspectives on substance use and related disorders.

The SPAB had six officers: president, secretary/treasurer, membership committee chair, journal editor, elections supervisor, and chair of the Bylaws and Constitution Review Committee. Table 15 lists the presidents of SPAB, beginning with the first election in 1979 and continuing through 1993, when the organization was absorbed into the new APA division on addictions. The SPAB's broadly conceived purpose, expressed in its brochure, was to "encourage scientific and professional communication among psychologists working in Prevention, Treatment, Research, Administration, [and] Education." By the mid-1980s, the society had more than 600 psychologists as members.

The maturation of the SPAB was evident in the development of its publications. In the late 1970s, Brenna Bry of Rutgers University edited an informal communication that was mailed to society members. This effort later evolved into a quarterly scientific journal under the able editorship of W. Miles Cox (1981–1994), who greatly expanded the scope and increased the quality of the publication. Originally titled *The Bulletin of the SPAB*, the journal was retitled *Psychology of Addictive Behaviors* in 1987. In 1992 the journal began publication and distribution under the auspices of the APA's special press, the Educational Publishing Foundation. To improve communication among the SPAB members, in 1990 a newsletter was

TABLE 15

Presidents of the Society of Psychologists in Addictive Behaviors
(1979–1993) and of the APA Division on Addictions (1993–2000)

Presidents of the Society of Psychologists in Addictive Behavior			
Years	Presidents	Years	Presidents
1979–1980	Faye J. Girsch	1987–1988	Curtis L. Barrett
1980–1981	Oakley S. Ray	1988–1989	George DeLeon
1981–1982	William R. Miller	1989–1991	Raymond F. Hanbury, Jr.
1982–1983	Chad D. Emrick		(2 terms)
1983–1984	G. Alan Marlatt	1991–1992	Dennis M. Donovan
1984–1985	Robert J. Pandina	1992–1993	W. Miles Cox
1985–1987	James L. Sorenson (2 terms)		
Presidents of the Division of Addictions			
Years	Presidents	Years	Presidents
1993–1994	Jalie A. Tucker	1997–1998	Robert A. Zucker
1994–1995	Raymond F. Hanbury, Jr.	1998–1999	Sandra A. Brown
1995–1996	Mark S. Goldman	1999–2000	Arthur T. Horvath
1996–1997	George DeLeon		

Note: Division 50 was approved in February 1993 as a candidate division of the APA during Miles Cox's term as SPAB president. He provided leadership for the new division until the August 1993 APA convention, when Jalie Tucker became president of Division 50 through the APA election process.

initiated under the editorship of Raymond F. Hanbury, Jr., who continued in this role until 1994, when Bruce S. Liese became editor of the newly titled *The Addictions Newsletter* for Division 50.

From 1988 through 1993, SPAB held an annual symposium in conjunction with the APA annual convention. These day-long, preconvention meetings served as a forum for psychologists to disseminate their knowledge to other psychologists who shared similar interests. Examples of presentation topics were "Motivational Model of Alcohol Use"; "Clinical and Legal Hazards of Failing to Address Substance Abuse Appropriately"; "Addictions and Family Law"; "Youth Gambling, Prevalance, Risk Factors, Clinical Issues and Social Policy"; "Eating Disorders"; "New Perspectives on Development and Treatment"; and "Relapse to Substance Abuse." The 1993 symposium papers on relapse were jointly contributed by members of the nascent Division on Addictions and by members of Division 28 (Psychopharmacology & Substance Abuse) and were published as a special section of Division 28's APA journal *Experimental and Clinical Psychopharmacology* (1996). Maxine Stitzer and Cox coordinated the symposium and served as section editors for publication of the papers on behalf of Divisions 28 and 50, respectively.

DEVELOPING SUPPORT FOR AN APA DIVISION
ON ADDICTIONS

Beginning in the late 1980s, members of the SPAB began laying the groundwork to establish a new division on addictions as part of the APA. The bases of need for such a division were several. First, psychologist members of the APA with interests in addictive behaviors were scattered throughout other divisions and did not have a "home" division within which their specialized interests could be expressed, developed, and promoted. For example, in 1993 when Division 50 was first approved as a candidate division of the APA, 10% or more of the new members also were members of the following divisions: Division 12 (Society of Clinical Psychology; 20.3%); Division 28 (Psychopharmacology & Substance Abuse; 11.0%); Division 29 (Psychotherapy; 23.1%); Division 38 (Health Psychology; 10.6%); and Division 42 (Psychologists in Independent Practice; 29.2%). The majority were clinical psychologists (61.5%). More members were employed in service delivery positions than in research or education, with the ratio being about 2.5 to 1 in favor of service delivery, but the great majority reported engaging in research, education, and practice to some extent.

Although Division 28 may have seemed to be an appropriate organization with which SPAB members could affiliate—and some of them did—Division 28's mission and identity then were, and continue to be, largely scientific in nature. Division 28 thus was not in a position to support vigorously the practice-oriented issues that were important to many SPAB members and to members of Division 42, who also were actively promoting the development of a division on addictions. Although practice-oriented issues continue to be an important part of Division 50's activities, as discussed later it would be an oversimplification to define the division's mission solely in terms of a practice agenda.

The rapid changes that occurred during the 1980s and 1990s as the United States moved from a "fee for service" to a "managed care" model of health care delivery provided a second, powerful impetus for developing a division on addictions. Mental health and substance abuse services, collectively known as "behavioral health" services, have been particularly targeted by the cost-containment strategies used by managed care plans. Although more covered individuals now have a behavioral health benefit as part of their health care plan, the scope of benefits typically is quite limited, especially in relation to benefits for medical conditions (the "parity" problem), and managed care companies continue to reduce the scope of behavioral health benefits and to lower reimbursement rates for providers. In the case of substance abuse service providers, subdoctoral addictions counselors far outnumber doctoral specialists, and some managed care plans either have reduced reimbursement rates to those paid to subdoctoral counselors or have failed to recognize, and thus to reimburse, doctoral professionals as legitimate providers.

Independently practicing doctoral psychologists in lucrative, urban, managed care markets (e.g., New York) have been particularly hurt economically by these changes. Therefore, it was no accident that these psychologists spearheaded the initiative to develop a division on addictions from within the APA, while the SPAB pursued the initiative from outside the APA. Jack G. Wiggins, Jr., a former APA president (1992) and a leader in Division 42, appointed Herbert J. Freudenberger, an independent practitioner in New York City, to chair the Ad Hoc Committee on Alcoholism and Substance Abuse of Division 42—Independent Practice—which later was instrumental in gaining approval from the APA Council of Representatives for a division on addictions. Other committee members lived in the New York City area and included George De Leon, R. Hanbury, Jr., Edward Schwab, and Barbara C. Wallace.

The committee met monthly from 1989–1993 and addressed a number of issues. First, a series of regional conferences were being held throughout the country, known as the Primary Care/Substance Abuse Linkage Initiative—Office of Treatment Improvement (Department of Health and Human Services—Alcohol, Drug Abuse and Mental Health Administration). Psychologists were the only professional group in attendance who did not have a position paper on substance abuse from their primary national professional organization. The ad hoc committee developed a statement on alcohol and other drug abuse that was adopted as APA policy by the Council of Representatives on February 29, 1992 (see Fox, 1992, pp. 922–923). The document was intended to guide the APA's activities in addressing the enormous societal problems of alcohol and other drug abuse and covered issues related to prevention; assessment, diagnostic, and treatment services; research; and education.

Second, the committee developed a strategy and a rationale for the creation of a division on addictions that was presented to the APA Council of Representatives on February 26, 1993, by Freudenberger, who then was a Division 42 Council representative. The presentation, titled "Why a Division on Addictions?" articulated the need for a "home base within APA" for psychologist experts on addiction. This base would encompass all aspects of substance abuse research, prevention, and treatment, so that the APA would have a "channel" for participating in national dialogues and initiatives concerned with substance abuse and other addictive behaviors. The full text of the presentation was published in the inaugural issue of the Division 50 newsletter (Summer 1993). Along with the presentation, the Council received a petition to establish a new division on addictions that had been signed by more than 700 APA members, which exceeded the requisite 1% of the APA members and fellows required to establish a new division. Daniel L. Yalisove had coordinated the collection of signatures for several years. The majority of signatories were members of the SPAB, which then had a membership of about 700 and formed the nucleus of the new division.

The Council of Representatives unanimously approved the petition, and Division 50 became a "candidate division" of the APA following Freudenberger's presentation. Division 28 did not oppose the formation of Division 50, which was viewed as a practice division that would complement Division 28's scientific focus.

The name of the new division (Addictions) was not well-received by some members of the SPAB, however, particularly by applied researchers and behaviorally oriented practitioners. They preferred the term "addictive behaviors," which better reflects the major focus of contributions to research and practice made by psychologists and which is in the name of the SPAB's (and now Division 50's) journal. The putative clinical utility of the term "addiction" in positioning psychologists in the medically oriented health care marketplace apparently weighed heavily in the choice. There also was some concern that the SPAB's membership base and broadly conceived agenda encompassing research, practice, and education was being cooped in service of the more limited practice agenda of independent practitioners who were being hurt financially by managed care. As discussed next, these issues proved resolvable, and there was near universal delight in achieving divisional status in the APA under the leadership of Freudenberger's committee. The division officially became operational and part of the APA at the annual convention in August 1993, held in Toronto, Canada. Because the division maintained the necessary membership base required to obtain permanent status for the next two years, in 1995 Division 50 became a fully recognized division of the APA.

ORGANIZATION (1993–1999)

When Division 50 was approved by the APA Council of Representatives in February 1993, an immediately pressing organizational issue concerned the role that the SPAB and its then current officers would have in the new division. Cox was then president of the SBAB, and Jalie A. Tucker was president-elect. Although both of these scientist–practitioner, academic clinical psychologists had been active in the SPAB, particularly in developing the journal (with Cox as editor and Tucker as an associate editor), neither were members of Division 42. This created some resistance within the latter constituency to the then-current SPAB officers assuming comparable roles in the new division. Moreover, new elections had to be held in the spring of 1993 as part of the regular APA election process. Through a series of telephone calls, including group conference calls, a slate of candidates was developed that was acceptable to both constituencies. Tucker was elected president and Daniel R. Kivlahan was elected secretary–treasurer, which continued their roles from the SPAB. Hanbury was elected president-elect, and Freudenberger, G. Alan Marlatt, and Curtis L. Barrett were elected as the three members-at-large of the Division 50 executive committee. Marlatt and Barrett were past presidents of the SPAB. Freundenberger also was elected to serve a three-year term as Division 50's APA Council representative once the division secured a seat on Council during the next apportionment ballot. Beginning in August 1995, Division 50 has consistently held one seat on the Council of Representatives. Freudenberger was succeeded by Tucker in 1998.

By satisfying the different stakeholder groups in the new division, the rapid resolution of this organizational issue forged essential alliances and an inclusive identity for Division 50 that continues to the present. The division is dedicated to providing a home for practitioners, scientist–practitioners, and even a few basic scientists who are concerned with addictive behaviors and who want to promote activity not only in their respective primary domains but at the interface of science, practice, and public policy. Probably above all else, Division 50 values the professional diversity of its members and wants to advance the development and dissemination of interventions for addictive behaviors that are guided by the best available scientific evidence. This commitment to maintaining diversity of perspective and to promoting the interface of science and practice is reflected in the officers of the division (summarized in Tables 15 and 16), who include psychologists who are variously employed in academic psychology departments, medical schools, substance abuse research institutes, Veterans Administration medical centers, rehabilitation hospitals, inpatient substance abuse treatment programs, therapeutic communities, and independent practice settings. The many channels of knowledge and experience that flow into the division from its diverse membership are a distinguishing characteristic and a source of strength as well as occasional conflict.

During the division's first year of existence (1993–1994), Tucker, with input from the executive committee, developed and implemented a committee structure to serve this agenda. Committee chairs were appointed, who then selected committee members with the executive committee's input and oversight. The original standing committees, which have been continued with a few modifications, included the bylaws, education and training, science advisory, nominations and elections, membership, and fellows and awards committees. The work of the bylaws committee is largely done, but the other committees remain active. Because the scope and responsibilities of the education and training committee grew very rapidly (for reasons

TABLE 16
Division on Addictions Executive Officers, Convention Program and
Standing Committee Chairs, Editors, Liaisons, and Representatives

	Executive Officers		
Years	Secretary–Treasurer		
1993–1996	Daniel R. Kivlahan		
1996–1998	Arthur T. Horvath		
1998–2000	Gregory T. Smith		
Years	Members-at-Large	Years	Members-at-Large
1993–1995	G. Alan Marlatt	1996–1997	Sandra J. Brown
1993–1996	Herbert J. Freudenberger	1997–1999	Kenneth E. Leonard
1993–1999	Curtis L. Barrett (2 terms)	1999–2001	Kim Fromme
1995–1998	Jerome J. Platt	1999–2000	Daniel R. Kivlahan
Years	APA Council Representative		
1995–1997	Herbert J. Freudenberger		
1998–2000	Jalie A. Tucker		
	Convention Program and Standing Committee Chairs		
Years	APA Convention Program Chairs	Years	APA Convention Program Chairs
1993–1994	Alan R. Lang	1997–1998	Kim Fromme
1994–1995	Jon Morganstern	1998–1999	Michael Sayette
1995–1996	Gregory T. Smith	1999–2000	Mariela Shirley
1996–1997	Arthur Horton		
Years	Bylaws		
1993–1995	Stephen E. Schlesinger		
Years	Continuing Education	Years	Continuing Education
1997–1998	Jerome J. Platt	1998– —	Robert W. Elliott
1997–1998	Robert G. Thompson		
Years	Education and Training		
1993–1996	Sandra A. Brown		
1996–1998	Mark B. Sobell		
1998–2000	Mark Meyers		
Years	Fellows and Awards		
1993–1997	Robert A. Zucker		
1997–1998	James L. Sorensen		
1998– —	Peter E. Nathan		
Years	International Membership		
1995–1997	W. Miles Cox		
1997– —	G. Alan Marlatt		
Years	Membership	Years	Membership
1993–1995	James L. Sorensen	1997–1999	Joy Schmitz
1995–1997	Janice G. Williams	1999–2001	Arthur Horton

(continued)

TABLE 16 *(continued)*

Years	Nominations and Elections	Years	Nominations and Elections
1993–1996	Gerard J. Connors	1997–1999	Lisa Najavits
1996–1997	Elsie R. Shore	1999–2001	Fred Rotgers

Years	Science Advisory
1993– —	Vincent J. Adesso

Editors

Years	Psychology of Addictive Behaviors	Years	Psychology of Addictive Behaviors
1981–1994	W. Miles Cox	1999– —	Thomas Brandon
1994–1998	Susan J. Curry		

Years	The Addictions Newsletter
1990–1994	Raymond F. Hanbury, Jr.
1994– —	Bruce S. Liese

Liaisons and Representatives

Years	Liaison to Division 12 (Clinical Psychology)
1993–1994	G. Alan Marlatt
1997– —	Holly Waldron

Years	Liaison to Division 28 (Psychopharmacology and Substance Abuse)
1993– —	Rudy E. Vuchinich

Years	Liaison to Division 38 (Health Psychology)
1993–1999	David B. Abrams

Years	Liaison to the APA Office of Substance Abuse
1993–1999	Kenneth E. Leonard
1999– —	Jon Morganstern

Years	International Liaison, APA
1995–1998	G. Alan Marlatt
1996–1998	Jerome Platt

Years	Graduate Student Representative to Division 50 Executive Committee
1993–1998	Linda A. Dimeff
1998–1999	Susan Tate
1999– —	Tamara Bryan and Goldie Millar

Note. Executive officers are elected for 3-year terms, except for the president (1-year term). All others are appointed by the president or executive committee, which is composed of all elected officers (president, president-elect, past president, secretary–treasurer, three members-at-large, and the APA Council representative).

described in the next section), in 1997 a separate standing continuing education committee was established. Ad hoc committees also have been formed, including one to develop a Diplomate in addictive behaviors under the auspices of the American Board of Professional Psychology (ABPP; Arthur Horton, chair) and another to promote psychologists' involvement in treatment and research on gambling (Curtis Barrett, chair), which is rapidly emerging as a serious, national addictive behavior problem.

Also beginning in 1993, liaisons were appointed to establish relations and promote communication with other divisions and groups in the APA who had related interests. (These are summarized in Table 16.) As described in the next section, the liaison activities with Division 28 (Psychopharmacology & Substance Abuse) have been and continue to be important for advancing the interests of both divisions in relation to several larger developments within the APA. Finally, as summarized in Table 17, Division 50 began selecting fellows for the division. Most "charter" fellows inducted in 1994 were fellows in other APA divisions. Fellows inducted in subsequent years included a mix of new fellows selected initially by Division 50 and others who were already fellows of other divisions. The division also began giving awards for outstanding service to the division and for excellence in graduate student research presented as part of the Division 50 convention program (See Table 17). Finally, two Division 50 members, Freudenberger and Peter E. Nathan, have received awards from the American Psychological Foundation and from the APA, respectively, for their exceptional professional contributions.

MAJOR ACTIVITIES (1993–1999)

This section summarizes activities in which Division 50 has participated since its inception. Several were initiatives of the APA that included input from Division 50, whereas others were generated within the division to advance its goals.

College of Professional Psychology

At its February 1994 meeting, the APA Council of Representatives narrowly approved a resolution to establish a national College of Professional Psychology, which "shall have the authority to issue certificates of proficiency to [licensed] health services providers in psychology" (see DeLeon, 1994, pp. 625–626). At the time, such certificates gave practitioners a measure of protection with respect to managed care organizations, which were refusing to reimburse services rendered by uncertified providers. As described earlier, this situation was especially acute in the case of substance abuse treatment,

TABLE 17
Division on Addiction Fellows and Award Recipients (1993–2000)

Fellows

David B. Abrams	Raymond F. Hanbury, Jr.	Ovide F. Pomerleau
John P. Allen	Dorothy K. Hatsukami	Barbara J. Powell
Thomas F. Babor*	Stephen T. Higgins	Oakley S. Ray*
Allan Barclay	Arthur Horton, Jr.	Kenneth Sher
Curtis L. Barrett	George J. Huba, Jr.	Saul Shiffman*
Howard T. Blane*	Ronald M. Kadden	D. Dwayne Simpson
Sandra A. Brown	M. Marlyne Kilbey	Linda C. Sobell*
Vivian B. Brown	Alan R. Lang	Mark B. Sobell*
Donald Calsyn	Kenneth E. Leonard	James L. Sorensen*
Jerome F. X. Carroll	Bruce S. Liese	M. Duncan Stanton*
Marilyn E. Carroll	Richard H. Longabaugh*	Maxine L. Stitzer
R. Loraine Collins	G. Alan Marlatt*	Jose Szapocznik
Gerard J. Connors	Barbara S. McCrady*	Ralph E. Tarter*
M. Lynne Cooper	William R. Miller*	Jalie A. Tucker*
W. Miles Cox*	Peter M. Monti*	Rudy E. Vuchinich*
Robert J. Craig	Peter E. Nathan*	Barbara C. Wallace
George De Leon	Michael D. Newcomb*	Jack G. Wiggins, Jr.*
Dennis M. Donovan	Timothy J. O'Farrell	Sharon C. Wilsnack
Patrick M. Flynn	Oscar A. Parsons*	Charles Winick
Raymond D. Fowler	Elizabeth C. Penick	Alice M. Young
Herbert J. Freudenberger*	Michael G. Perri*	Robert A. Zucker*
Meyer D. Glantz	Robert O. Pihl*	Joan E. Zweben
Mark S. Goldman	Jerome J. Platt*	

Award Recipients

Years	Division 50 Distinguished Service Awards	Years	Division 50 Distinguished Service Awards
1995	Jalie A. Tucker	1996	Herbert J. Freudenberger
1996	Sandra A. Brown	1997	Carlo C. DiClemente

Years	Division 50 Student Research Awards
1994	Michael G. MacLean, Arizona State University (Advisor: David MacKinnon) "Relationship between coping skills and alcohol use in adolescence"
1995	Joan Simmons, University of Kentucky (Advisor: Gregory Smith) "Expectancies for eating, dieting, and thinness in adolescent girls" Jack Darkes, University of South Florida (Advisor: Mark S. Goldman) "Disinhibition and the prediction of drinking"
1996	Linda Meyerholtz, Bowling Green State University (Advisor: Harold Rosenberg) "Psychometric assessment of the SASSI-2 with college students"
1997	Cathy A. Simpson, Auburn University (Advisor: Rudy E. Vuchinich) "Delayed reward discounting in social drinkers and problem drinkers"
1998	Estee Shapiro, The University of Texas at Austin (Advisor: Kim Fromme), "Differential determinants of young adult substance abuse and sexual behavior"

Years	APA and APF Awards Received by Division 50 Members
1999	Herbert J. Freudenberger, American Psychological Foundation Gold Medal Award for Life Achievement in the Practice of Psychology
1999	Peter E. Nathan, APA Board of Professional Affairs Award for Distinguished Professional Contributions, Distinguished Contributions to Knowledge

*1994 Charter Fellows

and, for this reason, it became the first area of practice designated for proficiency certification by the college.

Division 50 thus found itself at the center of a major APA initiative during its first year of existence, while it was still organizing. In hindsight, it seems clear that the interest of Division 42 (Psychologists in Independent Practice) in developing a division on addictions was in response to these larger developments in the APA and in the health care marketplace. Although sympathetic to the financial impact of managed care on practitioners, the scientist–practitioner constituency of Division 50, particularly treatment researchers, was concerned that the college certification process reflect the contemporary research base on effective interventions for substance use disorders, rather than perpetuating dominant but poorly supported treatment approaches. Division 28 (Psychopharmacology & Substance Abuse) shared these concerns. This was not merely an academic position but one that would well-serve consumers of substance abuse services by providing them with the best available interventions. It also would help psychologists compete more effectively in the health care marketplace by integrating their comprehensive mental health training and research skills with their expertise in substance abuse treatment.

The college initially resisted the involvement of treatment experts from Divisions 50 and 28, who collaborated to gain "a place at the table" as the college developed the substance abuse proficiency certificate. Tucker, then president of Division 50, and Alice M. Young, then Division 28's Council representative, laid the foundation for involving the two divisions in the college and succeeded in having nonvoting liaisons appointed from each division. The college liaisons, Sandra A. Brown for Division 50 and Maxine L. Stitzer for Division 28, did the bulk of the work on the certificate process on behalf of both divisions and orchestrated the involvement of other experts at appropriate points. For example, Barbara S. McCrady, another expert treatment researcher, coordinated the preparation of the content domains covered by the proficiency exam. On the college side, David A. Rodgers, a member of the College Board of Governors, and Vicki V. Vandaveer, who was chair of the college when most of the work on the substance abuse certificate was completed, provided critical support for the involvement of the expert groups. The final product, which balanced practical concerns with scientific viability, was satisfactory to the different stakeholder groups in the divisions and in the college, and, in 1996, the college offered the proficiency certificate exam to the APA membership. As of 1999, 2732 psychologists have been certified and, as planned originally, the exam content is being updated as new knowledge becomes available.

One final strange twist in the college process occurred during President Hanbury's term in 1994–1995. Even though the Council of Representatives had already designated substance abuse treatment as a proficiency, Division

50 was asked after the fact to prepare an application to have the content area recognized as a proficiency by the Joint Interim Committee for the Identification and Recognition of Specialties and Proficiencies (JICIRSP; Edward Bourg, chair, APA Education Directorate). The JICIRSP was the precursor to the current standing APA committee (Committee for the Recognition of Specialties and Proficiencies in Professional Psychology, or CRSPPP) that has authority to designate content areas as proficiencies or specialties in psychology. The college may then select from among areas so designated for which it wishes to develop certificates.

In collaboration with Division 28, Division 50 prepared the application and, as required by the JICIRSP guidelines, designated itself as the professional group responsible for the proficiency. However, because JICIRSP was an interim committee, it did not have the authority to designate Division 50 as the responsible petitioner, even though the division contributed extensively to the college proficiency certificate. Thus although Division 50 is widely regarded as the de facto petitioner and will lay claim to the proficiency through CRSPPP when the seven-year renewal cycle arrives, the substance abuse treatment proficiency is presently an "orphan" of the APA, having been authorized directly by a vote of Council and not subjected to the CRSPPP review process. As of 1999, it remains the only certificate offered by the college.

Convention and Continuing Education Programs

The dissemination of knowledge about addictive behaviors through convention and continuing education programs has been a keystone of Division 50's activities since its inception and continues a tradition of scholarly exchange among psychologists that was established in the SPAB. Every year beginning with its initial eligibility in 1994 to be part of the APA convention program, Division 50 has filled its allotted program hours with a full offering of symposia, poster sessions, and invited addresses. In 1994, Alan R. Lang, the division's first program chair, received nearly 100 submissions; in all subsequent years, the program chairs (see Table 16) received more than 100 submissions, allowing acceptance of high-quality presentations. Increasingly over time, select Division 50 program offerings have been cosponsored by other divisions, including Divisions 6 (Behavioral Neuroscience & Comparative Psychology), 25 (Experimental Analysis of Behavior), 28 (Psychopharmacology & Substance Abuse), 29 (Psychotherapy), 38 (Health Psychology), and 42 (Psychologists in Independent Practice).

Two highlights of Division 50's convention programs merit mention. In 1998, under the leadership of Division 50 President Robert Zucker and Program Chair Kim Fromme, Division 50 collaborated with Division 28 and the NIAAA to host a miniconvention. Titled "Alcohol and Addiction Research: Achievements and Promise in Behavioral Science," the miniconvention presentations covered alcohol and other drug-related research, prevention, and treatment activity. Enoch Gordis, NIAAA director, gave a keynote address and received a National Recognition Award for Contributions to Behavioral Science Research from the APA. In 1997 Division 50 President De Leon organized a day-long, preconvention symposium titled, "The Addictions in Psychology: Commonalities Across Substance Abuse, Gambling, Sexual Addictions and Eating Disorders" that included presentations on substance abuse and other addictive behaviors. The symposium advanced acceptance of the notion that there are "addictions without substances."

The consistent breadth of Division 50 programming, on topics ranging from practice issues to applied and basic research, reflects the diversity of member interests and expertise, as well as the division's commitment to promoting the scientific study of addictive behaviors and the interface between science and practice. However, Division 50 has encountered organizational obstacles within the APA with respect to its participation in both practice and science activities, especially regarding convention programming. The APA designates divisions as either practice divisions (e.g., Division 50) or science divisions (e.g., Division 28) and has no category for divisions such as 50 that are intimately involved in both science and practice. Early on, this created considerable problems for Division 50 program chairs. For example, in 1994 when Lang attended the winter meeting for program chairs at the APA in Washington, DC, he found that Division 50 could not participate in an already planned Science Weekend component on addictions and, more generally, that "The Science and Practice Directorates of APA ... had a hard time accepting our division because we harbor the apparently heretical idea that science and practice should inform one another" (Lang, 1994, p. 5).

Over time, this situation has improved and, in 1999, several Division 50 symposia and invited addresses were listed in the "More science programming" section of the Science Directorate's "Focus on Science" convention program. This positive change may reflect growing sensitivity within the APA of the value of promoting the science–practice interface, as well as Division 50's persistence in pursuing it in its program offerings and other activities. The many program collaborations between Divisions 50 and 28 (Psychopharmacology & Substance Abuse) also have been helpful, as has the inclusion of basic science presentations in Division 50's convention programs. For example, in 1999, George Koob of the Scripps Research Institute gave an invited address on "The Dark Side of Drug Addiction: The Neurobiology of Hedonic Dysregulation and Allostatis" that was sponsored by Division 50 (Brown, chair) and cosponsored by Divisions 6

(Behavioral Neuroscience & Comparative Psychology) and 28 (Psychopharmacology & Substance Abuse).

To offer applied educational activities to practitioners, in 1997 a standing Continuing Education (CE) Committee was established apart from its heretofore parent committee, the Education and Training Committee. Brown had chaired the latter committee since its inception in 1993 and recognized that the scope of its activities, which had long been dominated by the college proficiency certificate process, precluded sufficient attention being paid to the CE needs of practitioners. During her term as Division 50 president (1998–1999), she made obtaining approval from the APA for Division 50 to be a CE provider a priority. Under the leadership of CE committee chair Robert Elliott, Division 50 was approved by the APA as a CE sponsor effective March 26, 1999. The division will offer its first CE programs at the APA convention in 2000.

Journal Activities

Under the sequential editorships of Cox, Susan Curry, and Thomas Brandon, the *Psychology of Addictive Behaviors* has grown rapidly in visibility and quality. For example, between 1995 and 1998, the number of manuscripts submitted annually increased from 61 to 101, an increase of 66%. The rejection rate increased from 60% to 71% over the same period. Today the journal has approximately 2000 individual and institutional subscribers, and it is becoming one of the better specialty journals in the area of addictive behaviors.

Involvement in the APA Psychopharmacology Training Initiative

The importance of psychopharmacology in treating behavioral and psychological disorders increased dramatically during the 1970s and 1980s. In recognition of psychologists' growing involvement in the psychopharmacological aspects of practice, in 1990 the APA board of directors appointed the Ad Hoc Task Force on Psychopharmacology to explore the possibility of psychoactive drug prescription privileges for psychologists. The 1992 report of the task force advocated that a subset of psychologists obtain prescription privileges and articulated the more general training needs of professional psychologists in psychopharmacology. The task force report specified three overlapping levels of training:

- *Level 1* training would provide basic, didactic knowledge about the biological basis of neuropsychopharmacology; the loci and mechanisms of psychoactive drug action; and the psychopharmacology of drug classes that typically are used to treat psychological disorders. Given the importance of psychopharmacology in contemporary mental health services, the task force argued that all professional psychologists should receive Level 1 training, preferably as part of predoctoral graduate education.

- *Level 2* training would be at the internship or postdoctoral level and would prepare psychologists to participate collaboratively with physicians and other health professionals in medication management and in the integration of psychopharmacological and psycho-social interventions. Level 2 training would be more intensive than Level 1 and would involve practica and internship experiences as well as coursework.
- *Level 3* training also would be postdoctoral and would prepare psychologists for prescription authority. This level of training would be commensurate with that of other health professionals who have independent prescription privileges.

In response to the task force report, in 1994 the APA's Board of Educational Affairs (BEA) formed the Working Group on Psychopharmacology Education and Training, which also received some financial support from the Center for Mental Health Studies/Substance Abuse and Mental Health Services Agency (Department of Health and Social Services). All divisions of the APA were invited to nominate individuals to serve on the working group, the members of which were selected by the BEA. The working group had 14 members who represented a wide range of interests in psychopharmacology, including basic behavioral pharmacology and neuroscience research, Level 2 and Level 3 clinical practice, pharmacotherapy efficacy research, education, ethno-pharmacology, consumer issues, and rural health. M. Marlyne Kilbey, a past president of Division 28 (Psychopharmacology & Substance Abuse) and fellow of Divisions 28 and 50, chaired the BEA working group, and Rudy E. Vuchinich, also a fellow in both divisions, served as a working group member representing Division 50. The working group was charged with developing model curricula for Level 1 and Level 2 training. Developing recommendations for Level 3 training was assigned to the Committee for the Advancement of Professional Psychology (CAPP), the members of which have completed their assignment in a way that complements the BEA working group's recommendations for Levels 1 and 2.

After several meetings at APA headquarters, in December 1995 the BEA working group produced a report that articulated a curriculum for Level 1 training in psychopharmacology. In March 1997 the group produced the curriculum for Level 2 training in psychopharmacology. This documented the general goals, procedures, and content for Level 2 training and specified curricular modules for the areas of child/adolescent, older adult, adults with serious mental illness, and mental retardation and developmental disabilities.

Finally, in 1998 and 1999 Vuchinich participated in an interdivisional committee that developed a document to petition CRSPPP to recognize psychopharmacology as a proficiency. This interdivisional committee, which received some financial support from the APA, also was chaired by Kilbey and had representatives from Divisions 28 (Psychopharmacology & Substance Abuse; Frank Holloway), 31 (State Psychological Association Affairs; Jack Wiggins), and 42 (Psychologists in Independent Practice; Morgan Sammons). Acceptance of the document by CRSPPP (now pending) will allow the College of Professional Psychology to develop an exam and credential that recognizes practicing psychologists who are competent to provide clinical services in the area of medication management (a Level 2 activity). This is not equivalent to prescription authority but would expand the scope of psychological practice in the area of psychopharmacology.

APA Office of Substance Abuse (OSA)

Addiction-related issues raised with the APA (primarily the Practice Directorate) by external organizations are referred to OSA, which then requests expert input from Divisions 50 or 28 (Psychopharmacology & Substance Abuse). Input on major initiatives coordinated by liaison officer Kenneth Leonard during the initial years of Division 50 included (a) providing input, particularly concerning treatment, to a collaborative working group established by the American Bar Association (the Drug Crisis Working Group and later the Special Committee on Drug Crisis), which issued a report titled "New Directions for National Substance Abuse Policy"; (b) providing assistance via OSA to the federal Center for Substance Abuse Treatment for the development of Treatment Improvement Protocols; (c) reviewing the Draft Supplement of the American Society of Addiction Medicine Patient Placement Criteria (Leonard was a field reviewer and coordinated the division's response); and (d) reviewing a survey proposal from the National Task Force on the Future of Addictions Treatment, which was convened by the National Treatment Consortium for Alcohol and Other Drugs for purposes of producing a "white paper" on the future of addictions treatment.

Resolution on Mandatory Minimum Drug Sentencing Regulations

At its August 1998 meeting, the APA Council of Representatives approved a resolution supporting the restoration of reasonable boundaries in drug sentencing guidelines, phasing out mandatory minimum sentencing laws at the state and federal levels for drug-related offenses that do not involve drug trafficking or harm to others, and promoting proper emphasis on prevention, early intervention, and treatment. The resolution (see Levant, 1999, p. 638) was introduced by Division 32 (Humanistic Psychology), and the final version was cosponsored by Divisions 50, 28, 27 (Society for Community Research and Action: Division of Community Psychology), and 36 (Psychology of Religion). Tucker and Young, Council representatives for Divisions 50 and 28, respectively, helped craft the text of the final approved resolution. The APA board of directors had recommended that the Council reject the initial version.

CONCLUSION

During its brief history, Division 50 has become a channel for the confluence of research and practice on addictive behaviors. The division's professional diversity has allowed it to participate effectively in a wide range of scientific and professional activities important to its membership, the broader field of addictive behaviors, and the APA. Practice issues will continue to be an important part of Division 50's agenda, but the long-term viability of that agenda will be facilitated by intimate guidance from the scientific evidence on addictive behaviors. The reciprocity of practice and science has not been idle rhetoric in this division, which has demonstrated in several situations (e.g., with the college certificate and with the development of the psychopharmacology curriculum) how scientific knowledge can be exploited to advance constructively the pressing needs of practitioners in today's managed care environment. Fostering the positive evolution of the science–practice interface is not a simple matter and involves knowledge of, and sensitivity to, a complex and dynamic set of practical, scientific, economic, and political variables.

There are several developing issues that are crucial to psychology where this kind of skill is needed and where Division 50 will likely continue to play a role, in collaboration with other professional groups. One such area is obtaining prescription privileges for psychologists and ensuring that they have the necessary training and knowledge to function effectively in prescribing and managing medications. Division 28, with the assistance of Division 50 and other groups, has been a critical contributor to articulating the knowledge base necessary for competent prescription authority. These educational requirements must find their way into prescription authority legislation so that the public welfare is protected and psychology as a whole is protected from the negative consequences of incompetent practitioners.

Another area of urgent need concerns current U.S. drug control policies that emphasize reducing the drug supply through interdiction and criminal penalties and that have contributed to an underemphasis on prevention and treatment. Division 50 members will continue to play a role in expanding access to effective interventions for persons in need and to disseminate knowledge about effective interventions to other health care professionals and to paraprofessionals working in community and school settings. Expanding the base of substance abuse services is critical to slowing the HIV epidemic (National Institutes of Health, 1997) and to bringing services to the under-served majority of individuals with addictive behavior problems who never find their way into specialized treatment programs. Prevention and early intervention will be key components in an expansion of services.

Gambling is a final area that deserves greater national attention and that intersects with Division 50's interests and expertise. During the past decade or so, there has been explosive growth across the country in the kinds of gambling and opportunities for it, ranging from traditional casinos to state-sponsored lotteries to video poker to on-line gambling on the Internet. The prevalence of gambling disorders in adults has increased over the past two decades, and adolescents now have a higher prevalence of gambling disorders than adults (Shaffer, Hall, & Bilt, 1999). Gambling is rapidly emerging as a serious national addictive behavior problem, and Division 50, through the leadership of Curtis Barrett, is working to promote psychologists' involvement in addressing the problem, including their research involvement with the National Center for Responsible Gaming.

These three areas of priority involvement for Division 50 are national in scope, exceed the boundaries of psychology, and involve components that demand the attention of psychologists with expertise on addictive behaviors, psychopharmacology, and other drug-related fields. Historically, problems of addiction have not been well studied, widely treated, or sufficiently funded with respect to research opportunities or coverage in health insurance plans, and they remain stigmatized and marginalized compared to many other health and mental health problems (Fink & Tasman, 1993). The presence of two thriving divisions, 50 and 28, that can collectively address these problems in the arenas of practice, science, and public policy is a positive development for the APA and one that holds promise for realizing the vision articulated in Freudenberger's multifaceted argument to the Council for why the APA needs a division on addictions.

REFERENCES

American Psychological Association. (1992, July). *Report of the Ad Hoc Task Force on Psychopharmacology of the American Psychological Association* (M. A. Smyer, chair). Unpublished manuscript.

De Leon, P. H. (1994). Proceedings of the American Psychological Association, Inc., for the year 1993: Minutes of the annual meeting of the Council of Representatives, August 19 and 22, 1993, Toronto, Ontario, Canada, and February 25–27, 1994, Washington, DC. *American Psychologist, 49,* 586–635.

Fink, P. J., & Tasman, A. (Eds.). (1993). *Stigma and mental illness.* Washington, DC: American Psychiatric Association.

Fox, R. E. (1992a). Proceedings of the American Psychological Association, Inc., for the legislative year 1998: Minutes of the annual meeting of the council of Representatives, February 20–22, 1998, Washington, DC, and August 13 and 16, 1998, San Francisco, CA, and minutes of the February, June, August, and December 1998 minutes of the Board of Directors. *American Psychologist, 54,* 605–671.

Fox, R. E. (1992b). Proceedings of the American Psychological Association, Inc., for the year 1991: Minutes of the annual meeting of the Council of Representatives, August 14 and 17, 1991, San Francisco, and February 29 to March 1, 1992, Washington, DC. *American Psychologist, 47,* 893–934.

Kessler, R. C., McGonagle, K. A., Zhao, S., Nelson, C. B., Hughes, M., Eshleman, S., Wittchen, H., & Kendler, K. S. (1994). Lifetime and 12-month prevalence of *DSM-III-R* psychiatric disorders in the United States: Results from the national comorbidity study. *Archives of General Psychiatry, 51,* 8–19.

Lang, A. R. (1994). Reflections on a convention past. *Division on Addictions Newsletter, 2,* 5–6.

Levant, R. F. (1999). Proceedings of the American Psychological Association, Inc., for the legislative year 1998: Minutes of the annual meeting of the Council of Representatives, February 20–22, 1998, Washington, DC, and August 13 and 16, 1998, San Francisco, CA, and minutes of the February, June, August, and December 1998 minutes of the Board of Directors. *American Psychologist, 54,* 605–671.

Manning, W. G., Keeler, E. B., Newhouse, J. P., Sloss, E. M., & Wasserman, J. (1991). *The costs of poor health habits: A RAND Study.* Cambridge, MA: Harvard University Press.

National Institutes of Health. (1997). *Interventions to reduce HIV risk behaviors* (NIH Consensus Statement No. 15(2), pp. 1–41). Bethesda, MD: Author.

Shaffer, H. J., Hall, M. N., & Bilt, J. V. (1999). Estimating the prevalence of disordered gambling behavior in the United States and Canada: A research synthesis. *American Journal of Public Health, 89,* 1369–1376.

Secretary of Health, Education, and Welfare. (1971). *First Special Report to the U.S. Congress on Alcohol and Health* (DHEW Publication No. [ADM] 74-68), U.S. Department of Health, Education, and Welfare, Alcohol, Drug Abuse, and Mental Health Administration. Washington, DC: U.S. Government Printing Office.

Sitzer, M. L., & Cox, W. M. (Eds.). (1996). Special section: Relapse to substance abuse: Recent findings from basic and clinical research. *Experimental and Clinical Psychopharmacology*, *4*, 3–60.

U.S. Department of Health, Education, and Welfare and U.S. Public Health Service, Center for Disease Control. (1964). *Smoking and health: Report of the advisory committee to the Surgeon General of the Public Health Service* (DHEW Publication No. PHS1103). Washington, DC: U.S. Government Printing Office.

NAME INDEX

Numbers in italics refer to listings in reference sections.

Branch, C. H. H., *135*
Branden, N., 96
Brandon, T., 170, 176
Bray, C. W., 13, 14, 29
Brenman, M., 61, 64, *81*
Breuer, J., 60, *81*
Brieland, D., 37
Broedling, L., 22
Bronstein, R., 144
Brown, B., 129
Brown, S. A., 164, 169, 172, 173
Brown, S. J., 169, 175, 176
Brown, V. B., 172
Brucker, B., 39, 47
Brunswick, E., 119, *133*
Bruyere, S. M., 39, 44, 47, *54*
Bry, B., 163
Bryan, A. I., 12, 29
Bryan, T., 170
Buckelew, S., 47, 49, 51, *55*
Buell, G. J., 48, *54*
Buelna, 77
Bugental, 88–89, 101, 102, 106, *110*
Bühler, C., 86, 89, 104
Butters, N., 141, 142, 143, 144, 146–147, 155
Byrd, 49
Byred, E. K., *55*

Cadwallader, T. C., 2, 8
Calsyn, D., 172
Cammack, S., 48, *54*
Campbell, A., 149
Campbell, C. H., 22
Campbell, D. E., 75, 129
Campbell, R. C., 22
Campise, R. L., 22
Canter, D. V., 126
Capafons, A., 77, 82
Caplan, B. M., 39, 45
Capshew, J. H., 9, 11, 29
Card, J. J., 129
Cardena-Buelna, E., 82
Cardeña, E., 68, 76, 77
Carney, R. M., 18, 24, 26, 29, 31
Carroll, M. E., 172
Carroll, J. F. X., 172
Carter, L., 14
Cermak, L. A., 141, 147, *159*
Chambers, R. M., 14
Chan, F., 47, 49, *54*

Chaves, J. F., 59, 62, 66, 67, 75, *83*
Cheek, D., 76
Chelune, G., 142, 143
Chenven, H., 37
Chilman, C., 116
Christensen, J. M., 14, 19
Chubon, R. A., 44, *54*
Clemens, S. L., 60, *81*
Clinton, W., 18
Coe, W. C., 59, 62, 67, 73, *81*, *83*
Collins, R. L., 172
Combs, A. W., Jr., 106
Conger, J. J., 139, *159*
Conn, J., 66
Connors, G. J., 170, 172
Conway, D., 122
Cooper, L., 66
Cooper, M. L., 172
Copeland, D. R., 67
Corrigan, J. D., 39, 52, *54*
Costa, 137, 138, 139, 142, 148, 151, 155, *159*
Council, J. R., 5, 67, 71–72, 76, 79, 80, 82
Cox, W. M., 163, 164, 167, 169, 170, 172, 176, *181*
Crabtree, A., *82*
Craig, E., 102
Craig, R. J., 172
Craik, K., 120, 124, 128, *133*
Crawford, H. J., 67
Crawford, M. P., 14, 22, 23, 29
Crewe, N. M., 38, 39, 47
Cripe, L., 143, 149, *159*
Criswell, J. H., 37
Criswell, E., 85, 107
Cronin, C. J., 10, 29
Crosson, B., 150
Crown, B., 94
Cruikshank, W. M., 37
Crutchfield, R., 117
Cullum, M., 143
Cummings, J., 155
Curry, S. J., 170, 176
Cvetkovich, G., 128, 129
Czerlinsky, T., 39

Dailey, J. T., 14
Darkes, J., 172
David, H. P., 113, 115, 116, 117, 119, 128, *133*
De Leon, G., 166, 172, 175, *181*

Geldard, F. A., 13, 14
Gellman, W., 37, 44, *55*
Gendlin, E., 102
Georgoulakis, J. M., 26, 31
Gerton, M., 76
Gibbons, D., 90, 91
Gifford, R. D., 128
Gill, M. M., 61, *81*
Giorgi, A., 85, 87–88, 102, 106, 107, 108,
    111
Girsch, F. J., 164
Glantz, M. D., 172
Gleuckauf, R., 39
Gluck, J. P., 49, 51, *55*
Glueckauf, R. L., 48, *55*
Goldberg, S. L., 14, 21, 27
Goldin, G. J., 45, *55*
Goldman, M. S., 164, 172
Goldstein, K., 50, 88
Goldstein, G., 137, 141, 142, 143, 144,
    149, *159*
Gonick, M. R., 42, , *54*
Goodglass, H., 141, 142, 151
Gordis, E., 175
Gordon, W. A., 45, 47, 48–49, 50, *55*,
    64, 66
Gottfredson, G. D., 130, *134*
Gottsegen, G., 85, 93, 94, 95, 97,
    111
Gough, H. G., 116, 117, *133*
Grafton, F., 23
Graham, K. R., 67
Graham, S., 90, 91, 95, 97, 109
Gravitz, M. A., 5, 60, 67, 79, *82*
Green, G. W., 37
Greenberg, I. M., 23
Greene, R. Y., 48, *56*
Greening, T., 6, 103–104, 106
Greenwald, H., 66
Greenwald, J., 129
Grether, W., 14, 19
Griffith, J. E., 14, 24
Gruber, K., 9
Gruenewald, D., 66
Grzesiak, R. C., 38, 39, 47
Gugel, R. N., 38
Guze, H., 64, 65, 66, 80

Hackman, R., 12
Hall, G. S., 2

Hall, M. N., 180, *181*
Halpern, F., 109
Hammeke, T., 143
Hamsher, K., 143, 151
Hanbury, R. F., Jr., 7, 164, 166, 168, 170,
    172, 173
Harari, C., 85, 91, 94, 95–96, 97, 100,
    101, 106, 109, *111*
Hardin, G., 114, *133*, *134*
Harley, J. P., 149, *160*
Harper, D. C., 39, 53, 56
Harrell, T. W., 12
Harris, J. H., 22, 26, 31
Harris, C. B., 22
Hartlage, L., 142
Harvey, S. M., 115, 128, 129, *133*
Hathaway, S., 138
Hatsukami, D. K., 172
Heaton, R., 142, 143, 144, 153, 154
Hebb, D. O., 158, *159*
Heilbronner, R., 151
Helmreich, R., 120
Hendlin, S. J., *111*
Herek, G., 18, 19, 24, 31
Heron, W., 66
Hibbard, M. R., 49, 50, *55*
Hibler, R. J., 14
Hicks, L., 116
Higgins, S. T., 172
Hildreth, J., 93, *111*
Hilgard, E. R., 3, 8, 9, 11, 29, 59, 60,
    61–62, 63, 64, 65, 66, 67, 75, 76,
    82, *82*, 83
Hilton, R., 97
Holahan, C. J., 120, 129, *133*
Holland, J. L., 130, *134*
Holloway, F., 178
Holsopple, J. Q., 12
Hom, J., 143
Horevitz, R. P., 69, 70–71, 75, *82*
Hornyak, L. M., 71
Horton, A., Jr., 169, 171, 172
Horvath, A. T., 164, 169
Houston, J., 102
Howard, G. S., 114, *134*
Huba, G. J., Jr., 172
Hughes, M., *181*
Hull, C. L., 61, *82*
Humphreys, L. G., 14
Hunt, W. A., 13
Huxley, A., 104

Ince, L. P., 38, 48, *56*
Inouye, D. K., 17, 21, 28
Ittelson, W. H., 120, *134*

Jacobs, D. F., 37, 38, 46, 47, *56*
Jaggi, C., 23
James, L., 22
James, H., 33
James, W., 60, 82, 107, *112*
Janowitz, M., 25
Jansen, M. A., 38, 45
Jeffrey, T. B., 14, 22
Jenkins, J. G., 12, 13, 14, 19, 27, 31
Jobe, J. B., 14, 18, 20, 21, 24, 27, 31
Johnson, L., 5, 43
Johnson, R. C., 22
Jones, E. I., 14
Jordan, J. E., 37, 38
Jordan, S., 59
Jourard, S., 96, 104

Kadden, R. M., 172
Kagehiro, D., 129
Kamenske, G., 118
Kaplan, E., 141, 142, 144
Kardiner, A., *82*
Katz, N., 75
Keeler, E. B., 161, *181*
Keiffer, M., 116
Kelly, E. L., 13
Kelly, G., 89
Kelty, M., 116, 119, 128
Kendler, K. S., *181*
Kerr, N. J., 38, 42, 46, 47, *56*
Kessler, R. C., 161, *181*
Kewman, D. G., 52, *56*
Kihlstrom, J. R., 76
Kilbey, M. M., 172, 177, 178
Kirsch, I., 6067, 72, 73, 77, 82, 83
Kivlahan, D. R., 168, 169
Klee, J., 94
Klesch, J. J. K., 22
Kline, M. V., 59, 61, 64, 65, 66, 67, 75, 77
Klove, H., 138
Knapp, B., 92, 94, 97
Knapp, D. J., 14, 24, 26, 31
Knapp, R., 89
Kobrick, J., 21
Koob, G., 175
Krasner, J. D., 109, *111*

Krause, J., 47, 49, *56*
Kreutzer, J., *55*
Krippner, S., 67, 80, 85, 96, 97, 101, 107
Krueger, G. P., 14
Kutcner, 45

Laing, R. D., 87, 102, 104, 107
Lam, C. S., 49, *54*
Lang, A. R., 169, 172, 174, 175, *181*
Larson, P., 5
Laskow, G., 17, 22
Laung, P., 47
Laurence, J. R., 14, 76
Leitner, L., 106
Leonard, K. E., 169, 169, 169, 172, 178
LeShan, L., 94
Leung, P., 39, 53, 54, *56*
Levant, R. F., 17, 26, 31, 179, *181*
Levit, R., 22
Leviton, G. L. 41, 42, 45, *54, 55, 56*
Levitt, E. E., 5, 59, 64, 66, 67, 68, 69, 72, 75, 77–78, 78–79, 80, 82
Levitts, P., 151
Levitts, R. A., 151
Lewin, K., 42, 48, 119, *134*
Lichtenberg, P., 47
Liese, B. S., 164, 170, 172
Limburg, C. C., 12, 31
Lindner, H., 66
Liss, M., 52, *56*
London, P., 64, 66, 80
Longabaugh, R. H., 172
Louttit, C. M., 11–12, 13, 31
Lueng, 49
Lynn, S. J., 67, 75, 77, 80–81, 82, 83
Lyons, A., 103
Lyons, J. D., 20, 27

Mackie, R. R., 14
MacKinnon, D. W., 60, 172
MacLean, M. G., 172
Mahran, A. M., 6, 63–64, 65–66, 66–67, 75
Mahrer, A., 85, 96, 102, *111*
Malec, J. F., 149, *160*
Malthus, R. T., 115, *134*
Manaster, A., 94, 97
Mangelsdorff, A. D., 14, 22, 23, 31
Manning, W. G., 161, *181*
Marcotte, A., 6, 143, 144, 146, 154
Marcuse, F., 64

White, R., 141, 142, 143, 144
White, R. W., 60, 83, 89
White, W. P., 113, 116, 120, 121, 122, 123, 125, *134*, *135*
Whitehouse, F. A., 37
Whitely, J. M., 36, 43, *57*
Wick, E., 72, 75, 78, 82
Wicker, A. W., 128
Wickless, C. 67, 68, 80
Wickramasekera, I., 67, 80
Wiggins, J. G., Jr., 70, 166, 172, 178
Willems, E., 120
Williams, D., 26, 31
Williams, J. G., 169
Wilmoth, G. H., 129
Wilsnack, S. C., 172
Winick, C., 172
Winkel, G., 120, 124, *134*
Winter, D. D., 114, *135*
Wiskoff, M. F., 14, 21, 22, 27
Wittchen, H., *181*
Wohlwill, J., 120, 124, 126, *135*
Wolfers, H., 116
Wolfle, D., 13

Wong, D., 49, *54*
Woody, R., 64
Wootin, A., 22
Wrenn, C. G., 12, 13, 31, 32
Wright, B. A., 36, 37, 40, 41, 42, 45, 46, 47, *55*, *57*
Wright, E., 75
Wright, G. N., 38, 46, 47, 48, *57*
Wright, L., 109
Wright, M. E., 37, 45, *57*, 64, 76

Yalisove, D. L., 166
Yeates, K., 143, 146
Yerkes, R. M., 2–3, 9–10, 11, 27
Young, A. M., 172, 173, 179
Young, P. C., 60
Yuker, H. E., 47, 48, *57–58*

Zamansky, H., 66
Zaretsky, H. H., 38, 39, 47, 48, 55, 56
Zeidner, J., 10, 32
Zhao, S., *181*
Zucker, R. A., 164, 169, 172, 174–175
Zweben, J. E., 172

SUBJECT INDEX

Managed care, 52
Medicare/Medicaid, 43–44, 51, 150–151
Military psychology. *See* Division 19;
　　Homosexual issues
Minimum drug sentencing regulations,
　　178–179
Minority issues, 149–150

National Academy of Neuropsychology,
　　150
National Council on the Psychological
　　Aspects of Disability (NCPAD),
　　5, 35–36
National Council on the Psychological
　　Aspects of Physical Disability
　　(NCPAPD), 36
National Institute on Alcohol Abuse and
　　Alcoholism (NIAAA), 162, 175
National Institute on Drug Abuse
　　(NIDA), 162
National Research Council, 2, 10
National Society of Crippled Children
　　and Adults, 34
NCPAD. *See* National Council on the
　　Psychological Aspects of Dis-
　　ability
Neuropsychology. *See* Division 40
Neurorehabilitation. *See* Division 22
NIAAA. *See* National Institute on Alco-
　　hol Abuse and Alcoholism
NIDA. *See* National Institute on Drug
　　Abuse

Office of Substance Abuse (OSA), 178
Operation Desert Storm, 24

PAA. *See* Population Association of
　　American
Personality. *See* Division 32
Philosophical sources. *See* Division 32
Pop psychology, 87
Population. *See* Division 34
Population Association of America
　　(PAA), 115

Psychopharmacology Training Initiative,
　　176–178

Rehabilitation Act of 1973, 5
Rehabilitation psychology. *See* Division
　　22

Saybrook Institute and Conferences, 89,
　　98, 107
Society for Clinical and Experimental
　　Hypnosis (SCEH), 62, 64
Society for the Psychological Study of
　　Social Issues (SPSSI), 10
Society of Experimental Psychologists, 2
Society of Psychologists in Addictive
　　Behavior (SPAB), 163, 165–166
Society of Psychologists in Substance
　　Abuse, 163–164
SPAB. *See* Society of Psychologists in
　　Addictive Behavior
SPSSI. *See* Society for the Psychological
　　Study of Social Issues

Task Force on Education, Accreditation,
　　and Credentialing of Clinical
　　Neuropsychologists, 139, 147–149,
　　150
Task Force on Environment and Behav-
　　ior, 113, 119–123, 124–125
Task Force on Psychology, Family Plan-
　　ning and Population Policy, 113,
　　114–119, 124–125
Task Force on the Use of Computer
　　Technology in Evaluation and Re-
　　habilitation in Neuropsychology,
　　148–149

VA. *See* Department of Veterans Affairs
Vietnam War, 27, 116

War. *See* Division 19; Division 22; indi-
　　vidual wars by name
World Health Organization (WHO), 52
World Wars, 9–11, 27

ABOUT THE EDITOR

Donald A. Dewsbury was born in Brooklyn, New York, grew up on Long Island, and received an AB degree from Bucknell University in Lewisburg, Pennsylvania. After completing his PhD in psychology with Edward L. Walker, he spent a year as a postdoctoral Fellow at the University of California, Berkeley, with Frank A. Beach. Through much of his career he has been a comparative psychologist with a special interest in the evolution of reproductive and social behavior. In recent years, his interests have shifted so that he now works primarily in the area of the history of psychology, with a secondary interest in comparative psychology. He is the author or editor of 12 books, including *Comparative Animal Behavior* (1978) and *Comparative Psychology in the Twentieth Century* (1984). In addition, he has published more than 300 articles and book chapters. He is a Fellow of the American Psychological Association's Divisions 1, 2, 6, and 26, the American Association for the Advancement of Science, the American Psychological Society, and the Animal Behavior Society. He has served as president of the Animal Behavior Society and APA's Divisions 6 and 26. He is the historian for Divisions 1, 6, and 26, the Psychonomic Society, the Animal Behavior Society, and the Cheiron Society.